CONTENTS

INTRODUCTION

Since the last edition of this book was published lacunae in the statuary and monuments of London have been filled. We now have memorials to the Fleet Air Arm, The Royal Tank Regiment, the Gurkhas, and a statue of Britain's valued wartime ally General Wladyslaw Sikorski. Raoul Wallenberg, who saved many thousands of Jewish lives, is remembered in Cumberland Place; Westminster Abbey has ten modern martyrs on its west front.

In a lighter vein Sherlock Holmes again ponders crime in Baker Street, and Hodge the audacity of mice in Gough Square. Passers-by in Adelaide Street pause for 'A Conversation with Oscar Wilde'. At the Royal Hospital a Chelsea In-pensioner raises his stick in salute to past comrades and holds oak-leaves in memory of the hospital's founder, Charles II. The City, too, has newcomers, including the 'Market Trader' in Walbrook and there is a bas-relief of Michael von Clemm, a progenitor of this burgeoning financial centre, at Canary Wharf. Robert Milligan has returned to his old kingdom by the sugar warehouses at West India Dock, and the magnificent Hibbert Ship Gate can again be admired in nearby Hertsmere Park.

In the planning stage are memorials to the Australian Armed Forces, the Women of the Second World War (to replace Raleigh in Whitehall), Animals in War, Lloyd George and Sylvia Pankhurst, and the National Police Memorial (to be at the junction of Horse Guards' Parade and the Mall). The Royal Naval Division Memorial is to return to its former home near the Admiralty. Harry Potter may soon approach Platform $9^3/4$ at King's Cross station, on his way to Hogwarts Academy and lasting fame. A statue of Beau Brummel, the dandy, will stand in Jermyn Street.

In September 2001 it was announced that a commemorative sculpture by the Venezuelan sculptor Flor West is to stand outside Liverpool Street station. It will commemorate the ten thousand Jewish children who arrived in Britain through the station in the 1930s, refugees from Nazi persecution. Prospective foster parents stood on the platform to select the child they would care for. The sculpture will be in the form of a 9 foot glass suitcase (each child was allowed to bring one suitcase only), which will hold some of the objects that travelled in the original suitcases. A bronze figure of a girl will be seen peering into it.

Less happily, the empty plinth in Trafalgar Square is a problem unresolved. This important site is still dedicated to sculptures dismissed by one critic as 'ephemeral modern rubbish'. An inappropriate statue of Nelson Mandela was suggested in March 2001. In 2000 Margaret Purves QC proposed a memorial to holders of the Victoria Cross, of whom only twenty-four remain alive. A fine bronze model by Simon Dyer exists of Queen Victoria on horseback, investing with the very first VC Mate Charles Lucas, who in 1854, at risk of his life, threw a live bomb overboard from HMS *Hecla*. This bronze group links three strands – regal, naval and military, and equestrian – of the square's well-established character. Field Marshal Lord Bramall suggested that holders of the George Cross should also be included. Canada, Australia and New Zealand all have public memorials to their holders of the VC; Britain has not. Or why not a statue of Admiral Sir Bertram Ramsay? Without his organisational genius in Operation 'Dynamo' at Dunkirk and 'Neptune' on D-Day, Trafalgar Square might be a very different place. There is a fine model in the statue by Stephen Melton, unveiled in 2000 at Dover Castle.

The May Day anti-capitalist riots of 2000, when Winston Churchill's statue

MARGARET BAKER

DISCOVERING

LONDON STATUES
AND MONUMENTS

A SHIRE BOOK

Front cover: *This statue of Sarah Siddons, based on the painting of her as 'The Tragic Muse' by Sir Joshua Reynolds, stands on Paddington Green by the Westway flyover.*

British Library Cataloguing in Publication Data: Baker, Margaret. Discovering London statues and monuments. – 5th ed. – (A Shire book) 1. Monuments – England – London – Guidebooks 2. Statues – England – London – Guidebooks 3. London (England) – Guidebooks I. Title II. London statues and monuments 725.9'4'09421 ISBN 0 7478 0495 8.

ACKNOWLEDGEMENTS
The author expresses her thanks to the following for their kind assistance:

The Beau Brummel Statue in St James's Trust (Mr Christopher Fenwick, Chairman)
The Brontë Society (Ms Ann Dinsdale)
Brooks's (Mr Graham Snell, Secretary)
The Canary Wharf Group plc (Ms Suzanne Wild)
The Cheshire Military Museum (Major [Ret'd] J. E. H. Ellis BA, Curator)
Chiswick Public Library (the Reference Librarian)
The Corporation of London (Ms Kate Williamson, Principal Planning Officer, Urban Design and Conservation)
The Corporation of London: the Guildhall Art Gallery (Ms Vivien Knight, Curator)
The Corporation of London: the Guildhall Library (Mr John Fisher, Keeper of Prints and Maps)
English Heritage, London Region (Mr Christopher Cook)
The Friends of War Memorials
Greenwich Tourist Information Centre (Ms Susan Jenkinson)
Hogarth's House, Chiswick (the Curator)
The Honourable Society of the Inner Temple (Brigadier Peter Little CBE, Sub-Treasurer)
The International Maritime Organisation (Ms Lesley Brook, Public Information Services)
Kent Arts and Libraries (the staff at Deal Public Library)
The Metropolitan Police Service (Inspector John Graham and Mr T. Dolphin)
The Museum of Docklands (Mr Chris Elmers, Director)
The Museum of Rugby, Twickenham (Mr B. A. King, Librarian)
The National Maritime Museum, Greenwich (Mrs L. Verity and Ms B. Tomlinson)
The National Trust (the Curator, Chartwell, Kent)
The Oscar Wilde Society
The Royal Army Medical Corps (Captain A. Walker)
The Royal Hospital, Chelsea (Major Martin Snow)
The Royal Marines Museum, Southsea (Mr M. G. Little, Archivist)
The Royal Naval Volunteer Reserve (HMS *President*)
The Royal Tank Regiment (Colonel [Ret'd] J. L. O. Longman)
The St James's Club (Mr Cyril Stein, Chairman)
The Scout Association (Public Relations Department)
Shakespeare's Globe, Bankside (Ms Bianca Basnett)
The Sherlock Holmes Society of London (Ms Heather Owen)
United Westminster Schools (Mrs Mary Dobson, Foundation Secretary)
The Wimbledon Lawn Tennis Museum (Ms Audrey Snell, Assistant Librarian)
The Worshipful Company of Brewers (Ms P. MacGibbon, Archivist)
The Worshipful Company of Mercers (Mrs Ursula Carlyle, Archivist and Curator)
Mr Tomasz Zamoyski (Initiator, General Sikorski statue)

Published in 2002 by Shire Publications Ltd, Cromwell House, Church Street, Princes Risborough, Buckinghamshire HP27 9AA, UK. Website: www.shirebooks.co.uk
Copyright © 1968, 1995 and 2002 by Margaret Baker. First published in 1968 as 'Discovering London's Statues and Monuments'. Second edition 1980. Third edition, completely revised, 1992, as 'London Statues and Monuments'. Fourth edition 1995. Fifth edition, revised and updated and published as a 'Discovering Handbook', 2002. Number 42 in the Discovering series. ISBN 0 7478 0495 8.
Margaret Baker is hereby identified as the author of this work in accordance with Section 77 of the Copyright, Designs and Patents Act, 1988.

Printed in Malta by Gutenberg Press Limited, Gudja Road, Tarxien PLA 19, Malta.

was defaced with graffiti, demonstrated that even statues and memorials in very public places are prey to vandalism. But many organisations are working and watchful on their behalf: English Heritage, who recently splendidly restored the Albert Memorial and Constitution Arch (with a permanent exhibition on the London statues and monuments in its care), Friends of War Memorials, the Imperial War Museum and local councils among them.

And what else of the future? A worthy candidate for City commemoration must be Robert Hooke (1635–1703), the natural philosopher and City Surveyor after the Great Fire, who helped his friend Wren with his plans for rebuilding and with the design of the Monument (which he called the 'Fish Street Pillar'). The greatest experimental scientist of the seventeenth century, a member of the Royal Society, with the widest interests, Hooke's array of inventions included the universal joint, the anchor escapement, the iris diaphragm, the balance spring and, with Boyle, the air-pump. His buildings ranged from Bethlehem Hospital to the gazebo overlooking Greenwich Park. Hooke lived most of his life at Gresham College, as Professor of Geometry from 1665. His *Micrographia* (1665), the first important study of microscopy, dealt with many new topics, including wheel-barometers, thermometers and lens-grinding. Samuel Pepys sat up to 2 a.m. reading it and declared it to be 'the most ingenious book that I have ever read'. Arguments with Newton (partly provoked by Hooke's difficult temper and ill-health) clouded Hooke's career. He is little remembered today. An IRA bomb in 1992 destroyed his memorial window at St Helen's, Bishopsgate, his parish church. The tercentenary of his death in 2003 would be an excellent moment for the City to recall a unique scholar.

Surely it must be time too for a fitting statue of Joseph Mallord William Turner, doyen of English romantic artists. Others of lesser stature, such as Millais, Rossetti and Reynolds, have several memorials; Turner has one small relief portrait on a plaque in Queen Anne Street and a façade statue or two. His interpretations of London events, such as *The Burning of the Houses of Parliament* (1834), *The Funeral of Sir Thomas Lawrence at St Paul's* (1830) and, of course, his immortal *The Fighting Téméraire*, deserve better. As Turner himself remarked of painting in general, this neglect is 'a rum thing'.

Perhaps, too, for the steps of Eros there should be a flower girl with her basket. The cry of 'Violets, lovely violets' was the last of the old cries of London heard within living memory. When Lord Shaftesbury (whose memorial is Eros) died, the 'girls' (many of them grandmothers) sent a wreath inscribed 'The loving tribute of the flower girls of London'.

What is certain is that there will be no lack of candidates to add to the selection in this book, which is, of course, by no means exhaustive. There are still many discoveries to be made.

Joseph Durham's William Hogarth, painter, caricaturist and engraver, is in Leicester Square.

Nelson's Column in Trafalgar Square.

1.
CHARING CROSS, TRAFALGAR SQUARE AND LEICESTER SQUARE

In Charing Cross station's forecourt is an **Eleanor Cross**, a Victorian replica of one erected here in 1291 by Edward I, marking the last resting place of the body of his queen, Eleanor of Castile, on its way from Lincolnshire to burial at Westminster. The original cross was removed by Parliament in 1647 as an idolatrous object. The replica, by E. M. Barry and Thomas Earp, was erected in 1863 by the London, Chatham & Dover Railway Company.

On a traffic island facing down Whitehall from Trafalgar Square is the statue of **Charles I** (1600–49) by the Huguenot sculptor Hubert le Sueur. It was cast in 1633, removed during the Commonwealth and sold to a brazier named Rivett to be melted down. He made souvenirs supposedly from the metal but actually hid the statue in his garden and produced it for triumphal re-erection at the Restoration in 1660.

The King, only 5 feet 4 inches tall, wished he were taller. The statue's specification required 'the figure of his Maj. King Charles proportionable full six feet'. During the Second World War the statue was moved for safety to Mentmore, Buckinghamshire, and in 1947 was re-erected with a new sword in the King's hand. The original disappeared in 1867 when a reporter climbed on the statue for a better view of a procession and grabbed the sword to steady

George IV and Charles I in Trafalgar Square.

himself; it fell into the crowd and was never seen again. The sculptor's name and date appear on one of the hooves. Each year on 30th January, the anniversary of the King's execution, wreaths are laid, including in January 2001 one from the King Charles Club of St John's College, Oxford, whose members had first attended divine service in the Banqueting House, Whitehall, from which the King stepped to his death.

Sir Robert Peel called Trafalgar Square 'the finest site in Europe'. It was laid out in 1829–41 to Sir Charles Barry's design to commemorate Lord Nelson's victory over the Combined Fleets of France and Spain at Trafalgar on 21st October 1805. The fluted Corinthian column is surmounted by a 17 foot 4 inch statue by E. H. Baily of **Horatio, Viscount Nelson, Duke of Brontë** (1758–1805), England's perennial folk-hero. The column of Devon granite was designed by William Railton and is a copy of one at the temple of Mars Ultor in Rome. The foundation stone was laid by Charles Davison Scott, the son of Nelson's secretary killed at Trafalgar. The four reliefs of Nelson's victories on the base, cast from French cannon captured at the battles of St Vincent, the Nile, Copenhagen and Trafalgar, are the work of Watson, Woodington, Ternouth and Carew. At the base are four 11 foot lions by Sir Edwin Landseer, added in 1867. Cannon from the *Royal George*, which sank at Spithead in 1782, furnished metal for the capital. Before the statue was put in place in 1843, fourteen people dined precariously on top of the column. At the four corners of the square are octagonal lamps, said to have come from the *Victory*, Nelson's flagship. Lamplighters once received extra wages for cleaning these 'battle lamps'. In the nineteenth century admiring crowds watched steeplejacks scale the column on Trafalgar Day to crown the admiral with laurel. Today wreaths are laid round the base of the column by the Fleet and the Nelson Society, and all over the world ships and establishments of the Royal Navy and Royal Marines hold Trafalgar Night dinners, at which the traditional toast to Nelson's 'Immortal Memory' is drunk.

Other statues in the square include that of **Sir Henry Havelock** (1795–1857) by William Behnes, the first to be made from a photograph. Havelock took part in the First Anglo-Burmese War and the First Afghan War and, when the Indian Mutiny broke out in 1857, commanded a mobile column of the 78th Highlanders and loyal sepoys. His force, weakened by casualties, arrived too late to save the British women and children of the Cawnpore garrison, whose

The lions below Nelson's Column were added in 1867. The lion model died; Sir Edwin Landseer had to work quickly with a decaying carcass.

Sir Henry Havelock in Trafalgar Square.

bodies, to the anguish and anger of the troops, they found butchered and thrown down a well. They moved on to Lucknow, where, after four assaults using fixed bayonets (and panicking the Indian elephants with their bagpipes), they saved the garrison. For their bravery they won six Victoria Crosses. Havelock was a pioneer in caring for his soldiers' welfare and introduced reading-rooms and canteens to the cantonments. Perhaps less popular was his Army Temperance Society, whose members were accorded the soubriquet 'Havelock's Saints'. There are twelve streets in London named after him.

General Sir Charles James Napier (1782–1853), who has a statue by George Cannon Adams (1855), fought in the Irish Rebellion (1798), at Corunna (1808), at Chesapeake (1813) and from 1841 in India, where he led the Scinde Force (Napier used this spelling of the word). It was a successful campaign and he announced his victory at Hyderabad in 1843 with the punning signal *Peccavi* (I have sinned: I have Scinde), a subtle joke, since Napier had been told not to take Scinde, but to wait. Thus it would seem military success and contrition were both covered. The only British regiment in the Honourable East India Company force was Napier's 22nd (Cheshire) Regiment and he was its Colonel at the time of the campaign. The regiment, raised in 1689 and unamalgamated, continues vigorously today. It took the Cheshire title in 1882. Napier was a popular commander; the most numerous contributions to the statue fund were from private soldiers. In politics he was a radical, supported Chartism and worked tirelessly for his troops, introducing married quarters and becoming the first British general to mention private soldiers in dispatches. Today The Cheshire Regiment's retired regular officers belong to the Peccavi Club, and the regimental march of the 22nd (Cheshire) Regiment is 'Who wouldna fight for Charlie'. Twenty London streets are named after him.

In the north-east corner of the square is an equestrian statue of **George IV** (1762–1830) by Sir Francis Legatt Chantrey. Because of problems with the bill the statue was not erected until 1843. The subject selected the pose – he rides bareback without stirrups – and the Roman costume. Rather a show-off, he boasted to the Duke of Wellington of an equestrian feat on the Devil's Dyke, near Brighton. 'I once galloped down there at the head of my regiment,' said the King. 'Very steep, Sir,' replied the Duke.

The bronze bust of **John Rushworth, first Earl Jellicoe** (1859–1935), the British admiral, is by William Macmillan and was erected in 1948. Jellicoe is especially remembered for his command of the Grand Fleet in the First World War and for his part in the battle of Jutland in 1916. The bust of **David, first Earl Beatty** (1871–1936), who accepted the surrender of the German Grand Fleet at Scapa Flow in 1918, is by Sir Charles Wheeler. To these was added in 1967 a bust by Franta Belsky of **Admiral Lord Cunningham,** first Baron Cunningham of Hyndhope (1883–1963), noted for his brilliant aggressive

Busts of naval commanders Jellicoe, Cunningham and Beatty keep company with Nelson in Trafalgar Square.

strategy in the Second World War and author of one of the most famous naval signals of all time, on 11th September 1943: 'Be pleased to inform their Lordships that the Italian Battle Fleet now lies at anchor under the guns of the fortress of Malta'.

On the first floor of South Africa House, on the east side of the square, is a stone statue of **Bartolomeu Diaz** (or Dias) by Coert Steynberg (1934). To the statue's right is a column with the date 1488 and 'DIAS', to the left are a globe and a ship's stern. John II sent Diaz, a leading Portuguese navigator, on a voyage of discovery. He sailed down the West African coast, the first sailor to do so, and doubled the Cape of Good Hope, which he called *Cabo Tormentoso*, the 'Cape of Storms'.

In front of the National Gallery on the north side of the square is a bronze statue by Grinling Gibbons of **James II** (1633–1701), in Roman dress. The second surviving son of Charles I, he was overthrown in 1688 by William of Orange, two years after the statue's erection. Some regard this as the finest outdoor statue in London. The commissioner and donor was Tobias Rustat, Yeoman of the Robes.

Also in front of the Gallery is a bronze copy of Jean Antoine Houdon's distinguished marble statue at Richmond, Virginia, of **George Washington** (1732–99), the first President of the United States of America. It was presented by the State of Virginia in 1921 and was unveiled by Judith Bower, daughter of the Speaker of the Virginia House of Delegates. Some twenty castings have been made of the original; there are replicas in Montevideo, Lima, San Francisco and Versailles. Washington is in military uniform but holds a walking stick; his sword and riding cloak are thrown over a pillar. The thirteen bound staves represent the thirteen states of the new union. The statue is exactly 6 feet 2 inches high, Washington's height in life.

In St Martin's Place, by the National Portrait Gallery, is a statue of **Nurse Edith Cavell** (1865–1915), shot at Brussels in 1915 for alleged spying and assisting the escape of British and French soldiers after the retreat from Mons. The statue (1920) is by Sir George Frampton. To many, the execution was judicial murder. British tribunals throughout the First World War avoided passing the death sentence on women. Cavell's famous words, 'Patriotism is not enough', were added in 1924, four years after the monument's unveiling by Queen Alexandra. Edith Cavell is well remembered; a service of thanksgiving

Above: The stone statue of Diaz (or Dias) on the first floor of South Africa House.

James II, by Grinling Gibbons, and George Washington, on the lawns of the National Gallery.

was held in October 2000 by her grave in Norwich Cathedral.

On the north side of the National Portrait Gallery is Sir Thomas Brock's statue (1910) of **Sir Henry Irving** (1838–1905), the actor–manager who rose to fame in 1874 when he played Hamlet for two hundred nights. He often played opposite Ellen Terry as his leading lady. He was the outstanding theatrical personality of his day, magnetic with a passionate and intense, rather than resonant, voice, and was the first actor to be knighted (an honour he resisted for twelve years). His last words on stage, playing Becket, were 'Into thy hands O Lord …'. He died that same evening. The Irving Society visits the statue on Sir Henry's birthday to lay a commemorative wreath but it is no easy task. Because of his great height Irving was known as 'The Elevator of the Stage'. In 2000 the wreath was hoisted on to the plinth with the undignified aid of a golf umbrella. At the ceremony on 11th February 2001, in a new approach, the author Michael Kilgarriff, himself over 6 feet 5 inches tall, scaled the statue with the help of an aluminium ladder he had dragged across Covent Garden from the Theatre Museum.

In Adelaide Street, behind St Martin's-in-the-Fields, is Maggi Hambling's statue of **Oscar Wilde** (1856–1900), playwright, poet and wit, author of *The Importance of Being Earnest, Lady Windermere's Fan* and 'The Ballad of Reading Gaol'. The bronze head of Wilde, who is depicted smoking a cigarette, rises from a granite sarcophagus, forming a bench on which passers-by are invited to sit for 'A Conversation with Oscar Wilde'. It bears one of his finest lines: 'We are all in the gutter, but some of us are looking at the stars'. The statue was unveiled on 30th November 1998 by Wilde's grandson, Merlin Holland, his great-grandson, Lucian Holland, and the actor Stephen Fry, who starred in the film about Wilde. In 1899, as he lay dying, Wilde said, 'I will

Nurse Edith Cavell in St Martin's Place.

Left: Sir Thomas Brock's statue of Henry Irving.

Below: Oscar Wilde. Passers-by may stop for 'A Conversation with Oscar Wilde' in Adelaide Street.

never outlive the century'. He was thinking of physical existence but in a wider sense he could not have been more wrong. His plays are constantly performed, his wit relished and his letters, edited by his grandson and published in 2000, enhance our understanding of a complex character. Wilde held strong views about statues: 'To see statues of our departed statesmen in marble frockcoats and bronze double-breasted waistcoats adds a new horror to death'. Would he have liked his own?

St Martin's Lane runs north from St Martin's Place to Seven Dials, the meeting place of seven streets. A pillar here, supporting a clock with seven faces, was taken down in 1773 in a search for treasure reputed to be hidden beneath it. Nothing was found. The pillar was later re-erected on Weybridge Green, Surrey, to commemorate the long residence of Frederica, Duchess of York, at Oatlands. As part of the William and Mary tercentenary celebration in 1989 a new **Seven Dials Pillar** was raised and unveiled by Queen Beatrix of the Netherlands. The architect, A. D. Mason, worked from Edward Pierce's original plans, and the cream Doric pillar, made by trainee masons, carries blue and gold sundials. The original pillar formed part of Master of the Mint Thomas Neal's speculative property plans of 1693–1710 to develop a high-class residential area. They failed and the district became a notorious haunt of thieves, only improved with the cutting of the Charing Cross Road in the late 1880s. Today, Neal's Yard and Thomas Neal's Shopping Centre recall the pillar's origins.

Leicester Square became derelict in the 1860s. The resident statue of **George I** (1660–1727) was in a parlous state: it lacked arms and legs, and the horse, also wanting a leg, was propped up on sticks. In September 1866 it was white-washed. A letter to *The Times* 'from the statue itself' complained that one coat would be inadequate for the winter; overnight, black dapples were added and the king was given a dunce's cap and a broomstick for a lance. Crowds flocked to view it. Shortly afterwards the rider disappeared and the horse was sold for scrap.

Leicester Square is now an ornamental garden, laid out in 1874 and refurbished in 1990–2. In the centre is a marble statue of **William Shakespeare** (1564–1616), a copy of Scheemakers on a base designed by James Knowles, and at the corners busts of **Sir Joshua Reynolds** (1732–92) by Henry Weekes, **William Hogarth** (1697–1764) by Joseph Durham, **Sir Isaac Newton** (1642–1727) by Calder Marshall and **William Hunter** (1718–83) by Thomas Woolner, all of whom are associated with the square by residence or otherwise.

Also here, in the centre of the entertainment industry, stands a statue of **Charles Spencer Chaplin** (1889–1977), the London-born film actor and comedian. Discovered by Mack Sennett in about 1913, Charlie Chaplin soon became famous for his 'little man' character, whose trademark baggy trousers, bowler hat, cane and little moustache are faithfully portrayed in the statue sculpted by John Doubleday and unveiled in 1981 by Sir Ralph Richardson.

The Seven Dials Pillar.

The marble statue of Shakespeare in the centre of Leicester Square commemorates the gift of the area to the public by a local MP.

William Hunter in Leicester Square.

Charlie Chaplin's statue stands in Leicester Square, facing Shakespeare.

At the junction of Whitehall Court and Whitehall Place is The Royal Tank Regiment's memorial.

2.

WHITEHALL AND HORSE GUARDS

Whitehall leads from Trafalgar Square to Westminster. At the junction of Whitehall Court and Whitehall Place, between Whitehall and Northumberland Avenue, is the memorial to **The Royal Tank Regiment**. The 9 foot bronze group depicts a Comet tank crew of *c*.1945. Five figures, of driver, co-driver, gunner, loader and tank commander, symbolise the close bond between crew members, each of whom is identified by the equipment he carries. The sculptor was Vivien Mallock, working from the original design by G. J. Paulin. At least 50,000 men have served in tanks and some 5000 have died in action. The statue commemorates all those who have served and who continue to serve. Major General Sir Ernest Swinton conceived the idea of the tank on 13th June 1900 during the Boer War, and tanks went on to break the stalemate of trench warfare and the dominance of the machine gun on the battlefields of the First World War. The plinth is embossed with an interpretation of the flag flown on General Elles's tank during the Battle of Cambrai in 1917: 'From mud through blood to the green fields beyond'. Brown, red and green are the regimental colours. The statue was unveiled on 13th June 2000 by Queen Elizabeth II, Colonel-in-Chief of The Royal Tank Regiment, 'to commemorate the sacrifices made by the Tank crewmen during the Twentieth Century'. The memorial site is significant: between the Old War Office, where the decision to procure the first tank was taken, and the Metropole Building, where Colonel Swinton set up his office to recruit the first tank crews in 1916.

Opposite the Old War Office is a statue of the Duke of Cambridge.

In Whitehall, opposite the Old War Office, is an equestrian statue of the **second Duke of Cambridge** (1819–1904) by Adrian Jones. The Duke, Commander-in-Chief of the British Army from 1856 to 1895, is shown in field marshal's uniform, with plumes and whiskers flying. He is perhaps best remembered for the striking statement, 'Change, at any time, for whatever purpose, is to be deprecated'.

Between the Old War Office and the Banqueting House is a statue of the **eighth Duke of Devonshire** (1833–1908) by H. Hampton (1910). The Duke became Minister of War in 1882 and was partly responsible for sending General Gordon to Khartoum and for the failure to rescue him from the siege of the city. More pleasantly, he was a generous landlord and benefactor and an intimate friend of Edward VII, who often stayed with him. A modest man, the Duke is remembered for saying, 'The proudest moment of my life was when my pig won first prize at Skipton Fair'.

The first Gurkha regiment was formed in Nepal in 1815 by the East India Company, and nearly two hundred years later the first major **Gurkha Memorial** was unveiled by Queen Elizabeth II on 3rd December 1997. The 7 foot high bronze, by Philip Jackson, of a Gurkha in the uniform of the First World War, in which a hundred thousand Gurkhas served in the British army, stands in Horse Guards' Avenue. Gurkhas have won a total of thirteen Victoria Crosses. The Queen, with the Duke of Edinburgh, who is their Colonel-in-Chief, inspected a hundred-strong guard of honour from the First Battalion, Royal Gurkha Rifles. In

A Gurkha soldier in First World War uniform forms the Gurkha Memorial in Whitehall.

Viscount Wolseley, in Horse Guards' Parade.

September 2001 it was announced that a defining moment in the relationship between the British Army and its Gurkha soldiers would be recorded in a 7 foot painting by Jason Askew, which will probably hang at regimental headquarters at Folkestone, Kent. In 1857 in the battle of Delhi, in the Indian Mutiny, the Gurkhas, who remained loyal to the Crown, fought alongside British troops. The painting shows the Gurkhas and the 60th Rifles (now The Royal Green Jackets) repelling the mutineers' attack on the strategic Hindu Rao House on the ridge. The battle, a keystone of Gurkha history, featured on the decorated truncheon given to the Gurkhas by Queen Victoria in 1863. Lieutenant-Colonel Craig Lawrence of the Royal Gurkha Rifles said the battle marked 'the beginning of the friendship between the Nepalese and British troops that has lasted to this day'. The battle, which is commemorated each 9th September, lasted three months and took the lives of 327 Gurkhas – over half the battalion – who fought with their traditional weapon, the large *kukri* knife.

Horse Guards' Parade is the scene of Trooping the Colour on the sovereign's official birthday. Its statues include **Garnet Joseph, first Viscount Wolseley** (1833–1913), who served in the Indian Mutiny and the Crimea, commanded the expedition attempting to relieve Gordon at Khartoum, and was Commander-in-Chief of the British Army from 1895 to 1900. He was the prototype of Gilbert's Modern Major-General in *The Pirates of Penzance*. As a colonel he wrote *The Soldier's Pocket Book*, which covered every campaigning eventuality, from snakebite to singing on the march, and was used worldwide. His equestrian statue is by Sir William Goscombe John. When Sir Garnet was winning his battles in Egypt, the army phrase 'All Sir Garnet!' came into common use, meaning that everything is going well.

The equestrian statue of **Frederick Sleigh, first Earl Roberts of Kandahar and Waterford VC** (1832–1914), is by Harry Bates. Roberts commanded the British troops in the Boer War and in 1901 followed Wolseley as Commander-in-Chief. He died from a chill at St Omer, France, at the beginning of the First

The Cadiz Memorial, in Horse Guards' Parade, was presented to the Prince Regent. The statue of Earl Roberts can be seen in the background.

World War. The Earl was a fine horseman. His horse Volomel was named after a chieftain he had defeated in Assam. This spirited Arab grey, as famous as his owner, went with Roberts to Afghanistan and at Queen Victoria's insistence was given the Kabul to Kandahar Star and the Afghan War Medal with four clasps. Roberts rode Volomel in the Diamond Jubilee procession in 1897. Sittings for the statue were made while both man and horse were alive; the likenesses are said to be excellent.

Nearby is the cast-iron **Cadiz Memorial**, a French mortar mounted on a Chinese dragon, presented by the Spanish government to the Prince Regent to commemorate the raising of the siege of the city by the Duke of Wellington in 1812. It was nicknamed the 'Regent's Bomb' and appeared in many irreverent cartoons.

On the south side of Horse Guards' Parade there is a statue of **Horatio, first Earl Kitchener of Khartoum and of Brooke in Kent** (1850–1916), by John Tweed (1926). Kitchener fought in the Sudan, Egypt and the Boer War and reorganised the British army to embrace voluntary recruitment.

Kitchener's statue by John Tweed has a barbed-wire backdrop, appropriate for the man who set up prisoner of war camps in South Africa.

19

After the Dardanelles campaign he fell from favour and died when the cruiser *Hampshire* was sunk by the Germans in 1916. A difficult man, he was noted for his unwillingness to be advised.

The 9 foot 5 inch bronze statue by Franta Belsky of **Lord Mountbatten of Burma** (1900–79) stands on Foreign Office Green overlooking Horse Guards from the south. It shows him in the uniform of an Admiral of the Fleet and was unveiled by Queen Elizabeth II on 2nd November 1983. 'Dickie' Mountbatten, a great-grandson of Queen Victoria, was in pre-war years a handsome, dashing naval captain and socialite and later a statesman, admiral and socialist. He was an outstanding figure in the Second World War, Chief of Combined Operations Command (1941–3) and Supreme Allied Commander in South-east Asia (1943–6), when the British retook Burma. He was appointed Viceroy of India in 1947, Governor-General 1947–8, and supervised the transfer of power from Britain to India and Pakistan. He was made an earl in 1947. He returned to his naval career, becoming First Sea Lord in 1955 and Chief of the Defence Staff, 1959–65. He was assassinated by IRA terrorists while boating near his holiday home in Ireland in August 1979. He was not without critics but his achievements were many. His wife, Edwina, was as famous in her field of welfare and relief work as her husband was in his.

Facing Horse Guards from the west, a 36 foot high, 170 ton cenotaph in Portland stone designed by H. C. Bradshaw commemorates the men of the **Guards Division** killed in the First World War. It has bronze statues by Gilbert Ledward of guardsmen of the five regiments – Scots, Welsh, Irish, Coldstream and Grenadier. The figures were cast from guns captured by the brigade and the memorial was unveiled by the Duke of Connaught in 1926. Members of the Household Division who died in the Second World War and 'In the Service of their Country since 1918' are also remembered. The inscription is by Rudyard Kipling, whose only son, John, in the Irish Guards, was killed at the age of eighteen at the battle of Loos.

Back in Whitehall is the Banqueting House of Old Whitehall Palace. Above the entrance is a lead bust of **Charles I** (1600–49) dating from about 1800. It is the best of three such busts found in about 1945 in a builder's yard in Fulham

Lord Mountbatten of Burma stands on Foreign Office Green.

This Guards Memorial, opposite Horse Guards' Parade, commemorates the men of the Guards Division who were killed in the First World War and later.

by Hedley Hope-Nicholson, secretary to the Society of King Charles the Martyr, and placed here in 1950. The sculptor is unknown. Through a window of the Banqueting House (the precise one cannot be identified) the King stepped to his execution on 30th January 1649, first handing his George (the Order of the Garter whose jewel shows St George) to the Bishop of London, saying enigmatically, 'Remember'. Wreaths are laid here on the anniversary of the execution, to which he walked across St James's Park, his dog, Rogue, running at his side.

Opposite the Banqueting House is an equestrian statue by A. F. Hardiman of **Douglas, first Earl Haig** (1861–1928), who commanded the British forces from 1915 to 1918 in the First World War but was later denigrated for his policy of attrition. Haig was founder and first president of the British Legion. When the statue was erected in 1937 horsemen were quick to point out that the position of the horse's hind legs suggested equine urination. The sculptor was presumably ignorant of such matters. More recently Earl Haig's military reputation has been freshly and far more favourably assessed. On 29th January 2001, the anniversary of his death, the Douglas Haig Fellowship placed 'In Memoriam' notices in the national newspapers.

Southwards down Whitehall is the lawn in front of the Ministry of Defence, known as Raleigh Green, named after the statue of Sir Walter Raleigh which stood here until October 2001, after which it was transferred to Greenwich. Still here are three heroes of the Second World War. Field Marshal the **Viscount Slim** (1891–1970), who led the Fourteenth Army from 1943 to 1945, fought a memorable

Douglas, first Earl Haig, awkwardly seated opposite the Banqueting House, Whitehall.

21

One of three heroes of the Second World War whose statues are on Raleigh Green, in front of the Ministry of Defence, is Field Marshal the Viscount Slim.

campaign to recapture Burma from the Japanese. The statue, by Ivor Roberts-Jones, was commissioned by the Burma Star Association, and shows Slim in battledress and a slouch hat, holding binoculars. Both subject and sculptor held the Burma Star. After his campaign with the Fourteenth Army, Slim was Commander of Allied Land Forces, South East Asia Command, and succeeded Montgomery as Chief of the Imperial General Staff, 1948–52. From 1953 to 1960 he was Governor-General of Australia. Around the plinth are the names of battles Slim fought, from Rangoon to the Chindwin.

Next is the statue of Field Marshal the **Viscount Alanbrooke** (1883–1963), Winston Churchill's chief military advisor during the Second World War, also by Ivor Roberts-Jones. General Sir David Fraser, Alanbrooke's biographer, pronounced him 'doyen of Churchill's generals', forming with Winston Churchill 'an incomparable partnership'. However, the field marshal's secret wartime diaries, published in unexpurgated form for the first time in May 2001, reveal a less harmonious picture. Although Alanbrooke's cautious,

painstaking and logical approach to wartime decisions did restrain Churchill's boisterous and impulsive genius to good effect, for much of the time the two men could hardly stand one another. Alanbrooke forthrightly expressed his views on his political masters and military colleagues, writing, for example, of de Gaulle's 'megalomania' and Mountbatten's 'half-baked thoughts', describing Beaverbrook as an 'evil genius' and judging Eisenhower to be 'as a general … hopeless'.

The third statue on Raleigh Green is a small spare figure in battledress with the famous two-badged beret, the statue of **Viscount Montgomery of Alamein** (1887–1976), sculpted by Oscar Nemon. During 1979 over £30,000 was raised by public subscription for the statue, much of it from men of the

Viscount Alanbrooke who was Winston Churchill's chief military advisor, can also be found on Raleigh Green.

Each November a national service of remembrance is held at the Cenotaph in Whitehall, when wreaths of poppies are laid.

John Tweed's statue of Robert, first Baron Clive of Bengal, can be found at the top of the steps in Horse Guards' Road.

Eighth Army who served under Montgomery in the North African campaign in the Second World War. The simple inscription, 'Monty', conveys something of the great affection his troops felt for him. In 1944–6 Monty commanded British forces in France and Germany and accepted the German surrender at Lüneburg Heath in 1945. After the war his posts included Deputy Supreme Commander Europe (NATO) from 1951 to 1958, but he will for ever be associated with the Eighth Army (Desert Rats) and their victories from Egypt to Tunis. The extraordinary sense of comradeship that marked the Eighth Army was evident at the Desert Rats' reunions, which even members of the Afrika Korps asked to attend. On the night of Monty's death, Sir Brian Horrocks, who as commander of the Thirteenth Corps in North Africa held part of the El Alamein line against the German Afrika Korps in 1942, broadcast an obituary: 'A showman, difficult, autocratic – yes *all* these! But can any other general equal his achievements? ... he was the greatest British general since Wellington ... with the passing away of the Victor of Alamein Britain has lost one of her really great soldiers'. The *Daily Mirror* had the final word: 'His troops loved him and he won battles. Could any better tribute be paid to any general?'

In the centre of the road in Whitehall, the **Cenotaph** commemorates the fallen of the First and Second World Wars. Designed by Sir Edwin Lutyens, it was first constructed in plaster as a saluting base for the Victory March of 19th July 1919, was rebuilt in Portland stone and unveiled on Armistice Day, 11th November 1920, as Britain's national memorial. An additional inscription commemorating the dead of the Second World War was unveiled in 1946 by George VI. On the Sunday nearest to 11th November each year a national service of remembrance is held here, attended by the monarch, statesmen, and representatives of the diplomatic corps, Commonwealth and armed forces, together with, since 2000, civilian organisations such as ENSA (Entertainments National Service Association), whose members entertained the troops.

King Charles Street leads from Whitehall to Horse Guards' Road. At the top of the steps is John Tweed's statue (1916) of **Robert, first Baron Clive of Bengal** (1725–74). Reliefs show Clive at Plassey, the siege of Arcot and reading the Grant of Bengal. This restless, suicidal but brilliant man first went to India with the East India Company, became a soldier and founded the British Empire there, which was to last for nearly two hundred years. Arcot (1751) was

Left: *Oscar Nemon, sculptor of the statue of 'Monty', is seen here with the plaster cast of his statue prior to the erection of the finished work.*

Below: *The finished statue of Montgomery stands on Raleigh Green.*

called 'the turning point in the Eastern career of the English'. In 1753 Clive came home with a personal fortune but squandered it and returned to India to become Governor of Bengal from 1757 to 1760. He became Baron Clive in the Irish peerage in 1762 and three years later was back in Bengal reorganising the administration. A campaign began against him and although a parliamentary enquiry exonerated him his health was broken. He took to opium and ultimately died from an overdose.

Tradition has it that the young **Charles Dickens** (1812–70) visited the Red Lion Inn at the corner of Parliament Street (the southern end of Whitehall) and Derby Gate, announced that it was his birthday and was kissed by the landlady, an incident he used in *David Copperfield*. On the second floor of the inn is a terracotta head of Dickens by an unknown sculptor, dating from about 1900.

Appropriately, Sir Winston Churchill's statue in Parliament Square faces the House of Commons.

3.
WESTMINSTER TO MILLBANK

The long frontages of the Houses of Parliament, built between 1840 and 1850 by Sir Charles Barry, are decorated with statues and royal arms of **British sovereigns** from pre-Conquest times to Queen Victoria. The sculptor is John Thomas.

In New Palace Yard, Westminster, a fountain by the Polish sculptor Valenty Pytel celebrated **Queen Elizabeth II's Silver Jubilee**. Of galvanised steel struts painted black, it has symbols of the continents – a unicorn (Europe), a lion (Africa), an eagle (America), a tiger (Asia), a kangaroo (Australia) and a penguin (Antarctica) – surmounted by St Stephen's Crown. It was unveiled by the Queen on 4th May 1977.

Parliament Square, laid out by Barry to set off his buildings, was successfully rearranged in the 1960s. The central island's group of statues includes that of **Benjamin Disraeli, first Earl of Beaconsfield** (1804–81), Conservative statesman, man of letters and favourite of Victoria. The statue is by Mario Raggi (1883). Twice Prime Minister, three times Chancellor of the Exchequer, Disraeli, a colourful figure in nineteenth-century politics, reorganised the Conservative party on modern lines. His dash was coupled with foresight. In 1875 he purchased (on his own authority) £4,000,000 worth of shares in the Suez Canal from the Khedive of Egypt, thus securing power and wealth for Britain. Queen Victoria was susceptible to his charm and included his favourite flower, the primrose, in her funeral wreath. Each 19th April, 'Primrose Day', the statue was decorated with primrose wreaths. London florists regularly ran out of the

The statue of Disraeli in Parliament Square was unveiled in 1883. The event was recorded in the Illustrated London News.

flower. Disraeli was nobody's fool and understood the worth of his talents, once saying (although presumably not to Victoria), 'You have heard me accused of being a flatterer. It is true. I am a flatterer. I have found it very useful. Everyone likes flattery: and when it comes to royalty you should lay it on with a trowel.' On his deathbed he declined to see Victoria: 'She would only ask me to take a message to Albert!'

The fourteenth Earl of Derby and Field Marshal Jan Christian Smuts in Parliament Square.

The fourteenth Earl of Derby (1799–1869), an unmemorable but worthy statesman, who with Disraeli reshaped the Tory party, has a statue by Matthew Noble (1874) with panels showing his inauguration as Chancellor of Oxford University. St Stephen's Chapel, meeting place of the House of Commons before the disastrous fire of 1834, is depicted on the plinth.

The statue of the South African soldier and statesman **Field Marshal Jan Christian Smuts** (1870–1950) by Jacob Epstein is a vivid example of this sculptor's representational work, erected in 1956.

Facing the House of Commons is a statue of **Sir Winston Churchill** (1874–1965), perhaps the best known in London. Churchill, a many-faceted personality, is warmly remembered as Britain's wartime Prime Minister. It is this aspect that Ivor Roberts-Jones expressed in his vigorous 12 foot bronze statue, unveiled by Lady Spencer Churchill in 1973. The bareheaded figure, striding out in buttoned-up military greatcoat and grasping a walking stick, reflects an indomitable personality. Churchill had already had an exciting career as a soldier and war correspondent in the Boer War when he moved to politics, first as a Conservative, then as a Liberal, returning to the Conservatives to be Chancellor of the Exchequer from 1924 to 1929. Although out of office between 1930 and 1938, he warned repeatedly of the dangers of appeasing Hitler and of Britain's unpreparedness to deal with Nazi aggression. In May 1940 he became Prime Minister (commenting later, 'I felt as if I were walking with destiny'); he remained Prime Minister until his defeat by the

Labour party in 1945. His courageous independence of thought, perhaps a handicap in earlier years, came into its own in wartime days and Churchill became an international leader, radiating hope to enemy-occupied countries and expressing the British people's determination to beat Hitler. He was the outstanding orator of the twentieth century. In 1945 Churchill moved to 28 Hyde Park Gate, his home for the rest of his life. In 1946 he toured the United States of America (where he made his 'iron curtain' speech). He was Conservative Prime Minister again in 1951–5, resigned through ill-health, and died in 1965. He is buried at Bladon, Oxfordshire, near Blenheim Palace, his birthplace.

Churchill's works *The Second World War* (1948–51) and *The History of the English Speaking Peoples* (1956–8) confirmed his literary stature. He received the Nobel Prize for Literature in 1953 and, a talented painter, was made a Royal Academician Extraordinary in 1948. In 1963 he received honorary American citizenship. In a unique honour, on 10th March 2001 the US Navy named its latest ship *Winston Churchill*. The navigating officer is to be a lieutenant commander of the Royal Navy while an officer of the US Navy is to carry out similar duties on HMS *Marlborough*.

Also on the paved walk is a statue of **Henry Temple, third Viscount Palmerston** (1784–1865), by Thomas Woolner, erected in 1876. Palmerston personified Victorian self-confidence at its peak and, although he was accused of jingoism, his bluff, adventurous foreign policy was highly successful. Much of his success came from sheer hard work. An omnibus driver who regularly drove up Piccadilly pointed out to his passengers Palmerston's head bent late over the desk in his window, with the words, ''E earns 'is wages: I never comes by without seein' 'im 'ard at it'. Something of a man about town, Palmerston was first nicknamed 'Lord Cupid', but after Canning's death in 1827 he toughened up, sending gunboats to protect British interests and taking a firm line with recalcitrant ambassadors. He was renamed 'Lord Pumicestone'. His apogee of popularity came in 1867 with the Don Pacifico affair. David Pacifico (1784–1854), a Gibraltarian living in Athens, demanded compensation from the Greek government when a mob destroyed his house in 1847. They jibbed. Palmerston sent a fleet to blockade Piraeus from January to April 1850 and the Greeks compromised. In his great speech to the House of Commons explaining his policy Palmerston said: 'As the Roman, in days of old, held himself free from indignity, when he could say *Civis Romanus sum*; so also a British subject, in whatever land he may be, shall feel confident that the watchful eye and the strong arm of England will protect him against injustice and wrong'. The doctrine echoes to this day. It was quoted as recently as August 2001, when British citizens resident in Zimbabwe were attacked by squatters, supporters of President Robert Mugabe's Zanu-PF Party. Later Palmerston was seen as a father-figure and called himself 'bottle-holder' to the world's squabbling nations. (A bottle-holder held the combatants' coats during a fight and offered a reviving bottle afterwards.) Palmerston was witty to the end: on his deathbed he joked, 'Die, my dear doctor? That's the last thing I shall do!'

Facing the Houses of Parliament is a statue by Matthew Noble of **Sir Robert Peel** (1788–1850) erected in the year that he died after falling from his horse on Constitution Hill. Peel was noted for his administrative ability and intellectual honesty. Wellington said of him, 'I never knew a man in whose truth and justice I had more lively confidence'. Peel stated his philosophy plainly when he said, 'As a minister of the Crown I reserve to myself, distinctly and unequivocally, the right of adapting my conduct to the exigency of the

The statue of Abraham Lincoln is a copy of one in Chicago.

George Canning, briefly Prime Minister, has a statue paid for by public subscription.

moment'. This flexibility gave him rein to develop free trade, introduce income tax on all incomes over £150 *per annum* and support the Anti-Corn-Law League after having spent years opposing it. Peel is chiefly remembered as the founder of the modern police force, whose officers were nicknamed 'Peelers' or 'Bobbies'. The latter name sticks to this day. Peel was an administrator, with little charm. One observer said that Peel's smile reminded him of the gleam of a silver plate on a coffin.

On the west side of Parliament Square the statue of **Abraham Lincoln** (1809–65), sixteenth President of the United States of America, is a copy of that by Augustus Saint-Gaudens in Chicago and was presented by the American people in 1920. Lincoln, bitterly opposed to slavery, was assassinated by John Wilkes Booth, a supporter of the Southern states, while visiting Ford's Theatre, Washington.

Also here is Westmacott's bronze statue of **George Canning** (1770–1827). Canning was Foreign Secretary and, after Lord Liverpool's death in 1827, Prime Minister and Chancellor of the Exchequer. The statue was shadowed; it fell in the sculptor's studio, killing his assistant, Vincent Gahagan. Amid the strains of office, Canning kept his sense of humour, sometimes sending diplomatic messages in rhyme. On 31st January 1826, during a row over customs duties, Sir Charles Bagot, British ambassador in the Hague, was intrigued to receive instructions from London which, when deciphered, read:

> In matters of commerce the fault of the Dutch
> Is offering too little and asking too much.
> The French are with equal advantage content,
> So we clap on Dutch bottoms just twenty per cent!

A statue of **Oliver Cromwell** (1599–1658) by Sir William Hamo Thornycroft stands outside Westminster Hall. Erected in 1899, it shows Cromwell in uniform, bareheaded, with Bible and sword, reflecting two modern views of him. Was he the pious saviour of English freedom or a ruthless dictator? Cromwell came to prominence in the English Civil War of 1642–8, creating the New Model Army and becoming the leading soldier in England, a remarkable achievement for a man without military training. With needless brutality he crushed the Irish Royalists and this was not easily forgotten. In the 1840s Prince Albert's 'Committee of Taste' denied Cromwell a niche at the new Palace of Westminster. But the publication in 1845 of Carlyle's eulogistic edition of Cromwell's *Letters and Speeches* helped to soften public opinion. Even so, in 1895 Irish MPs strongly opposed the Liberal Party's wish to vote £500 to the statue fund. In the end the Prime Minister, Lord Rosebery, made a gift of the statue. Admirers lay wreaths to Cromwell's memory each year.

Above: *Oliver Cromwell outside Westminster Hall.*

Below: *The bronze statue of Richard I, Coeur de Lion.*

At the north end of Old Palace Yard is the bronze statue of **Richard I**, Coeur de Lion (1157–99), England's most popular medieval king. The statue (1851) is the *chef d'oeuvre* of Carlo Marochetti (1805–68). The King's sword was bent by a bomb in the Second World War. Reliefs show Richard in battle and the archer who mortally wounded him being brought to the dying King to be pardoned (although he was treacherously flayed alive the moment the King died).

Across the road from Old Palace Yard is the national memorial to **George V**

(1865–1936) by Sir William Reid Dick (the King's Sculptor in Ordinary) and Sir Giles Gilbert Scott. The full-length figure, in the uniform of a field marshal, with Garter robes and Sword of State, was unveiled on 22nd October 1947 by George VI.

In Victoria Tower Gardens stands the bronze group of **The Burghers of Calais** (1915) by Auguste Rodin, a replica of the sculpture erected in Calais in 1895. In the fourteenth century the burghers surrendered themselves to Edward III, with halters round their necks, to save their town.

Mrs Emmeline Pankhurst (1858–1928), leader of the women's suffrage movement, frequently arrested and imprisoned for her beliefs, has a statue by A. G. Walker, erected in 1930 and unveiled by Stanley Baldwin. Her daughter, **Dame Christabel Pankhurst** (1881–1958), also a suffragette, is commemorated by a bronze medallion. One thousand women were imprisoned and many went on hunger strike. Women who had starved themselves almost to death were released and, under the 'Cat and Mouse Act', were re-arrested once they had recovered their health. The First World War changed everything. Women were eventually given the vote in 1918 (but only women aged thirty or more; equal voting rights with men were not passed until 1928). Touchingly, the band of the Metropolitan Police, who had arrested many of the suffragettes, played at the unveiling. Mrs Pankhurst was the last rioter to be confined in the special cell in St Stephen's Tower for agitators causing trouble in the Palace of Westminster.

Further south in the gardens is the **Buxton Memorial Fountain** by S. S. Teulon (1865), commemorating Sir Thomas Fowell Buxton (1786–1845), MP for Weymouth. In 1824 he became leader of the anti-slavery party, which worked to free slaves in the British dominions and elsewhere. The fountain was erected by Buxton's son Charles, also an MP.

The church of St Margaret, Westminster, in the shadow of Westminster Abbey, has another of the lead busts of **Charles I** found by Hope-Nicholson (see Chapter 2). It was bought by the rector, Canon Charles Smyth, who placed it in a niche on the external east wall of the church, to face Oliver Cromwell opposite. Cromwell's eyes are, appropriately, cast down. The sculptor is unknown.

In the east porch of St Margaret's is a stone bust of **Robert Lowe, Viscount Sherbrooke** (1811–92), MP for Kidderminster and later for Calne. His interests were diverse: he supported the public libraries bill, opposed decimal coinage and demanded full compensation for farmers affected by the Cattle Plague Act. An eloquent speaker, 'he neither flattered nor concealed the truth' but 'in force of sarcasm excelled all his contemporaries …'. Certain MPs he could not abide and he showed it, but the public were attracted by his good looks and his strange white hair and eyebrows. When he proposed a tax on matches he suggested as a motto for the box *'Ex luce lucellum'* – 'Out of light a little gain': the alarmed match manufacturers organised a march to Westminster from the East End of their women workers; the proposal was defeated. In addition to these varied activities Viscount Sherbrooke was 'an ardent advocate of bicycling' but not, it would seem, a very safe one. When, as Chancellor of the Exchequer, he was riding his penny-farthing bicycle at Kenley, Surrey, he somehow managed to run down and fatally injure a local greengrocer.

Ten statues of **modern martyrs,** sculpted by Tim Crawley, John Roberts, Andrew Tanser and Neil Simmons in French Richemont limestone, were unveiled on the west front of Westminster Abbey by the Archbishop of

Above left: *Rodin's The 'Burghers of Calais' in Victoria Tower Gardens.*

Above right: *The Buxton Memorial Fountain can be found in the southern part of Victoria Tower Gardens.*

Below left: *This statue to suffragette Mrs Emmeline Pankhurst was erected in 1930 and unveiled by Stanley Baldwin.*

Below right: *This bronze scroll commemorating the suffragette movement is in Victoria Street.*

Modern martyrs now occupy niches on the west front of Westminster Abbey, empty since the Middle Ages.

Canterbury, George Carey, on 9th July 1998. The niches for the statues had been empty since the Middle Ages. The martyrs, chosen from different continents, reflect 'the major areas of persecution and oppression' in the twentieth century. They are, from left to right: Maximilian Kolbe (a Catholic priest who aided Jews in Nazi-held Poland, killed in Auschwitz in 1941 after offering to take the place of a condemned man); Manche Masemola (a South African who converted to Anglicanism, killed at the age of sixteen by her animist parents in 1928); Janani Luwum (the Anglican Archbishop of Uganda arrested in 1977 on the orders of Idi Amin and murdered); Grand-duchess Elizabeth Feodorovna (the cousin of Tsar Nicholas II, thrown down a mineshaft by Bolsheviks in the Russian Revolution); Martin Luther King (Baptist minister and American civil rights campaigner, assassinated in 1969 by James Earl Ray); Oscar Romero (the Archbishop of San Salvador, who spoke out against the regime and was assassinated by a right-wing death squad in 1980); Dietrich Bonhoeffer (a German Lutheran theologian involved in the failed putsch against Hitler in July 1944 and executed a month before VE Day); Esther John (a Presbyterian evangelist in Pakistan, thought to have been killed by a Muslim relative); Lucian Tapledi (an Anglican in Papua New Guinea, who was killed by invading Japanese forces in 1942); and Wang Zhiming (a pastor in China, arrested in 1969 during the Cultural Revolution and executed in 1973).

Other **figures round the Abbey**, designed by Sir George Gilbert Scott and J. L. Pearson, include apostles, royal builders, archangels and those associated with many aspects of Christianity (such as Langham, the only abbot to become a cardinal and Archbishop of Canterbury).

West of the Abbey, by the Broad Sanctuary, a red granite column by Scott, with sculpture by J. P. Philip, commemorates the **Old Boys of Westminster School** who died in the Crimean War and Indian Mutiny.

Over the entrance to Caxton Hall, just off Victoria Street, are terracotta statues of **Queen Victoria** and **Edward VII**, dating from 1902.

Further down Victoria Street, where Broadway skirts New Scotland Yard, an upright scroll finished in cold cast bronze by Edwin Russell, erected in 1970, is inscribed: 'This tribute is erected by the **Suffragette Fellowship** to commemorate the courage and perseverance of all those men and women in the long struggle for votes for women who selflessly braved derision, opposition and ostracism, many enduring physical violence and suffering'.

Henry Purcell (1659–95), composer and organist, whose work was 'The flowering of the English Baroque', is commemorated at the corner of Broadway and Victoria Street. Organist at Westminster Abbey and the Chapel Royal, Purcell is perhaps best remembered for his opera 'Dido and Aeneas', for his

Glynn Williams's unusual depiction of Purcell was unveiled by HRH Princess Margaret in 1995.

settings of the songs from Shakespeare's *Tempest,* and for his celebratory odes. The sculpture, by Glynn Williams, is in the form of a face peering through leaves, reminiscent of the 'Green Man' carvings in English churches.

In the early eighteenth century, in an Anglican response to the rise of Dissent, charity schools were set up to provide elementary education and religious instruction for poor children aged between seven and sixteen, who left with money for apprenticeships. The **Blewcoat School** in Caxton Street was founded in 1688 for fifty poor boys; in 1713 thirty girls joined them. In a niche over the entrance is the figure of a charity boy in full-skirted blue coat with seven buttons, white bands and orange stockings, the uniform of 1709. The building is now a National Trust shop.

In Greycoat Place, south of Victoria Street, is the **Grey Coat Hospital**, founded in 1695, a charity school for forty boys and forty girls. The present building dates from 1701. In niches over the door, flanking the Coadestone Royal Arms, are eighteenth-century painted wooden figures of a girl and a boy in grey uniforms. The school still flourishes, now for girls only.

A stone bust of **the Reverend James Palmer** in an elegant architectural surround occupies a niche in the brick chimney of his almshouses at 42 Rochester Row, facing Vincent Square. These were established for six poor old men and six poor old women in Palmer's Passage in 1656 and re-erected in 1881 when Victoria Street was being built. The building of Victoria Street, from Victoria station to the Broad Sanctuary, was projected in 1844 but was not fully completed until the 1880s. The work entailed the clearance of much slum

The Reverend James Palmer's bust decorates his almshouses in Rochester Row.

property and 'Palmer's Village', named after James Palmer, who built several groups of almshouses there in the mid seventeenth century. Palmer Street, on the north side of Victoria Street, is named after him.

On 29th November 2000 the Duke of York unveiled a **cross** 50 feet high and 25 feet wide on the piazza of **Westminster Cathedral,** Victoria Street, to mark the beginning of the third millennium. It was the vision of Cardinal Basil Hume, who died in 1999, and its placing was an ecumenical project to which hundreds of donors, including the Queen, contributed. As the pinewood and steel cross was unveiled, trumpeters of The Life Guards sounded a fanfare. The Archbishop of Westminster dedicated it to Cardinal Hume's memory. Later it will be placed at Ampleforth Abbey in Yorkshire, where he had been Abbot.

In front of Westminster City School, Palace Street, stands a bronze statue by Frank Taubman of **Sir Sydney Hedley Waterlow**, Lord Mayor of London and first chairman of the school's governors from 1873, a position he held for thirty-three years. The statue was set up in 1901, during Sir Sydney's lifetime, and is a replica of the one in Waterlow Park, Highgate.

When Sir Sydney (1822–1906) gave his thirty-acre estate to London County Council, in recognition, a statue of him was set up in the park. In classic fashion Sir Sydney had risen from boy apprentice to head of his firm, Waterlow & Sons. He is remembered for 'indefatigable energy in developing the School property, of liberality and skill in administering the funds, of unwearied zeal in the cause of education ...' and his work helped to make Westminster City School one of the leading schools in London. Today, with Emanuel and Sutton Valence schools, it forms part of the United Westminster Schools. There is a minor variation between the statues; in Waterlow Park, Sir Sydney holds the keys of the park in his left hand; in Westminster, a document. In both he holds an umbrella, a unique feature among London statues.

'Lioness and Lesser Kudu' in Upper Grosvenor Gardens.

At the end of Victoria Street, north-east of the station, **Little Ben,** a 30 foot standing clock in the shape of Big Ben, stood until removed for road widening. It was replaced to commemorate the marriage in 1981 of the Prince of Wales and Lady Diana Spencer.

Facing Victoria station across Buckingham Palace Road is a copy of the statue at Cassel, France, of **Marshal Ferdinand Foch** (1851–1929) by G. Mallisard. It was unveiled by the then Prince of Wales in June 1930 and commemorates France's most famous general and Allied leader of the First World War, who was made a field marshal of Britain and given the Order of Merit. On the plinth are Foch's words: 'I am conscious of having served England as I served my country'.

At the corner of Grosvenor Gardens and Hobart Place stands the memorial by John Tweed (1924) to the officers and men of **The Rifle Brigade** who fell in the two world wars. It depicts on the left a rifleman of 1806, an officer of 1800 to the right, surmounted by a rifleman of the First World War. The Rifle Brigade, now part of The Royal Green Jackets, celebrated its bicentenary in 2000. Twenty-seven Riflemen have won the Victoria Cross.

In the gardens behind the Rifle Brigade is Jonathan Kenworthy's powerful bronze **Lioness and Lesser Kudu,** commissioned by the Duke of Westminster 'to mark the opening of Upper Grosvenor Gardens to the people of Westminster, 13th June 2000'.

On the wall of the **Belgian Embassy**, 103 Eaton Square, is a plaque with the inscription: 'Here many Belgians volunteered during World War Two to fight with their allies on land, sea and air, to liberate their country. Those who gave their lives will not be forgotten.' This

The statue of Marshal Ferdinand Foch faces Victoria Station.

Mozart as a child with violin and bow, in Orange Square.

plaque was unveiled by Her Majesty Queen Elizabeth the Queen Mother on 21st June 1964.

Wolfgang Amadeus Mozart (1756–91) was born in Salzburg and travelled with his father to Germany, Paris and London, his infant talents acclaimed. A bronze statue by Philip Jackson of the composer as a child holding his bow and violin stands in Orange Square, at the junction of Ebury Street and Pimlico Road, Belgravia. Here in 1764, at the age of eight, he composed his first symphony.

At the south end of St George's Drive, at the junction with Denbigh Street, south-east of Victoria station, is William Fawke's statue of **Thomas Cubitt** (1788–1855), master builder and developer. The statue, which stands on a site donated by the Sanctuary Housing Association, shows Cubitt at work with bricks and the tools of his trade. It was unveiled by the Duke of Westminster on 23rd May 1995. After a voyage to India as a journeyman carpenter (he was a carpenter's son), Cubitt set up in London as a housebuilder, the first man to undertake the whole project himself. After building villas in Highbury and elsewhere, he leased land from the Duke of Bedford in 1824 and built such properties as Woburn Place, Gordon Square and Tavistock Square. Aware of the fashion to move west, he leased the 'Five Fields', Chelsea, with adjacent land, developing Belgrave Square, Lowndes Square and Chesham Place, and filling the vast area between Eaton Square and the river, now Pimlico. Queen Victoria consulted Cubitt about alterations to Osborne House, and he also worked on Buckingham Palace and other Crown properties. His interests were wide: from charitable work to sewage problems; from smoke emission and the Building Act to embanking the Thames (he paid for 3000 feet of this work near Belgravia himself). He negotiated the purchase of property for the Great Exhibition of 1851 and when its success seemed threatened provided financial backing. He

The statue of Thomas Cubitt, builder and developer, shows him at work with bricks and tools.

The statue of William Huskisson in Pimlico Gardens.

was a thoughtful employer; when in 1854 his premises burned down and he lost £30,000, his first words on hearing this dire news were: 'Tell the men they shall be at work again within a week and I will subscribe £600 towards buying them new tools'. His will, generous to charity, was the longest on record, covering 386 Chancery folios and thirty skins of parchment. *The Builder*, in its obituary, accurately described him as 'a great builder and a good man'.

East of Vauxhall Bridge, in Pimlico Gardens by the river, is a statue of **William Huskisson** (1770–1830), MP for Liverpool, the first man to be killed by a railway train. The statue, by John Gibson, shows Huskisson in Roman senatorial dress (described by Sir Osbert Sitwell as 'boredom rising from the bath'). The accident occurred at the opening of the Liverpool & Manchester Railway on 15th September 1830. The Duke of Wellington, Sir Robert Peel and Huskisson were among the crowd of guests when the engines stopped to take in water at Parkside. Huskisson strolled with others along the line. As they returned to their seats a second train drew up, a door swung back and Huskisson was thrown under the wheels. His thigh crushed, he murmured, 'I have met my death,' and died that night in Eccles parsonage. The Duke of Wellington, who did not like Huskisson, is said to have described the accident as 'an act of God'.

A statue of **Sir John Everett Millais** (1829–96), brush and palette in hand, which stood outside Tate Britain in Millbank, which (as the Tate Gallery) he helped to found, has been moved to the back of the building, at the junction of John Islip Street and Atterbury Street. Millais, a prodigy, the youngest ever pupil at the Royal Academy Schools in 1840, founded with Rossetti and

Sir John Everett Millais can be found at the back of Tate Britain.

40

Noble's statue of Sir James McGrigor, the Director-General of the Army Medical Department, faces Tate Britain.

Holman Hunt the Pre-Raphaelite Brotherhood. Under its influence he produced such works as *The Carpenter's Shop* (1850). Millais then turned himself into a fashionable genre painter, forsaking Pre-Raphaelite principles with works such as *The Boyhood of Raleigh*, *The Order of Release* and *Bubbles*. When *The Graphic* published a print of his *Cherry Ripe* (for which his children were models) 160,000 copies were sold within a week. To august sitters such as Gladstone, Disraeli and Carlyle he showed a cheerful, confident face. When Cardinal Newman attended for this purpose and hesitated before mounting the 'throne', Millais encouraged him with 'Jump up, jump up, you dear old boy!' He was knighted in 1895, the first artist to be so honoured, became President of the Royal Academy in 1896 and died during his year of office. He said, 'One day the inspiration comes. And then it goes. It's all stomach,' – words which will strike a familiar chord with all artists.

When Sir Henry Tate, the sugar baron, financed the building of Tate Britain (formerly the Tate Gallery) and gave his collection of paintings to it, he required that there be a **Britannia** over the portico, flanked by a **lion** and a **unicorn**.

In Atterbury Street, by the side of the Tate, is the former Royal Army Medical Corps building with Noble's statue of **Sir James McGrigor** (1771–1858), Director-General of the Army Medical Department (1815–51). A bollard behind the McGrigor statue was presented to the RAMC by the City of Westminster. It stood at the head of the river steps and was used by barges, which until 1867 moored here to load prisoners sentenced to transportation to Australia. Millbank prison stood on this site; it was closed in 1890 and demolished in 1903.

Alfred Mond (1868–1939) was a Liberal MP and cabinet minister, and when head of Mond Chemicals helped to found Imperial Chemical Industries (ICI) in 1926. Created **Baron Melchett** in 1928, he was ICI's first chairman. ICI built their headquarters on Millbank, facing Lambeth Bridge, in 1929 and, instead of a keystone over the centre window on the seventh floor, set a projecting bust of Lord Melchett, four-times life-size, together with heads of illustrious chemists and ICI directors.

4.
CHELSEA AND BATTERSEA

On a brick surround, opposite Chelsea Bridge, is a memorial, erected in 1905, to the men of the **6th Dragoon Guards, the Carabiniers**, who died in the Boer War. Adrian Jones's bronze plaque consists of a mounted officer and three troopers, a trophy of flags and the regimental badge surmounted by a plumed helmet.

In the Figure Court of the Royal Hospital, Chelsea, an institution for old and invalid soldiers built by Wren in 1682–92, is a statue by Grinling Gibbons of **Charles II** (1630–85), the hospital's founder, in Roman dress. Like James II's statue in Trafalgar Square, it was commissioned by Tobias Rustat, Yeoman of the Robes. On 29th May, Charles's birthday, 'Oak Apple Day', the statue is wreathed in oak leaves to commemorate the King's hiding in the Boscobel Oak on 6th September 1651, during his flight after the battle of Worcester. Parliamentary troops searched the surrounding woods but the leaves hid the King and saved the monarchy. On this day the pensioners wear sprigs of oak leaves, receive double rations and give three cheers for 'Our Pious Founder' and for 'the Sovereign'.

On 4th May 2000, at the north front of the Royal Hospital, the sixth Duke of Westminster unveiled a statue of a **Chelsea In-pensioner** to mark the new millennium and over three hundred years of the hospital's history. The bronze statue, of heroic size, is by Philip Jackson and complements that of Charles II. The gift of the sixth Duke of Westminster (himself a brigadier in the Territorial Army) and the Westminster Foundation, it depicts an in-pensioner in the famous full-dress scarlet uniform coat and tricorne hat; he raises his stick in salute to past comrades and holds an oak branch, symbolising the link with Charles II. No particular pensioner was used as a model; the sculptor wanted a

The plaque on the Carabiniers' memorial, Chelsea.

composite of the some three hundred veterans at the hospital and 'tried to capture the heroism, military bearing and enthusiasm for a life well lived'. The pensioners, all former soldiers and non-commissioned officers, took a great interest in all aspects of the statue project.

The Royal Hospital exemplifies tradition but tradition can be waived. In November 2001 it was announced that the hospital would soon admit its first female pensioners. Until recently only the Union Flag and the Royal Ensign (during royal visits) have ever flown from the hospital's flagstaff. An exception to the rule occurred in October 2001 when United States General Henry Shelton was knighted at the hospital. The Stars and Stripes flew again on 22nd November 2001 in memory of the terrorist attacks of 11th September. A hospital spokesman explained: '... the hospital governor, General

Sir Jeremy Mackenzie, ... decided to fly the flag again on Thanksgiving Day, in sympathy with the American people'.

In the hospital grounds a granite obelisk (1853) by Cockerell commemorates the 255 officers and men of the 24th Regiment who died at the **battle of Chillianwallah** on 13th January 1849 in the Second Sikh War. After Sir Hugh Gough's decisive victory of Goojerat the Sikhs finally came under British rule. In May 1999 a wreath-laying ceremony by the 2nd Battalion, Royal Regiment of Wales, marked the 150th anniversary of the battle. On that day the obelisk was, by chance, in the middle of a flower show tent: Chelsea Flower Show is held annually in the hospital grounds.

The Chillianwallah Column in the grounds of the Royal Hospital, Chelsea.

This statue of Sir Hans Sloane in Chelsea Physic Garden is a replica; the original is now in the foyer of the British Museum.

The Boy David (above left) and the bronze nude, Atlanta, (above right) on the Chelsea Embankment by the Albert Bridge.

In Chelsea Physic Garden, established by the Apothecaries' Company in 1676, is a replica of a robed and wigged statue of **Sir Hans Sloane** (1660–1753) by John Michael Rysbrack (1737), now in the foyer of the British Museum. Sloane, physician and naturalist, presented the garden's site to the company in 1722 on condition that two thousand distinct plants grown there be presented ('well dried and preserved', in annual instalments of fifty) to the Royal Society, of which he was President, 1727–40. Seeds and plants from the garden are used worldwide in research. The first cedars grown in England were planted here, and in 1732 cotton seed was sent to America to found the Southern plantations.

The completion of Sir Joseph Bazalgette's **Chelsea Embankment** in 1874 is commemorated by two lamp columns with cherubs and cornucopias, one on the river wall by Cadogan Pier east of the Albert Bridge, the other at the end of Old Church Street.

In the gardens facing Cadogan Pier is **The Boy David** by E. Bainbridge Copnall, replacing a statue by Francis Derwent Wood that was stolen in 1963. By the other side of the bridge a bronze nude, **Atlanta** by Derwent Wood, was erected in 1929 as a tribute to the artist (who died in 1926) from his friends, particularly those in the Chelsea Arts Club.

Also in these gardens, opposite 16 Cheyne Walk, his former home, is a memorial fountain to **Dante Gabriel Rossetti** (1828–82), designed by J. P. Sedding, with a bronze medallion by Ford Madox Brown (1887). Rossetti, artist

Left: *Dante Gabriel Rossetti by Cheyne Walk.*

Below: *Thomas Carlyle, 'the sage of Chelsea', can be found in Cheyne Row.*

and poet, is depicted with palette and books, linking his gifts as poet, painter and a principal founder of the Pre-Raphaelite Brotherhood. The fountain was unveiled by Holman Hunt. Rossetti kept a menagerie in his back garden, seriously annoying his neighbours. It included a bull, a white peacock, a kangaroo and a raccoon. His wombat had a taste for ladies' hats. When one visitor lost her hat, Rossetti was unsympathetic, merely remarking: 'Poor wombat. *Very* indigestible.' As a consequence local house leases still expressly forbid the keeping of such creatures.

In Oakley Street, at the north end of the Albert Bridge by Pier House, is a life-sized figure of a **Boy with a Dolphin** (1975), by David Wynne. It is inscribed, 'In memoriam Roland David Wynne 1964–1999'. Roland had acted as model for the sculpture. The piece is regarded as Wynne's best work. Another work, 'Girl with a Dolphin', in St Katherine's Way, treats the same theme, but less successfully.

In Cheyne Row, west of Albert Bridge, is a statue of **Thomas Carlyle** (1795–1881), essayist and historian, by Boehm. Erected in 1882, 'an uncanny likeness', it shows Carlyle seated on his study chair, books piled beside him, looking thoughtfully across the Thames. Thomas Carlyle and his wife moved to London in 1834 and lived at 24 Cheyne Walk (now a National Trust property with Carlyle relics), where in 1837 he wrote *The French Revolution*, the work which brought him fame and membership of a literary circle including John Stuart Mill and Leigh Hunt. Carlyle's critics accused him, with some

Sir Thomas More, outside Chelsea Old Church where he worshipped. By L. Cubitt Bevis, it was unveiled in 1969 by the Speaker of the House of Commons.

justification, of an obsession with violence and a contempt for the rights of individuals, but his vibrant rhetorical prose broke completely with the dry style of earlier historians, causing one of them to remark: 'As a picturesque historian Carlyle has no equal'. At 24 Cheyne Walk there is a Portland stone **medallion of Carlyle** by C. F. A. Voysey and B. Creswick (1901).

The statue of **Sir Thomas More** (1478–1535) stands outside Chelsea Old Church, where he worshipped with a humility that prompted him to sing in the choir dressed in an ordinary surplice. 'God's body, my Lord Chancellor, a parish clerk?' said the Duke of Norfolk when he saw him. More, a brilliant, civilised and witty Renaissance scholar, and author of *Utopia* (1516), was one of a group embracing Erasmus and John Colet. He succeeded Wolsey as Lord Chancellor, 1529–32. His relationship with Henry VIII was at first jovial and intimate but he (like Becket) proved to be an obdurate Chancellor, strongly disagreeing with the King's wishes to divorce Catherine of Aragon, to relax the heresy laws and to enhance royal supremacy. In 1532 More resigned, incurring Henry's fury for refusing to sign the compulsory oath conceding these points. He was imprisoned in the Tower, tried, found guilty of treason, and executed on 6th July 1535. He was buried in the Tower chapel of St Peter ad Vincula and his head, as befitted a 'traitor', was tarred and nailed up on London Bridge. But it has long been a tradition that Margaret Roper, his daughter, secretly retrieved the head for burial at St Dunstan's, Canterbury. He was canonised by the Catholic Church in 1935 and in September 2000 the Pope announced that More was to become patron saint of politicians, of whose arts he was no mean exponent.

In 1712 Sir Hans Sloane purchased the Manor of Chelsea and on his retirement from medical practice settled on his estate here. He and his wife are buried in the churchyard and behind the More statue is a large **urn**, under a canopy supported by columns, by Joseph Wilton, put up by Sloane's daughters. Sloane presented six chained books to Chelsea Old Church, the only chained books in any London church.

Between the More statue and the Embankment is a 10 foot grey marble drinking-fountain commemorating **George Sparkes**, a judge at Madras in the service of the East India Company, who died in 1878. It was erected by his widow in 1880.

Opposite Chelsea Old Church are **Roper Gardens**, opened in 1964. Part of this land was a marriage gift from Sir Thomas More to his favourite daughter Margaret when she married William Roper in 1544. A bronze plaque records the story.

In Roper Gardens is a statue entitled **Awakening**, a full-size bronze nude girl on a tall plinth, by Gilbert Ledward (1880–1960). The girl holds up her hands as though waking from sleep.

Also here is a 4 foot carved relief of a figure by **Jacob Epstein**, commemorating the years 1909–14, when he lived and worked 'in a studio on this site'. The relief was unveiled on 3rd June 1972 by Admiral Sir Caspar John, son of Augustus John, the artist.

In the Roper Gardens lawn in front of an appropriately chosen flowering Japanese cherry tree is a marble plaque commemorating **Guni Koizumi** (1885–1965), 'Father of British Judo'.

In King's Road, opposite Oakley Street, a graceful obelisk, its inscription effaced by age, commemorates **Andrew Millar**, the Scottish bookseller of the Strand, who published Johnson's *Dictionary* in 1755. The obelisk (*c.*1760)

stands on Dove House Green, an open space planned by the Chelsea Society to mark Queen Elizabeth II's Silver Jubilee in 1977 and the society's fiftieth anniversary. It had been part of the old burial ground given to the people of Chelsea by Sir Hans Sloane.

Battersea Park extends along the Thames from Chelsea Bridge to Albert Bridge. A memorial to the **24th (East Surrey) Division** by Eric Kennington stands here. Kennington's friend, the poet Robert Graves, himself a captain in The Royal Welsh Fusiliers, acted as model for one of the soldiers shown standing close together as if in a trench, symbolic of comradeship.

Sloane's monument at Chelsea Old Church.

48

Robert Graves, the poet, acted as a model for the 24th Division memorial in Battersea Park.

The memorial, erected in 1924, is a rare First World War memorial in modern style. It is in the eastern part of the park towards Chelsea Bridge, by the path to the bandstand, and is the focus of wreath-laying on Remembrance Sunday.

Close by is a memorial to the 5397 **Australian Air Crew** lost in action over Europe during the Second World War. It has a carved crest and was unveiled on 16th May 1995 by the Air Force Advisor to the Australian High Commission.

Nearby is another memorial, with a bronze map of the **Anzac battlefield** in the Gallipoli Campaign, commemorating those who lost their lives in the failed expedition of 1915. Australian and New Zealand troops played a major role in the battle and suffered heavy casualties, provoking strong criticism of Winston Churchill, who was blamed for the failure. He resigned from the Cabinet in November 1915.

In 1985 a **Peace Pagoda** was built in Battersea Park, overlooking the Thames, by a Japanese order of Buddhist monks, using Canadian fir and Portland stone. It was one of a chain built round the world and dedicated to the search for international harmony and peace.

The Peace Pagoda in Battersea Park.

5. AROUND THE MALL AND ST JAMES'S PARK

The Mall leads from Trafalgar Square to Buckingham Palace. **Admiralty Arch**, by Sir Aston Webb, was opened in 1910 as part of the national memorial to Queen Victoria. On the left beyond the arch is a statue by Sir Thomas Brock, set up in 1914, of **Captain James Cook RN** (1728–79). Cook was the son of a Yorkshire labourer and began seafaring in the East Coast coal trade, transferring to the Royal Navy in 1755 and rising rapidly. His charting of the St Lawrence allowed big ships to approach Quebec and aided Britain's conquest of Canada. He spent several years charting the Newfoundland and Nova Scotia coasts and between 1768 and 1779 made three voyages to the Pacific and Australasia, then little known, using *Endeavour*, *Adventure* and *Discovery*, 'cat-built' Whitby colliers of a kind he knew well. He was the first navigator to cross the Antarctic Circle. He sailed up the west coast of North America seeking the North West Passage. His navigation skills were legendary; his intelligent use of antiscorbutics kept his crews healthy. After his second voyage the Royal Society made him a Fellow and gave him the Copley Gold Medal. On his third voyage he called at Tahiti with a gift from George III to the islanders of live cattle and poultry, discovered the Sandwich or Hawaiian Islands and sailed up to the Bering Strait, then back to Hawaii to refit. He was received as a god, as prophesied in legend, but disputes arose about water and the theft of

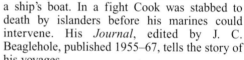

a ship's boat. In a fight Cook was stabbed to death by islanders before his marines could intervene. His *Journal*, edited by J. C. Beaglehole, published 1955–67, tells the story of his voyages.

Across the Mall is the **Royal Marines Memorial** by Adrian Jones to those who fell in the China and Boer Wars. It was erected in 1903. The battle scenes are by Sir Thomas Graham Jackson: one shows the Chinese attack on the Peking legation; the other, the action at Graspan in South Africa. A defiant marine with bayonet and rifle protects a fallen comrade. The memorial was enhanced and refurbished as the national memorial to Royal Marines killed in all conflicts and was unveiled by the Duke of Edinburgh, Captain General of the Royal Marines, on 29th October 2000.

By St James's Park on the other side of the Mall is the **Royal Artillery South African War Memorial** by W. Robert Colton (1910), commemorating the one thousand who fell in 1899–1900. A figure of Peace restrains a great horse; bronze panels show garrison and mountain artillery and the names of the fallen.

In the Mall stands Captain Cook, in un-seamanlike pose with his foot on a coil of rope.

The Guards' Monument in Lower Regent Street has figures cast from captured guns.

Back through Admiralty Arch, at the junction of Cockspur Street and Pall Mall East is a statue (1836) of **George III** (1738–1820), the first of the Hanoverians to identify firmly with Britain. In the Speech from the Throne in 1760 he declared: 'Born and educated in this country, I glory in the name of Briton'. The sculptor was Matthew Cotes Wyatt (1777–1862), son of James Wyatt the architect. The King ('Farmer George') was an agricultural innovator who wrote for farming papers under the pseudonym Ralph Robinson. He was an excellent horseman: he is depicted riding Adonis, for twenty years his favourite horse, and is wearing a riding wig, with pigtail. The combination of this and the Arab's plumed tail earned the statue the nickname 'Pigtail and Pumphandle'. The king knew how to get the best from this much-loved horse. When riding Adonis at Windsor, he turned to Lord Winchilsea: 'I know his worth and treat him accordingly. That's the right way, Winchilsea'.

At the foot of Lower Regent Street is the **Guards' Monument** of 1859 by John Bell, commemorating the 22,162 guardsmen who fell in the Crimean War. The monument has figures of guardsmen cast from captured Russian guns. The guns piled at the back were used at the siege of Sebastopol. To the right is a statue (1862) by John Foley of **Sidney Herbert, first Baron Herbert of Lea** (1810–61), Secretary for War during the Crimean campaign, and to the left his friend **Florence Nightingale** (1820–1910), renowned for her work in the hospital at Scutari, where she was called the 'Lady of the Lamp' because

The statue of Florence Nightingale (left) by Sir Arthur George Walker is decorated with plaques (above) showing her at work.

Pallas Athene stands outside the stately Athenaeum Club in Waterloo Place.

of the lamp she carried on night rounds. Her statue, by Sir Arthur George Walker, has plaques showing her interviewing officers, attending a meeting of nurses and arranging transport for the wounded.

The stately Athenaeum Club at the south-west corner of Waterloo Place was founded in 1824 for 'scientific and literary men and artists'. Over the entrance stands the gilded figure of **Pallas Athene** by E. H. Baily. She was to have been the only decoration for the building designed by Decimus Burton, but J. W. Croker, founder member and MP, wanted a frieze. Using £2000 subscribed by members for the purchase of an icehouse, he ordered one from John Henning with figures from the Parthenon. A rhyme circulated:

> I'm John Wilson Croker,
> I do as I please,
> You asked for an icehouse,
> I gave you a frieze.

The national memorial to **Edward VII** (1841–1910), an equestrian bronze (1921) by Sir Bertram Mackennal, the Australian sculptor, stands in the centre of the southern part of Waterloo Place.

To the east is a statue of **Captain Robert Falcon Scott** (1868–1912), the Antarctic explorer, given by officers of the Fleet in 1915. It also commemorates Oates, Bowers, Wilson and Evans, his companions on his final journey. The statue, by Lady Scott, shows the explorer in Antarctic dress, ski sticks in hand. Scott organised a series of expeditions and in 1910 sailed in the *Terra Nova* in an attempt to be the first to reach the South Pole. His party was beaten by

Edward VII in Waterloo Place, Pall Mall.

Captain Robert Falcon Scott, the Antarctic explorer, and Baron Lawrence, hero of the Indian Mutiny, are in Waterloo Place.

the Norwegian Amundsen and, disheartened and dogged by bad weather, they died on the homeward journey. Their papers were recovered and were published in 1913, together with Scott's 'Last Message to the Public': 'Had we lived I should have had a tale to tell of the hardihood, endurance and courage of my companions which would have stirred the heart of every Englishman. These rough notes and our dead bodies must tell the tale.' His wife still received the title Lady Scott, as her husband would have been knighted had he returned.

Next to Scott is a statue by Marochetti of **Sir Colin Campbell, Baron Clyde** (1792–1863), the son of a Glasgow carpenter who rose to high rank in the army, fought at Chillianwallah, commanded the Highland Brigade in the Crimea and, when appointed Commander-in-Chief by Palmerston, succeeded in suppressing the Indian Mutiny in a few months. He was dubbed the Saviour of Lucknow.

At the corner is **John Laird Mair, first Baron Lawrence** (1811–79), by Sir Joseph Edgar Boehm (1882). Lawrence entered the Indian Civil Service in 1829 and worked round Delhi. When news of the Mutiny reached him he raised an army of 59,000 and, after a three-month siege, captured Delhi. He was

created baronet on his return home and in 1863 became Governor-General of India. He was later raised to the peerage. The statue's inscription, 'How youngly he began to serve his country, how long continued', comes from *Coriolanus*.

This plaque on Sir John Franklin's statue shows his funeral on the ice.

Near the Athenaeum is **Sir John Franklin** (1780–1847), the Arctic explorer who discovered the North West Passage to the Pacific but died on the voyage. One plaque shows Franklin's funeral on the ice and the other (inaccessible) an Arctic chart and his two ships, *Erebus* and *Terror.* All the crew, from Franklin himself down to the boy seaman, David Young, are named: none was to return. Victorian England went into mourning. Franklin's ships were stuck in the ice for two winters and there were few clues as to the fate of the remainder of the expedition who died trying to make their way southwards over land. A decade after Franklin's disappearance Captain Francis McClintock of the *Fox* found the first mortal remains of the enterprise – a few bleached bones, knives and guns, buttons, spoons and sealing wax, copies of *The Vicar of Wakefield* and the *New Testament.* Examination of further bodies found in the 1980s revealed a high lead content. Did they die from poisoning by lead solder on food cans? In summer 2000 the Royal Canadian Mounted Police patrol vessel *Nadon* successfully negotiated the passage from west to east, finding clear water, not ice, and with the help of Inuit hunters discovered six more graves of expedition members. Franklin's statue, by Matthew Noble, was erected in 1866.

Also here is **Sir John Fox Burgoyne** (1782–1871), the natural son of General John Burgoyne and the opera singer Susan Caulfield. He joined Wellington in Portugal in 1809, fought with success at the sieges of Badajoz and Ciudad Rodrigo, and later in the Crimea, and became a field marshal in 1869.

The statue of **George Nathaniel, first Marquess Curzon of Kedleston** (1859–1925), by Sir Bertram Mackennal faces his former home at Carlton Gardens. Curzon, Viceroy of India, was often criticised for his rigid, autocratic ways, although his fine oratory was admired. In 1919 he became Foreign Secretary, a post he held with distinction. In 1923 he hoped to become Prime Minister in succession to Bonar Law but the honour went to Stanley Baldwin, and Curzon never recovered from his disappointment. He was India's most resplendent viceroy. At the Delhi Durbar of 1913 a parade of elephants carried rajahs, maharajahs, nawabs and sultans, with Lord and Lady Curzon riding in a silver howdah. But Curzon's aloof manner caused problems. His mode of addressing the House of Commons was compared to 'a divinity addressing black beetles' and rhymes rather unkindly mocked him:

My name is George Nathaniel Curzon,
I am a most superior person.
My face is pink, my hair is sleek,
I dine at Blenheim once a week.

Sir Bertram Mackennal's statue of Curzon stands opposite the Marquess's former home in Carlton Gardens.

General de Gaulle's statue by Angela Conner can also be found in Carlton Gardens.

The cross of Lorraine and de Gaulle's words of 8th June 1940 – 'France has lost a battle but has not lost the war' – appear on the memorial on the wartime **headquarters of the Free French Forces** at 4 Carlton Gardens.

Here, too, stands Angela Conner's statue of **General Charles André Joseph Marie de Gaulle** (1890–1970), Free French leader, statesman and President of France (1958–69). At 6 feet 5 inches, with the soubriquet '*La Grande Asperge*', de Gaulle symbolised French patriotism after the fall of France. His time in London was controversial. Churchill once fumed: '*Bloody* de Gaulle! He had the impertinence to tell me that the French regard him as the reincarnation of Joan of Arc. I found it very necessary to remind him that we had to burn the first!' De Gaulle resented his dependence on Britain and the United States. Antagonisms persisted. He passionately opposed British membership of the Common Market and in 1966 withdrew France from NATO. Finally, his prominence undermined by industrial and student unrest, he resigned in 1969.

There are probably more statues of **Queen Victoria** (1819–1901) in the world than of any other person. A regal-looking marble statue by Sir Thomas Brock (1897) under the porchway of the National Portrait Gallery Annexe at 15 Carlton House Terrace is one of them. It used to be in the Constitutional Club. Victoria succeeded to the British throne in 1837 at the age of eighteen and reigned for sixty-three years. She married her cousin Albert of Saxe-Coburg-Gotha (1819–61) and bore him four sons and five daughters. Either directly or by marriage she was related to most of the royal houses of Europe. The Industrial Revolution, the rise of the middle classes, social reform, scientific and medical advances, the apogee of empire, a distinctive artistic and architectural style, and a sense of union and security never again experienced marked

A stout Queen Victoria, once in the Constitutional Club and now on Carlton House Terrace, has had her chipped nose repaired.

At Duke of York Steps by The Mall the 'Grand Old Duke of York' on his column surveys the old War Office. Sir Richard Westmacott, the sculptor, received a fee of £7000 for the statue.

the period known as 'Victorian'. Victoria was a personality from the beginning. Of her first Privy Council meeting, only two hours after she succeeded, the Duke of Wellington commented: 'Five feet high, but she not only filled her chair but the room'.

At the south end of Waterloo Place rises one of London's most spectacular monuments, the **Duke of York's Column**, erected in 1833, with a bronze statue by Sir Richard Westmacott of Frederick Augustus, Duke of York and Albany (1763–1827). The statue, 13 feet high, weighs 7 tons and is of Aberdeen granite. A stairway of 169 steps (although not open to the public) leads to the top of the column. It was said that the Duke had taken refuge from his creditors and that his bills could be 'spiked' on the lightning conductor. The monument cost £30,000, raised by stopping one day's pay from every officer and man in the army, of which he was Commander-in-Chief from 1798. Although exonerated from blame, he resigned in 1809 after his mistress, Mary Anne Clarke, was found to be trafficking in army commissions, but he was reinstated in 1811. His reforms, such as vaccination against smallpox, the provision of greatcoats for soldiers and the founding of the Duke of York's Royal Military School (still flourishing in Dover), earned him the name 'the Soldier's Friend'.

Under a tree to the west of the column is the tombstone of **Giro**, the German ambassador's terrier, inscribed *Ein treuer Begleiter* ('a faithful companion') and dated February 1934. The German embassy was at 9 Pall Mall until 1939.

Steps lead down from Carlton House Terrace past the statue of **George VI** (1895–1952) by William Macmillan. The King is shown in the Garter mantle over the undress uniform of an Admiral of the Fleet.

The statue of George VI by William Macmillan.

Edward VII and Queen Alexandra lived at Marlborough House until he succeeded to the throne. Her memorial is in the garden wall; water flows behind the grating.

The setting was designed by Louis de Soissons and the statue was unveiled in 1955.

Across Pall Mall, in St James's Square, is a rococo equestrian statue of **William III** (1650–1702) by J. Bacon the Younger. In 1724 Samuel Travers left funds 'to purchase and erect in St James's Square, an equestrian statue in brass to the glorious memory of my master King William III'. The plinth was installed but because of a problem with the legacy no statue appeared until 1808. William met his death at Hampton Court when his horse stumbled over a molehill (shown under the horse's hooves). Jacobites toasted 'the little gentleman in the velvet jacket'.

This bronze medallion of Queen Mary is on the garden wall of Marlborough House.

Against the railings at the north-east corner of the square is the memorial to **WPC Yvonne Fletcher**, shot during the siege of the Libyan Embassy in April 1984.

At Norfolk House, 31 St James's Square, a bronze plaque (1947) marks General Eisenhower's use of the house as **Allied Forces Headquarters** in 1942 and 1944. Another plaque (1990) marks the **centenary of Eisenhower's birth**.

Marlborough Road leads from Pall Mall back to the Mall, and in the wall of Marlborough House an Art Nouveau memorial (1926) commemorates **Queen Alexandra** (1844–1925), consort of Edward VII. The couple lived here as Prince and Princess of Wales, and it was the widowed Alexandra's home from 1910. The memorial fountain is by Sir Alfred Gilbert.

Also on the garden wall, facing the Mall, is a bronze medallion by Sir William Reid Dick of **Queen Mary** (1867–1953), consort of George V. It was erected in 1967. Queen Mary was noted for her unchanging Edwardian fashions and hairstyle, her characteristic 'toque' hats and her collection of antiques.

At the west end of the Mall, in front of Buckingham Palace, is the mainly white marble **Queen Victoria Memorial** (of which the Mall itself forms a part). A distillation of later Victorian taste, it was designed by Sir Aston Webb, with sculptures by Sir Thomas Brock, and was set up in 1911. The central pedestal is crowned by a gilded and winged Victory with Courage and Constancy at her feet. At the base on the east side is a seated figure of Victoria, 13 feet high. On the other sides groups represent Motherhood, Justice, Peace and Progress, Science and Art, Industry and Agriculture, and Naval and Military Power. The whole is 82 feet high; 2300 tons of marble were used in all. Sir Thomas Brock was made a Knight Commander of the Bath on the platform during the unveiling. The Queen wears her wedding ring on her right hand as she did in life, to please Albert's German taste. The Victorian Society laid a wreath at the memorial on 22nd January 2001, to mark the centenary of the Queen's death.

The Canadian Memorial by Pierre Granche in Green Park by Constitution Hill, unveiled by Queen Elizabeth II on 3rd June 1994, commemorates the million Canadians who came to Britain to fight in the two world

Field Marshal Earl Alexander of Tunis is in front of the Guards' Headquarters, Birdcage Walk.

Queen Anne, outside 13 Queen Anne's Gate since 1708 at least, is one of London's most charming statues.

wars. Some 110,000 gave their lives. The memorial of Nova Scotia rose granite is inscribed 'From Dangers Shared, Our Friendship Prospers' and also commemorates the bonds of wartime years. In two parts, symbolising the two wars, the memorial bears bronze maple leaves in flowing water, suggesting a Canadian stream. A stone compass rose aligns the memorial with Halifax, Nova Scotia, the embarkation port from which many of the men left, and a port vital to the Atlantic supply line.

Across St James's Park, a statue of **Field Marshal Earl Alexander of Tunis** (1891–1969), Colonel of the Irish Guards 1946–9, is appropriately sited in front of the Guards' Headquarters, Birdcage Walk. The bronze statue by James Butler shows Alexander in campaign kit of sheepskin jacket, high boots and binoculars. He was an outstanding military figure of the Second World War, led the rearguard action at Dunkirk and the retreat from Burma, and was Commander-in-Chief in North Africa in 1942. In 1943–5 Alexander was overall commander in the Sicilian and Italian campaigns. After the war he was an exceptionally popular Governor-General of Canada and, less happily, Minister of Defence in Churchill's government 1952–4. He resigned in 1954.

Between the Guards' Headquarters and Horse Guards' Road, an alleyway leads to Queen Anne's Gate, one of London's handsomest streets. A weathered statue of **Queen Anne** (1665–1714) has stood outside Number 13 since 1708 at least. It was made by Francis Bird for the portico of St Mary-le-Strand, one of the earliest of the fifty churches designed by order of Queen Anne (always, as her friend Sarah, Duchess of Marlborough, remarked, 'religious without affectation'), but it was never erected there. Bird also made the first statue of Anne outside St Paul's Cathedral and that in the market place at Kingston-upon-Thames.

6.
PICCADILLY AND BOND STREET

In Piccadilly Circus the **Shaftesbury Memorial** (1893) by Sir Alfred Gilbert, a fountain surmounted by a winged archer, is universally known as Eros, although the sculptor intended it to depict the Angel of Christian Charity, with perhaps a pun on Shaftesbury's name since the archer is 'burying a shaft'. It was the first statue to be made of aluminium and was so light that Gilbert carried it across his studio. It commemorated the seventh Earl of Shaftesbury (1801–85), the reformer and philanthropist. Warm-hearted Shaftesbury, when he realised that the end of his life was approaching, said, 'I cannot bear to leave the world with all the misery in it'. A focus for celebrations, the statue was reinstalled on 26th May 1993 following year-long repairs required when a reveller swung on Eros's supporting leg.

On the south side of Piccadilly is St James's Church, built by Sir Christopher Wren in 1684 and his only West End church. It was rebuilt after wartime bombing with a memorial garden dedicated to the 'courage and fortitude of the people of London'. A fountain by A. Hardiman commemorates **Julian Salter Elias, Viscount Southwood** (1873–1946), the philanthropist and newspaper-owner, who paid for the laying out of the garden.

In the quadrangle of Burlington House, home of the Royal Academy and other learned institutions, is a statue (1931) of **Sir Joshua Reynolds** (1723–92), brush in hand. It is considered to be the best work of Alfred Drury. Reynolds, a Devonian who came to London and stayed for life, was the first President of the Royal Academy and founder of its schools. The most fashionable portraitist of his day, he painted Dr Johnson, Garrick, Gibbon and the Duchess of Devonshire, among two thousand others, and was regarded as the English successor to Van Dyck. His writings are still of value and his kindly good sense was legendary. In a discourse to the Royal Academy's students in 1769 he famously said: 'If you have great talents, industry will improve them; if you have but moderate abilities, industry will supply their deficiency' – wise words for anyone at the outset of a career. But his ebullient working style caused some

The Shaftesbury Memorial in Piccadilly Circus is universally known as Eros.

alarm. Lady Burlington confessed, 'I sometimes thought he would paint me and not the picture'.

The remodelled façade of Old Burlington House (1719) was again remodelled by Smirke in 1872–4 when the top storey was decorated with statues of **Pheidias, Leonardo, Flaxman, Raphael, Michelangelo, Titian, Reynolds, Wren** and **William of Wykeham**. In the loggia is a memorial to 2003 members of the **Artists Rifles, 28th Battalion, The London Regiment** killed in the First World War.

There are hundreds of small statues decorating the façades of London buildings, some 370 on the Houses of Parliament alone, and many more on other public buildings, including the former Museum of Mankind on the south side of Burlington Gardens, which series includes **Newton, Bentham, Milton, Harvey, Galileo, Goethe, Leibnitz, Linnaeus, Hunter, Hume, Davy, Adam Smith, Locke** and **Bacon.**

When William Fortnum, a footman in

Sir Joshua Reynolds in the quadrangle of the Royal Academy.

Adam Smith is one of several façade figures overlooking Burlington Gardens.

'The Allies' in New Bond Street is a favourite spot for tourists who can be photographed sitting betwen Roosevelt and Churchill.

the service of Queen Anne, retired from royal service he opened a grocer's shop with his friend Hugh Mason, who owned a small shop in St James's Market. It was called Fortnum & Mason. They imported exotic foods through the East India Company and provided supplies to officers in the Peninsular and Crimean Wars. Fortnum & Mason was Queen Victoria's grocer of choice; during the Crimean War she sent the firm's concentrated beef to Florence Nightingale for use in her hospital. In 1886 Mr Heinz called and they stocked his complete range of canned goods. In 1964 an articulated clock was set over the main entrance. Designed by Berkeley Sutcliffe and sculpted by P. J. Bentham, it carries eighteenth-century figures of **Mr Fortnum and Mr Mason**, who on the hour turn and bow to each other.

President Franklin D. Roosevelt and Sir Winston Churchill chat companionably on a bench near Aspreys, the jewellers, at 165 New Bond Street. The sculpture, entitled **The Allies**, by the American sculptor Lawrence Holofcener, erected by the Bond Street Association and unveiled in May 1995, commemorates fifty years of peace since the end of the Second World War.

Over the entrance to the saleroom of Sotheby's, the auctioneers', at 34–5 New Bond Street, a diorite sculpture of the Egyptian goddess **Sekhmet** dates from about 1600 BC. There have been 175 of these images found; some are in the British Museum.

In 1887 Wellington's equestrian statue by Wyatt was moved from the arch at Hyde Park Corner and taken to Aldershot. It was replaced by the smaller one by Boehm below.

7.
Hyde Park and Belgravia

Opposite Apsley House at Hyde Park Corner at the west end of Piccadilly, once known as Number 1, London, since it was the first house inside the Hyde Park

turnpike gate, is a bronze statue by J. E. Boehm of **Arthur Wellesley, first Duke of Wellington** (1769–1852). The Duke rides Copenhagen, the horse that carried him for over sixteen hours at the battle of Waterloo. He was honourably retired to the Duke's country home, Stratfield Saye, and eventually buried with full military honours. The horse's tombstone bears the words:

God's humbler instrument, though meaner clay
Shall share the glory of that glorious day.

At Hyde Park Corner the Duke of Wellington by Boehm rides Copenhagen, his mount at Waterloo.

Copenhagen was a personality in his own right. On the night of Waterloo, as the Duke dismounted wearily after a gruelling day, Copenhagen lashed out so vigorously that he nearly achieved what Napoleon had so conspicuously failed to do. Forty horses were needed to drag the horse's stone figure to the site. The Duke is guarded by a Grenadier, a Royal Highlander, a Welch Fusilier and an Inniskilling Dragoon, their figures cast from twelve French cannon captured in Wellington's battles. He faces Apsley House, his former home, now the Wellington Museum, where during his lifetime, on the anniversary of the battle,

his officers dined with their commander in the Waterloo Chamber. The 'Iron Duke', usually remembered exclusively for his military achievements, and greatly admired by his troops (one infantry captain said, 'We would rather see his long nose in a fight than reinforcements of ten thousand any day'), had a gentler side. A small boy was crying because he was leaving for school and was concerned about the welfare of his pet toad in his absence. The Duke promised to investigate and in due course the boy received a letter: 'Field Marshal the Duke of Wellington

Above: *The Wellington Arch by Decimus Burton now houses an exhibition about London's statues.*

The Machine Gun Corps Memorial at Hyde Park Corner.

presents his compliments to Master – and has the pleasure to inform him that his toad is well'. A report commissioned by English Heritage and published in March 2001 suggested that Wellington's statue be moved north to a more prominent position close to Apsley House as part of a £20 million project to transform the traffic maelstrom into 'an attractive oasis for London', reintegrated into the city's parks. The consultants recommend that Hyde Park Corner be reshaped into a 'grass amphitheatre' with terraced seating, new footpaths and viewing terraces. More trees, turf and hedges would mitigate the noise and fumes from the traffic.

The figure at Hyde Park Corner of David (1925) holding Goliath's sword is by Francis Derwent Wood. It forms the **Machine Gun Corps Memorial** and has the inscription: 'Saul hath slain his thousands but David his tens of thousands'.

The **Wellington (or Constitution) Arch** by Decimus Burton was moved here in 1882–3. A large statue of Wellington by Wyatt used to stand on the site but it was removed to Aldershot. The Arch is topped by 'Peace in her Quadriga' (1912). The sculptor, Captain Adrian Jones, a cavalry officer in the 3rd Hussars for twenty-three years, was also a qualified veterinary surgeon. His modelling of horses was particularly successful. In the 1950s the Arch was the smallest police station in London (two sergeants, ten constables and a cat) but after this maintenance was haphazard. English Heritage undertook a complete cleaning and repair programme, which finished in November 2000, and the Arch is now open to the public with viewing galleries below the Quadriga, access to some of the rooms and a permanent exhibition of London statues, monuments and war memorials in the care of English Heritage. The work of restoration was far-reaching (for example, fifteen of the forty-five lion masks were renewed at a cost of £2500 each). The bronze finish of the Quadriga gleams again: cleaning revealed the names, on the wings, of the four men who cast the group in 1912. The model for Peace was Beatrice Stuart, the foremost artists' model of her day, who sat for Sargent and Augustus John. The model for the chariot driver was the eleven-year-old son of Lord Michelham, the donor. The Diana, Princess of Wales, Memorial Walkway passes through the Arch.

Opposite the Arch, at the top of Constitution Hill, is the memorial to

One of the figures on the Royal Artillery War Memorial.

The bronze statue of Achilles in Hyde Park.

Commonwealth Troops, comprising two pairs of inscribed columns and a rotunda, erected in 2002.

Close by is the moving **Royal Artillery War Memorial** (1925) by Charles Sargeant Jagger and Lionel Pearson, a massive construction that takes the form of a huge gun with bronze figures on four sides and the inscription: 'Here was a Royal Fellowship of Death'. The gun is a howitzer used in siege work and is so positioned that a shell from it would, given sufficient charge, land on the Somme battlefield in France, where the Royal Artillery lost so many men in the First World War. The memorial, regarded by many as the greatest work of British sculpture of the twentieth century, was cleaned and given a light coat of wax in 2001, to protect it from traffic fumes and dirt. This is the first move in a major restoration programme.

In Hyde Park itself, on the left of the ring road from Hyde Park Corner to Marble Arch, is the colossal bronze **Achilles Statue** ('The Ladies' Trophy') by Sir Richard Westmacott. Erected in 1822, it is a copy of a horse-tamer on the Monte Catallo in Rome, and not Achilles. It was paid for by the women of England to commemorate the Duke of Wellington, but the subscribers were shaken on its delivery by the statue's unabashed nudity. Achilles was cast from cannon captured in the Peninsular War and, although not intended as a likeness, visitors expected the face to be Wellington's. One Napoleonic veteran, depressed by the great quantity of Wellingtoniana everywhere, exclaimed with relief when he saw it: *Enfin, on est vengé!*

To the right, on another traffic island, is a statue of **Lord Byron** (1788–1824) by Richard C. Belt (1880), which shows Byron meditating on a rock, accompanied by his dog Boatswain. The marble for the statue (*rosso antico*), weighing 57 tons, was given by the people of Greece. A friend of Byron remarked that it did not resemble the poet in the least, but whatever its defects in this respect the statue is the focus of a wreath-laying by the Byron Society. (Dr Johnson would have understood the sculptor's difficulty. In 1776 he commented: 'a fellow will hack half a year at a block of marble to make something in stone that hardly resembles a man – let alone achieves a reasonable likeness'.)

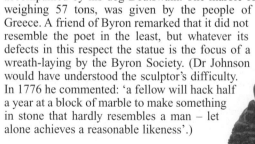

Lord Byron and his dog 'Boatswain'.

The Queen Elizabeth Gate, Hyde Park.

At the east end of Hyde Park is a memorial stone to the victims of the Holocaust.

The Queen Elizabeth Gate, Hyde Park, near Apsley House, was erected by public subscription to mark the ninetieth birthday of Queen Elizabeth the Queen Mother in 1990. The sculptor was David Wynne, the designer Giuseppe Lund. The gate, with stainless steel curlicues, pink roses and leaping salmon, has as a centrepiece a bright red lion and a white unicorn. Critics responded with such judgements as 'romantic candyfloss' and 'three-dimensional knitting'.

The **Cavalry Memorial** (1924), moved to Serpentine Road in 1961, commemorates cavalry regiments that served in the First World War, including the Yeomanry and those of Australia, Canada, New Zealand and South Africa. The regiments are listed, St George holds his sword aloft over the dead dragon, and round the plinth is a frieze of cavalrymen. This is another work of Captain Adrian Jones, who used as models suits of fifteenth-century armour for horse and man in the Wallace Collection. An annual commemorative service is held here, attended by former cavalry and successor regiments.

The memorial to Queen Caroline, who created the Serpentine.

In a grove of birches by the Dell, at the east end of Hyde Park, a memorial to victims of the **Nazi Holocaust** bears a quotation from the Book of Lamentations: 'For those I weep, streams of tears flow from my eyes, because of the destruction of my people'. The memorial was erected in 1983.

Caroline of Anspach (1683–1737), queen consort of George II, was a handsome, intelligent woman with a strong interest in landscape gardening. In 1730 she arranged to have the Westbourne, rising on Hampstead Heath and entering the Thames at Chelsea Bridge, dammed and widened to form the Serpentine. Her memorial urn is, appropriately, by the path, south of the east end of the Serpentine.

George Lansbury (1859–1940) is commemorated by a medallion by H. Wilson Parker (1953) on the pavilion on the south side of the Serpentine. Lansbury, a pacifist and Labour politician, founded the *Daily Herald*. He opened the London parks for games and introduced public bathing at the Serpentine – 'Lansbury's Lido'. The medallion was unveiled in 1953 by Clement Attlee and bears the inscription: 'He made this bathing shore for our enjoyment'. Each year stalwarts enjoy a Christmas dip here even if they have to break the ice first.

North of the Serpentine lake boathouse is a memorial erected by **Norwegian seamen**. A granite pre-Cambrian rock, nearly 7 feet high, on three smaller stones is inscribed: 'This boulder was brought here from Norway, where it was worn and shaped for thousands of years by forces of nature – frost, running water, rock, sand and ice, until it obtained its present shape'; and on the front: 'This stone was erected by the Royal Norwegian Navy and the Norwegian Merchant Fleet in the year 1978. We thank the British people for friendship and hospitality during the Second World War. You gave us a safe haven in our common struggle for freedom and peace.' When Norway was forced to surrender to the Germans in 1940 a large proportion of her vast fleet of merchant ships – greatly to Britain's benefit – sailed for British ports and with the Royal Norwegian Navy continued the battle alongside Britain.

To the north of the Serpentine the bird sanctuary is adorned by the figure of Rima by Jacob Epstein, which commemorates **William Henry Hudson** (1841–1922), author and naturalist. In Hudson's book *Green Mansions* Rima is a Spirit of Nature. Epstein's gross symbolism aroused such feeling that on at least two occasions the sculpture has been tarred and feathered. The figure was unveiled by

'Lansbury's Lido' was the name the public gave to the bathing place on the Serpentine, established by George Lansbury.

Epstein's Rima, commemorating W. H. Hudson, was controversial.

Stanley Baldwin, who unlocked the bird sanctuary gate with a silver key.

In the north-east of the park a black and white pebble **mosaic tree** surrounded by direction pointers and laid out in 2000 commemorates the struggle for political enfranchisement in the nineteenth century. When a tree was burnt down during the Reform League riots in 1866 the remaining stump became the Reformers' Tree, a notice board for political demonstrations and a gathering point for Reform League meetings. Prime Minister James Callaghan planted a new oak tree on 7th November 1977 on the spot where the Reformers' Tree was thought to have stood. In the early-Victorian period Hyde Park became a place for public meetings. At first these were banned by the police but at the huge rally of 1866 the crowd tore up hundreds of yards of iron railing, swarmed into the park and a serious riot followed, and the authorities became more conciliatory. In 1872 the Commissioner of Works designated a spot some

150 yards from the Reformers' Tree as a place for such assemblies: Speakers' Corner by Marble Arch has been a London attraction ever since.

Further south, on the Park Lane side of the park, opposite Mount Street, is the **Joy of Life fountain** by T. B. Huxley-Jones (1963). This was given by the Constance Fund, set up in 1944 by Mrs Constance Goetze in memory of her husband, a great benefactor to Regent's Park.

The Fund also set up in 1954 the fountain at the western end of Green Park, on the eastern side of Hyde Park Corner. The **Diana Fountain**, by E. J. Clack, has three granite basins, with twisted bronze branches rising to support the figure of Diana, a girl holding a leash, with a greyhound beside her.

The Diana Fountain in Green Park.

FOR A LIFE DEVOTED TO THE PUBLIC GOOD

Prince Albert, painted black in 1914 and now newly gilded, sits within his memorial facing the Albert Hall.

8.
KNIGHTSBRIDGE AND KENSINGTON

The statue of **Sir Robert Grosvenor KG, first Marquess of Westminster** (1765–1845), at the corner of Wilton Crescent and Grosvenor Crescent was commissioned by Gerald Cavendish, the sixth and present Duke of Westminster. It was sculpted by Jonathan Wylder in 1998 and includes two talbot dogs, part of the Grosvenor arms.

Opposite is Belgrave Square, where, in the north-east corner, stands a statue of **General Don José de San Martin** (1778–1850). It is signed 'Juan Carlos Ferraro, Buenos Aires 1993' and inscribed: 'Founder of the Argentine Independence. He also gave freedom to Chile and Peru.' The statue, the gift of the Argentine-British community in Argentina to the people of London, was unveiled on 2nd November 1994 by the Duke of Edinburgh.

In the south-east corner of Belgrave Square is a statue by Hugo Daini of **Simón Bolívar** (1783–1830), who devoted his life to the causes of freeing the South American countries from Spanish domination. With British aid he succeeded. Bolivia was named after him. The statue was erected in 1974 by the Council of Latin America and unveiled by James Callaghan, the Foreign Secretary. Bolívar had been called the George Washington of South America. On the plinth are the arms of the South American countries and the words: 'I am convinced that England alone is capable of protecting the world's precious rights as she is great, glorious and wise'.

In the south-west corner of Belgrave Square stands a statue of **Christopher Columbus** (?1447–1506) by Tomas Bauselos, erected by a committee of Canning House to mark the five hundredth anniversary of the 'encounter of the two worlds'. After months of peril and, at the end, mutiny, Columbus discovered America on 12th October 1492 (unless the Viking settlement at L'Anse aux Meadows, Newfoundland, has prior claim), first touching land at San Salvador (perhaps the modern Watling Island) in the Bahamas. He also discovered Cuba and Haiti and made three subsequent voyages, reaching Dominica on the first and landing on the mainland of America on the last.

The fifty-two members of the **Women's Transport Corps** (FANY) who died in the Second World War have their memorial on the north outer wall of St Paul's Church, Wilton Place. Thirteen died as secret agents in occupied Europe; two received the George Cross and six the Croix de Guerre. The memorial consists of a stone plaque with the red and blue badge of the service. A smaller plaque commemorates 'Odette', a renowned agent. Nearby a plaque lists the **old boys of St Paul's School** killed in the First World War.

The first Marquess of Westminster and his hounds survey his London estates. His foot rests on a milestone inscribed 'Chester 197 miles', home of the Grosvenor family.

Simón Bolívar overlooks the area of London closely associated with embassies from South American countries.

Heads decorate several Knightsbridge buildings at first-floor level: at Number 55 is **Edward VII**; at 59, **Queen Alexandra**; at 69, **Lord Roberts of Kandahar**; at 87, **William Temple**, Archbishop of Canterbury (1827–1902) and the **third Marquess of Salisbury** (1830–1903). All date from 1902; their sculptor is unknown.

In Hans Crescent, by the side of Harrods, is a memorial to **Stephen Dodd**, **Noel Lane** and **Jane Arbuthnot**, Metropolitan Police officers killed here by a terrorist bomb in December 1983. The stone stands between two windows of the famous store.

At the Pont Street end of Hans Place a red granite fountain basin, a stone column and a bronze portrait medallion by Boehm (1886) commemorate **Major General Sir Herbert Stewart** (1843–85), who commanded part of the expedition to relieve Gordon at Khartoum, and also Stewart's son Geoffrey, of the Coldstream Guards, killed in France in 1914.

A statue by Chavalliaud of **Cardinal John Henry Newman** (1801–90) stands in front of the Brompton Oratory, Brompton Road. In high Italian taste, it would have pleased Newman, who converted to Roman Catholicism in 1845 and later introduced the Institute of the Oratory to England. He was the founder of the Oxford Movement and author of the favourite hymn 'Lead Kindly Light'.

The Victoria and Albert Museum began soon after the Great Exhibition of 1851 and developed over a number of years. In 1899 Queen Victoria laid the foundation stone of the new building, the last important public engagement of her reign. The building was opened by Edward VII in 1909. Over the main entrance are statues of **Victoria** and **Albert** by Alfred Drury and **Edward VII** and **Alexandra** by W. Goscombe John. Around the building are statues by

Christopher Columbus's statue is in Belgrave Square.

72

Appropriately, Prince Albert presides over the entrance to the Victoria and Albert Museum.

students of the Royal College of Art of British painters, including **Millais, Leighton, Watts, Reynolds** and **Hogarth**; of sculptors including **Foley, Chantrey, Flaxman** and **Grinling Gibbons**; of architects, including **Barry, William Chambers, Wren** and **Inigo Jones**; and craftsmen, including **William Morris, Wedgwood, Chippendale, Tompion** and **Caxton**.

A **memorial to Soviet citizens** murdered on their return to the USSR during the Second World War stands in Cromwell Gardens in front of the Victoria and Albert Museum. At the Yalta Conference of February 1943, attended by Churchill, Roosevelt and Stalin, it was agreed that Soviet citizens found in the western zones of occupation should be repatriated. Many of them were murdered on arrival. The memorial, 'Twelve Responses to Tragedy' by Angela Conner, erected in 1986, is in Hopton stone and takes the form of a 5 foot

column with a group of Slav heads. It replaced a monument put up in 1982 but destroyed by vandals, 'to whom the truth was intolerable'.

Few successful organisations escape their share of jokes and denigration and the Scouts are no exception. Yet what other international youth movement can claim to have inspired every rising generation for nearly one hundred years? Scouting is the largest such movement in the world, with 600,000 members in Britain alone, and an international membership of some 25 million. The movement was founded by **Lieutenant-General Robert Stephenson Smyth Baden-Powell** (1857–1941). His statue of Cornish granite by Donald Potter (himself a Scout) stands outside Baden-Powell House at the south end

The Cornish granite statue of Baden-Powell.

73

Angela Conner's sculpture of heads, in memory of Soviet victims of the Yalta Conference, is in the public garden opposite the Victoria and Albert Museum.

of Queen's Gate and was unveiled in 1961 by the Duke of Gloucester, President of the Scout Association. A smiling, bareheaded Baden-Powell is in Scout uniform and, as he liked to wear, a cavalry cloak. The famous Scout hat is in his hand. (The original hat is in the museum at Baden-Powell House.) Baden-Powell enjoyed an adventurous army career and had become a national hero in the defence of Mafeking, where he and his troops were besieged for 217 days by the Boers. At the age of fifty-one he founded the Boy Scouts, using lessons learnt in campaigning. In *Scouting for Boys* he explained his object: 'The Scouts' motto is founded on my initials. It is: BE PREPARED, which means, you are always to be in a state of readiness in mind and body to do your duty.' In 1910 he retired from the army to give his full attention to the growing movement, which attracted over a hundred thousand members in two years. For girls the parallel Girl Guides movement was formed. According to Lord Ventry, a lifelong supporter of Scouting, Baden-Powell 'did more for the youth of the world than all the politicians'. Many would agree with him. Baden-Powell was raised to the peerage in 1929, taking as his title Baron Baden-Powell of Gilwell (a scoutmasters' training centre). A versatile man, he sketched, wrote widely on military history, Scouting and sport, and exhibited sculpture at the Royal Academy in 1907.

The north end of Queen's Gate has an equestrian statue by Sir Joseph Edgar Boehm of **Robert Cornelis, first Baron Napier of Magdala** (1810–90), chiefly remembered for his capture of the fortress of Magdala in Abyssinia in 1868 after an exhausting 400 mile march lasting ten weeks.

Facing the Albert Hall is the **Albert Memorial** by Sir George Gilbert Scott (1872), the national memorial to Prince Albert of Saxe-Coburg-Gotha (1819–61), consort of Queen Victoria. The statue of the Prince by John Foley shows him holding the catalogue of the Great Exhibition of 1851. It was commissioned, paid for and unveiled by Victoria and is regarded as Foley's *chef d'oeuvre*. The whole monument, reminiscent of an Eleanor Cross, is perhaps the fullest expression of Victorian taste to be seen in England today. But over the years the memorial deteriorated: rain crept in, ironwork rusted, stonework and statues were stained, and mosaics fell apart, peppering passers-by. In 1998 English Heritage completed a lengthy restoration programme at a cost of £11.2 million. The memorial was repaired and the three-times-life-size figure of Albert (painted black in 1914 lest its gleam attract the attention of Zeppelins) was dressed again in 23$\frac{1}{2}$ carat gold leaf. For eight years the memorial was shrouded in sheeting; then, on 21st October 1998, the Queen, Albert's great-great-grand-daughter, unveiled the restored memorial with the words: 'I am delighted that Albert's memorial has been so lovingly and generously saved and that all who pass by will see him again as those who knew and loved him best wished him to be remembered'. The *Daily Telegraph* greeted him: 'Welcome back, Albert, you have been sadly missed'.

Behind the Albert Hall is a bronze statue of **Prince Albert,** designed in 1858 by Joseph Durham, as a memorial to the Great Exhibition of 1851, which he had created. It overlooks 'Albertopolis', the cluster of scientific and art institutions that he founded.

Busts of two important men in nineteenth-century mining history flank the entrance to the Imperial College of Science (the old School of Mines) in Prince Consort Road. **Sir Julius Wernher** (1850–1912) was a German who went to South Africa, made a fortune in gold and diamonds and was associated with Cecil Rhodes. He made England his home, became a philanthropist, was created a baronet in 1905 and left the then considerable sum of £5 million. In addition to his mining activities, Sir Julius was a notable collector of works of art. In July 2001 English Heritage and the Wernher Foundation, which cares for these paintings, furniture, porcelain and the largest collection of Renaissance jewellery in Britain, arranged for the collection to be displayed at The Ranger's

Busts of mining pioneers, Wernher (left) and Beit (right), flank the entrance to the old School of Mines in Prince Consort Road.

The statue of Sir Ernest Shackleton is on the building of the Royal Geographical Society.

House, Greenwich. It was originally housed at Luton Hoo, Bedfordshire. Wernher's bust by Paul Montford (1910) is matched by one (also by Montford) of his business partner, **Alfred Beit** (1853–1906), a fellow German who also became a British citizen. Their firm was Wernher, Beit & Company. Alfred Beit was reputed to have given over £2 million to charity.

At the corner of Exhibition Road and Kensington Gore, high on the buildings of the Royal Geographical Society, is a statue of **Sir Ernest Shackleton** (1874–1922), who received the Society's special gold medal after his party had reached in 1908 the farthest point south then attained in Antarctica. Here too is **David Livingstone** (1813–73), the African explorer, and in the forecourt a bust of **Sir Clement Markham** (1830–1916), 'geographer and life-long friend and historian of the Peruvian people', whose government erected this memorial. In 1860 he led an expedition to collect cinchona trees and seeds in the eastern Andes and arranged their acclimatisation in India, resulting in a supply of quinine for medicinal purposes at low cost. On 19th February 2001 the RGS announced that, thanks to a National Lottery grant, it plans to open its vast archive to the public. Its

This figure of Queen Victoria near Kensington Palace is by her daughter, Princess Louise.

treasures include a photograph of Shackleton's *Endeavour* trapped in the Antarctic ice on the 1914–16 expedition, and Livingstone's 1860 sketch of Victoria Falls.

Within Kensington Gardens, on the south side of Kensington Palace is a statue of **William III** (1650–1702), presented in 1907 by Emperor Wilhelm II of Germany.

Between Kensington Palace and the Broad Walk is a white marble statue (1893) of **Queen Victoria** by her daughter Princess Louise (1848–1939), a sculptor of talent, whose rank deprived her of recognition. She was taught by Sir Joseph Edgar Boehm and had the unpleasant experience of finding her tutor dead in his studio.

In June 2000 the **Diana, Princess of Wales, Memorial Playground** was opened in the gardens, north of Kensington Palace, at a cost of £1.7 million. It includes six play areas, a pirate ship and a tree house. The seats are sheep-shaped. Images from *Peter Pan* are etched into the 'Home Under the Ground' (which houses the attendants' office and the lavatories). The playground, entered past a Victorian drinking-fountain and the Elfin Oak, forms part of the 7 mile **Memorial Walkway**, through Kensington Gardens, Hyde Park, Green Park and St James's Park. Adults are barred from the playground unless accompanied by a child.

The **Elfin Oak** now stands within a cage. In 1915 Ivor Innes, the sculptor, began carving the stump of a six-hundred-year-old oak tree into the shapes of elves and fairies, Wookey the witch, with her jars of health, wealth and happiness, and Huckleberry the gnome, carrying a bag of berries up the Gnomes' Stairway to the banquet in Bark Hall. The oak, now a Grade II listed site, was recently restored. Spike Milligan, the comedian, raised £65,000 for the work and the restored Elfin Oak was unveiled by the Prince of Wales on 12th June 1997.

One of London's best-loved statues stands on the west bank of Long Water: **Peter Pan** by Sir George Frampton (1911), with mice, rabbits, squirrels and fairies. Sir James Barrie's play *Peter Pan* was first produced in London on 27th December 1904 with Nina Boucicault (who modelled for the statue) as the first Peter Pan. The play proved an instant success and has been produced ever since. The characters of Peter, Nana the dog-nurse, Tinker Bell, Wendy and Captain Hook remain a part of nursery life. Barrie himself commissioned the statue and arranged with the Commissioner of Works to have it erected overnight, 'as if by magic'. Barrie lived in Bayswater Road and used to walk in the gardens, where he met the Llewelyn Davies boys out with their nurse. They became the inspiration for the Lost Boys in the story. Adults may find fault, but the high gloss on the rabbits' ears speaks of loving caresses from generations of children's hands.

South of Peter Pan is a bronze 12 foot equestrian figure entitled **Physical Energy**, by G. F. Watts (1907), a replica of part of the memorial to Cecil Rhodes at Groote Schuur, near Cape Town.

In the Italian Gardens at the north end of Long Water (that part of the Serpentine in Kensington Gardens) is Calder Marshall's statue (1858) of **Edward Jenner** (1749–1823), who pioneered vaccination against smallpox. Jenner was a doctor in Berkeley, Gloucestershire, and became interested in the country belief that those who had suffered from cowpox were immune from smallpox. His research, which at first aroused opposition, interested the royal family. Vaccination gradually spread through England and Parliament voted Jenner a grant of £10,000. The statue was first erected in Trafalgar Square but

Above: *The Elfin Oak near the children's playground in Kensington Gardens was carved by Ivor Innes.*

Above: *Peter Pan, probably the best-loved statue in London, was erected in Kensington Gardens by private arrangement between J. M. Barrie and the Commissioner of Works.*

Below: *'Physical Energy' is by G. F. Watts who at the age of 47 married the sixteen-year-old Ellen Terry.*

The portrait medallion of Prince Albert.

Edward Jenner, by Calder Marshall, ended up in the Italian Gardens.

was sent to Kensington Gardens in 1862. There was argument over the site. *Punch* did not refrain:

> England …
> I saved you many million spots,
> And now you grudge one spot to me.

On the south wall of the Italian Gardens are portrait medallions of **Prince Albert** (wreathed in oak-leaves) and **Queen Victoria**.

Just outside the gardens, at the junction of Lancaster Gate and Bayswater Road, is a stone column with a kneeling boy and a bust of **Reginald Brabazon, twelfth Earl of Meath** (1841–1929). He fought in the Boer War and First World War and became a brigadier general. The inscriptions, 'One King One Empire' and 'To him the British Empire was a goodly heritage to be fashioned unto the Glory of God', explain the Earl's philosophy. The sculptor was Herman Cawthra (1934).

South-west of Jenner is a granite obelisk to **John Hanning Speke** (1827–64), the African explorer who discovered the source of the

The Earl of Meath's memorial stands at the junction of Lancaster Gate and Bayswater Road.

Forgotten today but remembered in Kensington Gardens, John Hanning Speke was famous for discovering Lake Victoria Nyanza.

Nile. Speke was to address the British Association in Bath but that morning accidentally shot himself while partridge shooting. His companion in Africa, James Grant, was writing his account of their expedition. He had the pages he was writing when the news arrived printed with black borders.

On the north wall of the primary school on the west side of Church Street, Kensington, are figures of children made for **St Mary Abbots Charity School** in 1712. The girl wears a blue dress with red bonnet and shoes, the boy a knee-length blue coat. He holds a scroll with the words: 'I was naked and ye clothed me'. By 1710 over a hundred such schools existed.

On the north side of Holland Park, Kensington, on a plinth in the centre of a small pond, is a bronze statue by G. F. Watts and Boehm of **Henry Fox, third Baron Holland** (1773–1840), a nephew of Charles James Fox. He is seated and holds a stick; he suffered badly from gout. Holland, an aristocratic radical, was internationally minded, pro-French, opposed to slavery, and 'perhaps the greatest host in English history'. His political ambitions made him a candidate for the post of Foreign Secretary, but it is said that Lord John Russell had the delicate task of explaining to him that the Cabinet flatly refused to work with a man whose wife opened his letters. Lady Holland – Macaulay said she had 'the air of Queen Elizabeth' – was both beautiful and masterful. Denied his wish, Holland took revenge by opening a species of alternative Foreign Service at Holland House, supporting the unconventional, the liberal and the progressive, if not the downright revolutionary. His salons were brilliant, 'the favourite resort of wits and beauties, painters and poets, scholars, philosophers and statesmen'. Last words may be indices of character. Lord Holland's were: 'If Mr Selwyn calls, let him in; if I am alive I shall be very glad to see him, and if I am dead he will be very glad to see me!'

At the junction of Holland Park and Holland Park Avenue is a statue by Leonard Moll (1988) of **St Volodymyr the Great, Prince of Russia**

These figures of children were made for St Mary Abbots Charity School in 1712.

St Volodymyr the Great was the founder of Christianity in Russia.

(960–1015), erected by the Orthodox Church to mark a thousand years of Christianity in Russia.

In Warwick Gardens, West Kensington, a 23 foot red granite column surmounted by a flambeau bears a medallion portrait of **Queen Victoria** by F. L. Florence, encircled by a wreath engraved with the words, 'Queen Victoria Empress'. The memorial was presented in 1904 by the loyal inhabitants of the Royal Borough of Kensington.

'He who defied the storm has been killed by a breeze', was the *Paris Soir* epitaph on **Sub-Lieutenant Rex Warneford**. On 6th June 1915 Zeppelin LZ37 left Belgium to attack London. Warneford, flying a Morane-Saulnier Parasol, intercepted, dropped his bombs on it and the Zeppelin exploded, the first airship ever to be shot down in aerial combat. On 8th June Warneford woke to a telegram from Buckingham Palace and the award of the Victoria Cross. A hero, feted with flowers and champagne in both France and England, on 16th June he visited a Paris nightclub. A cigarette girl gave him a spray of red roses from her tray, wishing that they would bring him happiness when he returned to England. He replied sadly, 'They will be for my grave, Mademoiselle. I shall not live to see England again.' His premonition proved correct. On a short flight next day the tailplane dropped off his aircraft and he was killed. The *Daily Express* sponsored a memorial to him in Brompton Cemetery, near West Brompton underground station. It depicts an airship under attack with a portrait of Warneford.

Near the western boundary of the cemetery is a tall monument to honour 2625 **pensioners of the Royal Hospital, Chelsea**, who were buried here in the years 1855–93. The battles in which they fought are listed, from Mysore to the Crimea. At each corner stands a roaring bronze lion by stacked cannon balls, and the monument is surmounted by a trophy of flags.

Halfway along the cemetery path which runs parallel to Ifield Road to the east of the cemetery, and in its oldest part, is the grave of **John Jackson** (1769–1845). Jackson was England's champion fighter from 1795 to 1803. After retirement he ran a boxing school, of which Lord Byron, the poet, was a pupil. The monument bears a relief portrait of Jackson on the right-hand side and is surmounted (as is that of his fellow pugilist, Tom Cribb, at Woolwich) by a sculpture of a large lion. Unfortunately the face of the lion, once a symbol of strength and pugnacity, has weathered so that it looks more surprised than fierce. The monument was paid for by the subscriptions of Jackson's admirers.

9.
Around Oxford Street

Facing Great Cumberland Place, on the south side of Bryanston Square, is an elaborate drinking-fountain, a memorial to **William O. H. Byrne** 'from a design by his widow'. Byrne was editor of the *Morning Post*, a London newspaper founded in 1772. At first successful, it fell on evil days about 1850 but recovered to be amalgamated with the *Daily Telegraph* in 1937.

In Great Cumberland Place is **Raoul Wallenberg**'s statue by Philip Jackson. Wallenberg, a Swedish diplomat, is depicted with his back against a wall made up of a hundred thousand *Schutzpasses*, one for each of the Hungarian Jews he saved from the Nazi Holocaust in the Second World War. These bogus passport documents gave Swedish citizenship to refugees, allowing them to leave for Sweden. He and his chauffeur were arrested by the Russians in 1945 for alleged spying. For decades there have been reports of sightings of Wallenberg. A Swedish–Russian investigation into his fate lasted ten years. The Russians continue to maintain that Wallenberg died, or was murdered, in captivity on 17th July 1947. However, on 12th January 2001 Goran Persson, the Prime Minister of Sweden, said that there was no evidence that Wallenberg was dead. The Swedish government has promised to increase efforts to determine his fate. His memorial was unveiled by Queen Elizabeth II on 26th February 1998 in a ceremony attended by many distinguished guests, including the President of Israel.

Marble Arch by John Nash was set up in 1827 as a triumphal entrance to Buckingham Palace, at a cost of £80,000. Chantrey's crowning statue of George IV, now in Trafalgar Square, was made for it but was never put up. The Arch was intended to symbolise the victories of Trafalgar and Waterloo but the concept changed and the panels represent the Spirit of England inspiring Youth, Valour and Virtue, and Peace and Plenty. The sculptors were Flaxman, Westmacott, Rossi and Baily. The superb bronze gates were by Samuel Parker. Too late, it is said,

Raoul Wallenberg's memorial in Great Cumberland Place.

they were found to be too narrow to admit the State Coach. The Arch was moved outside the palace and finally brought here in 1851.

At the junction of Bayswater Road and Oxford Street the 12 foot high **Tyburn gallows** stood for nearly six hundred years, with room for eight executions at once. Public executions took place at a spot marked today by a Portland stone slab with a cross and inscription, on the traffic island at the end of Edgware Road. The condemned were brought by cart from Newgate prison and the Tower. They included Perkin Warbeck, the pretender to the throne, executed in 1499, and Jack Sheppard, a notorious eighteenth-century highwayman and prison-breaker. Executions attracted enormous crowds: 200,000 attended Sheppard's hanging in 1724. Jonathan Wild created a sensation by picking the hangman's pocket as he adjusted the noose. Here, too, 105 Catholic martyrs suffered for their faith. In 1998, on the Feast of St Edmund Campion, Westminster City Council affixed a memorial plaque to the wall of the Shrine of the Sacred Heart and Tyburn Martyrs (whose nuns pray for the souls of the martyrs) at Marble Arch. It was hoped that this would draw pilgrims away from the traffic island at one of London's most hazardous intersections.

Grosvenor Square, south of Oxford Street, laid out by Sir Richard Grosvenor (ancestor of the Dukes of Westminster) is one of the earliest examples of landscaping of this kind. It has been nicknamed 'Little America'. The transatlantic association began early when John Adams, later President of the

Presidents Roosevelt and Eisenhower in Grosvenor Square.

United States of America, moved here in 1785, and by the Second World War the square was surrounded by American offices and institutions. Now the name is even more apposite, with Saarinen's vast embassy (1958–61), surmounted by a gilded eagle with a wing span of 35 feet by Theodor Roszak (1960). Sir William Reid Dick's statue of **President Franklin Delano Roosevelt** (1882–1945), America's wartime president, was unveiled by Mrs Roosevelt on 12th April 1948. The subscription list was open to British citizens only; contributors were limited to five shillings (25p) per person and the sum required was raised within twenty-four hours. An avenue of trees leads to the statue, which shows the President cloaked and leaning on a stick. Following the devastating terrorist attacks on New York, Washington and Pennsylvania on 11th September 2001, a book of condolence was opened by the United States ambassador William Farish and placed in a marquee in the garden by the statue of President Roosevelt. Long queues formed and in groups of one hundred the public was admitted to sign the book. Many also left cards and flowers at the statue's plinth emphasising the warm bonds between the British and American peoples, exemplified by the Roosevelt statue and other American memorials nearby.

The statue of **President Dwight David Eisenhower** (1890–1969) stands near Number 20 Grosvenor Square, his wartime headquarters. His office was the corner room on the first floor. In the 1980s the United States ambassador to Britain, Charles H. Price, and his wife noticed the lack of a statue of Eisenhower and raised funds among friends and associates in Kansas City, where Eisenhower had been raised. The statue, by the American sculptor Robert Dean, was unveiled by Prime Minister Margaret Thatcher and Charles H. Price on 23rd January 1989. Eisenhower is shown in uniform, in relaxed stance, hands on hips. On the marble surround is a chronology of his career, on the reverse the historic Order of the Day for 6th June 1944. Eisenhower was Commander of Allied Forces in North Africa, 1942–3; Supreme Allied Commander Europe, 1943–5; Chief of Staff, American Army, 1945; First Military Commander of NATO, 1950–2; and President of the United States of America, 1953–61, during which time the Korean War ended and the Civil Rights Act was passed. He was that rarest of presidents, one whose personal popularity was nearly as great on retirement as on the day he was elected.

Also in the square, the **American Eagle Squadrons' Memorial** by Elizabeth Frink consists of a Portland stone pillar surmounted by the American bald eagle. It commemorates the 244 American and 16 British fighter pilots who served in the three RAF Eagle Squadrons. Their names, with the inscription 'They served with valour', are listed.

In Carlos Place, which leads south from Grosvenor Square, by the Connaught Hotel, is a **fountain** with an over-life-size nymph (1973). The inscription reads: 'A gift to the City of Westminster from the President of the Italian Republic 20th November 1987'. Sponsored by the Italian Bank in London, it commemorates the friendship between Britain and Italy.

Here is Mount Street, where a white marble bust of **Queen Victoria** in a niche over the entrance to Number 121 is dated 1887 in celebration of the Queen's Golden Jubilee. Nearby, at the corner with Carpenter Street, is a companion bust of the **first Duke of Westminster**, who presented both pieces.

Mount Street leads into Berkeley Square. Here a white marble **nymph** with reeds and a pitcher decorates a fountain, restored in 1994. It is the work of Alexander Munro (1825–71) and was presented about 1858 by Henry, third Marquess of Lansdowne, who lived nearby in Lansdowne House.

At the south end of Hanover Square is a bronze statue of William Pitt the Younger.

At the south end of Hanover Square, facing St George's Church, is a bronze statue of **William Pitt the Younger** (1759–1806), statesman and Prime Minister, by Sir Francis Chantrey. The statue had a stormy early life. When it was erected the Whigs attempted to pull it off its plinth. When told Chantrey smiled: 'The cramps are leaded and they may pull till Doomsday'.

George III had a great liking for Pitt, 'The Great Commoner' and 'The Pilot Who Weathered the Storm'. When Pitt resumed office in 1804 he congratulated the King on looking in better health than when they had last met in 1801. 'That is not to be wondered at,' replied the King, 'I was then on the point of parting with an old friend; I am now about to regain one.' Pitt, who had become Prime Minister at the age of twenty-four, had an unerring touch with a phrase. At the Guildhall in 1805, after Trafalgar, he thanked the company for their plaudits, saying, 'England has saved herself by her exertions and will, as I trust, save Europe by her example'. Sadly, further disappointments were in store before Napoleon was vanquished. After the Allied defeat at Austerlitz in December 1805 Pitt said: 'Roll up that map of Europe, it will not be wanted these ten years' – a prophetic comment since victory at Waterloo still lay ten years ahead. These phrases have been much quoted since.

Across Regent Street a painted stone bust of **William Shakespeare** (1564–1616) leans from a window of the Shakespeare's Head pub in Foubert's Place, at the junction with Great Marlborough Street, just east of Regent Street. The bust dates from about 1910; the sculptor is unknown. The pub has no connection with the playwright and was named, it seems, after Thomas and John Shakespeare, landlords from 1735 to 1744.

Golden Square, further south in Soho, has a statue of **George II** (1693–1760), hand extended, by John van Nost the Younger,

This nymph-decorated fountain in Carlos Place was a gift of the President of Italy to the City of Westminster.

Alexander Munro's white marble nymph in Berkeley Square.

William Shakespeare leans from a window at the 'Shakespeare's Head', Foubert's Place.

erected here in 1753. Dickens described it as 'this mournful statue, the guardian genius of a little wilderness of shrubs'.

East of Golden Square, on St Peter's and St James's School (now Soho Parish School) in Great Windmill Street, is the stone bust of **Edward George Stanley, fourteenth Earl of Derby** (1799–1869) by an unknown sculptor. In 1860, as Prime Minister, Lord Derby laid the foundation stone of St Peter's Church, demolished in 1954, when the bust was moved here. St Peter's had connections with two other Prime Ministers, Gladstone and Lord Salisbury, who were regular worshippers. Rather incongruously, Lord Derby surveys a street famous for the Windmill Theatre, where nearly nude revues were staged; its proud wartime boast was 'We never closed'.

On the west wall of the tower of St Anne's Church, Wardour Street, a tablet with a sculpted crown commemorates **Theodore, deposed King of Corsica** – in fact, Baron Neuhoff, a German soldier of fortune, who is buried here. In 1730 he agreed to help the Corsicans, provided he could be their king. He

George II in Golden Square.

The stone bust of the Earl of Derby in Great Windmill Street.

accepted the crown in 1736, lived in high style, ran into debt and was hounded out within months. After two attempts to regain his kingdom he settled in England in 1749. He was quickly arrested for debt but obtained his liberty from King's Bench Prison by sacrificing all his effects to his creditors, including his claim to the Corsican throne. He was released but died a mere three days later. John Wright, an oilman of Compton Street, paid for his funeral, to save the monarch from a pauper's grave, saying that 'He was willing, *for once*, to pay the funeral expenses of a king'. A regal epitaph was supplied by Horace Walpole:

> The grave, great teacher, to a level brings
> Heroes and beggars, galley slaves and kings,
> Fate pour'd its lessons on his living head,
> Bestow'd a kingdom and denied him bread.

In the centre of Soho Square is a weathered statue of **Charles II** (1630–85) by Caius Gabriel Cibber, son of the actor–dramatist Colley Cibber. Soho Square was laid out in Charles II's reign.

Oxford Street leads west to Regent Street at Oxford Circus. To the north-west is Cavendish Square, which dates from 1717. Here there is a bronze statue by T. Campbell (1851) of **Lord William George Frederick Bentinck** (1802–48), politician, secretary to his uncle, George Canning, and a great sportsman, who would attend the House of Commons in hunting kit under his overcoat. He became leader of the Protectionist Party and opposed Peel. A racing man, his mare 'Crucifix' won the Oaks, the One Thousand Guineas and the Two Thousand Guineas. Every ship in the Port of London marked his death with flags at half-mast.

Also in Cavendish Square, an empty plinth bears the inscription: 'Equestrian statue of **Duke of Cumberland** 1721–1765, erected by Lieutenant General

William Strode 1770'. Cumberland was reviled by many in Scotland for his supposed harshness to Highlanders after the battle of Culloden in 1746. Yet in England stories of his generosity were told and he was admired. When he died an equestrian statue paid for by public subscription was proposed but nothing came of it. General Strode persisted and set one up in 1770. The *Dictionary of National Biography* states, without elaboration, 'It was taken down in 1868'. The plinth has survived unoccupied ever since.

At 22/23 Queen Anne Street, north of Cavendish Square, a stone plaque with a relief portrait commemorates **Joseph Mallord William Turner** (1775–1851), an ARA at the age of twenty-four and RA at twenty-eight, and one of England's most evocative artists. His mastery of air, light and contrast is clear in such works as *The Fighting Téméraire* and *Ulysses Deriding Polyphemus*. His philosophy was eloquently expressed in his last words, 'The sun is God'. Turner lived in Queen Anne Street and when Lord Howard de Walden rebuilt the house in 1937 he placed the plaque by W. C. H. King over the garage. It is sad that so brilliant an artist has no more impressive memorial. When the Houses of Parliament were destroyed by fire on 16th October 1834 Turner spent the whole night on the Thames in a boat making numerous sketches. A series of nine delicate and intensely fiery watercolours, 'The Burning of the Houses of Parliament', is now in Tate Britain. One shows what historians believe to be the moment when the roof of the House of Lords collapsed.

Thomas Woolner (1825–92), a leading Victorian sculptor, lived at 29 Welbeck Street, at the west end of Queen Anne Street, from 1860 to 1892. The house bears a plaque with a relief portrait of Woolner, who made the statues of Hunter in Leicester Square, John Stuart Mill on the Victoria Embankment, and Palmerston in Parliament Square – the last regarded as his most successful.

John Nash (1752–1835), the architect, is remembered at the church of All Souls, Langham Place, with a wall-bust by Cecil Thomas under the portico (1956). Nash built All Souls' to complete the vista of Regent Street in 1823–4. The needle-like spire, much admired today, was derided by Nash's contemporaries. After a parliamentary debate on the subject a cartoon appeared showing Nash impaled on the spire by the seat of his trousers. He rather relished the publicity and, refusing to be depressed, joked with his assistants: 'See, gentlemen, how criticism has exalted me!' No one had greater influence on the appearance of the London of his day. The gleaming white stucco façades and columns of Carlton House Terrace (1827–32) make it the most inspiring of Nash's works. Nash popularised stucco, a paste based on a powder of fired clay nodules from the Isle of Sheppey, which looked like stone but was vastly cheaper:

> Augustus at Rome was for building renown'd,
> And of marble he left what of brick he had found.
> But is not our Nash, too, a very great master?
> He finds us all brick and he leaves us all plaster.

In Portland Place, close to All Souls', is a monument to the philanthropist **Quintin Hogg** (1845–1903), founder of Regent Street Polytechnic in 1882. The statue (1906) by Sir George Frampton shows Hogg surrounded by a group of boys, endearingly shown, in knitted pullovers, one of whom holds a football. Hogg lived at 5 Cavendish Square and founded the Polytechnic to provide day and evening technical instruction. He is said to have started by teaching two crossing-sweepers from Trafalgar Square, who studied by the light of a tallow

Charles II by Caius Gabriel Cibber in Soho Square.

Below: *John Nash on the church of All Souls in Langham Place.*

candle stuck in an empty beer bottle. From this grew the Polytechnic. Hogg also organised cheap holidays abroad for members and helped them to obtain jobs. In 1902 the government implemented Hogg's idea and founded labour exchanges in the metropolitan boroughs. The memorial also commemorates Hogg's wife and members of the Polytechnic who died in the two world wars.

Further along Portland Place is the bronze equestrian statue of **Sir George White** (1835–1912), the defender of Ladysmith, by John Tweed (1922). Ladysmith was a chivalrous siege: Britain sent the Boers medical supplies; in return the Boers fired a shell into the compound on Christmas Day – full of Christmas puddings.

In Portland Place, at the corner of Weymouth Street, opposite the Polish Embassy, stands the statue of **General Wladyslaw Sikorski** (1881–1943), Prime Minister of the Polish Government and Commander-in-Chief of the Polish armed forces and the resistance movement from 7th November 1939 to 4th July 1943. The bronze statue, of heroic size, by Faith Winter, which shows General Sikorski in the uniform of a general of the Polish army, was

Quintin Hogg, the philanthropist, has a monument in Portland Place.

unveiled by the Duke of Kent (whose father was a close friend of the general) on 24th September 2000. The statue also commemorates the soldiers, seamen and airmen of the Polish armed forces and the resistance movement. Sponsors of the project, which was initiated by Tomasz Zamoyski and funded by public subscription, were the Polish Institute and General Sikorski Museum and the British–Polish Council. General Sir Charles Guthrie, Chief of the Defence Staff, was patron. At the unveiling the Duke read a message from the Queen Mother in which she recalled the great esteem in which she and King George IV held General Sikorski.

General Sikorski died on 4th July 1943 when the aircraft bringing him back from inspecting Polish forces in the Middle East crashed off Gibraltar. In 1993 his remains were re-interred in Wawel Castle, Cracow, Poland. The role played by the Polish armed forces in the Second World War is legendary. Battles in which they fought are listed on the plinth: the Polish campaign, the French campaign, Narvik, the Battle of Britain, the Battle of the Atlantic,

Poland's wartime leader was General Wladyslaw Sikorski. His statue stands in Portland Place.

Lord Lister, the 'father of antiseptic surgery' and (below) Sir George White, the defender of Ladysmith.

Tobruk, Monte Cassino, Falaise and Arnhem and the Warsaw uprising of the Polish Home Army.

Poland also made a vital contribution to the breaking of the German Enigma code. Marian Rejewski, a Polish mathematician and code breaker, worked on the problem from 1932 and succeeded in reconstructing an Enigma machine which the Polish secret service gave to Britain. This was handed over on the 'Golden Arrow' platform at Victoria station on 16th August 1939 at the celebrated meeting between Captain Gustave Bertrand of French Intelligence, and Colonel Stewart Menzies, deputy head of MI6, who was wearing a dinner jacket with the rosette of the *Légion d'Honneur* in his buttonhole. As captain Bertrand said, it was an '*Accueil triomphal*', for a gift that was an important component in Bletchley Park's mastery of the Enigma code. Bletchley Park, alias 'Station X', was the war section of the Government Code and Cypher School in Buckinghamshire.

Here too is **Lord Lister** (1827–1912), the surgeon and 'father of antiseptic surgery'. His bust by Brock is near his old home. Lister developed an early interest in gangrene and inflammation, studied and developed carbolic acid as an antiseptic and published his findings in *The Lancet* in 1867. His techniques revolutionised surgery; he became the first medical peer and was one of the twelve original members of the Order of Merit.

In Park Crescent, at the end of Portland Place is a statue by Sebastian Gahagan of **Edward Augustus, Duke of Kent** (1767–1820), father of Queen Victoria, his only child.

The International Students' Hostel at 1 Park Crescent has a memorial bust to **John Fitzgerald Kennedy** (1917–63), the youngest and first Catholic President of the United States, associated with social reform and the civil rights movement. The bust by Jacques Lipchitz (1965) is a copy of the one in the Library of Congress and Harvard Library. It was unveiled by President Kennedy's brothers, Edward and Robert.

Between 1839 and 1851 **Charles Dickens** (1812–70) lived in a house that

Above: *President Kennedy's memorial bust at 1 Park Crescent.*

Left: *In Park Crescent is the Duke of Kent, father of Queen Victoria.*

stood at the junction of Marylebone Road and Marylebone High Street. *The Old Curiosity Shop, Barnaby Rudge, Martin Chuzzlewit, David Copperfield* and *A Christmas Carol* were written here. On the wall of Ferguson House, Numbers 15 and 17 Marylebone Road, is a sculpted relief of Dickens and characters from his books by Eastcourt J. Clack (1960).

Tussaud's Waxworks have long been a London attraction, kept up to date with additions and deletions. On the east façade of the exhibition building in Marylebone Road is a fibreglass medallion of the founder, **Madame Marie Tussaud** (1760–1850). A Swiss from Bern, she was drawing mistress to Louis XVI's children and also inherited her uncle's waxworks. During the French Revolution she was brought freshly severed heads from the guillotine, including that of Marie Antoinette, and ordered to make death masks. She married a Frenchman named Tussaud but left him, came to England and, after touring, set up a permanent exhibition of waxworks in 1835. The original

This plaque to Dickens is in Marylebone Road.

The Great Detective

Sherlock Holmes, 'The Great Detective', wears deerstalker and cape at Baker Street station.

building was gutted by fire in 1925 but was rebuilt, and the medallion, by Arthur Pollen, was added in 1969. The Duke of Wellington was among the fans of the Chamber of Horrors: he asked to be informed when a new 'horror' was added. Dickens described Tussaud's as 'more than an exhibition ... an institution'. Its popularity endures today.

The creation of a statue of Sir Arthur Conan Doyle's immortal character **Sherlock Holmes** was long an ambition of the Sherlock Holmes Society of London. Now the statue stands outside Baker Street station in Marylebone Road, and is inscribed simply 'The Great Detective', a title by which Holmes is affectionately recognised from London to Sydney, from Tokyo to Cairo (where the stories were said to have been used as a police training manual). The 9 foot high bronze statue by John Doubleday was unveiled on 23rd September 1999 by Lord Tugendhat, Chairman of Abbey National plc, principal sponsors of the project. (Abbey National has been associated with Holmes since 1930, when its head office moved to 221 Baker Street – Holmes himself had rooms at 221b.) The statue was accepted on behalf of the people of Westminster by the Deputy Lord Mayor. A colourful pageant of characters from the novels followed, accompanied by a hansom cab and a Victorian horse-drawn omnibus, which proceeded from Lord's Cricket Ground to Baker Street. The project was supported by many well-wishers and Holmesian societies worldwide, including the Baker Street Irregulars of New York. John Doubleday also created the statue of Holmes at the Reichenbach Falls, Switzerland, where the detective pushed his arch adversary, Moriarty, over the Falls to his death. Thirty or forty letters a week are still addressed to Mr Holmes, requesting his help. All are faithfully answered by his secretary. On 14th February 2001 he even received a Valentine.

Further west, at 1 Dorset Square, was the office of the **Free French Forces** engaged in wartime Resistance work. A plaque unveiled in 1957 states that it was placed 'to commemorate the deeds of the men and women of the Free French Forces and their British comrades who left from this house on special missions to enemy-occupied France'. Sadly, many did not return.

10.
BLOOMSBURY, EUSTON AND CAMDEN TOWN

On the south side of Russell Square is a statue of **Francis Russell, fifth Duke of Bedford** (1765–1805), the great agriculturalist, builder of the square, and a large landowner in this area. (Russell is the family name of the Dukes of Bedford.) The statue by Sir Richard Westmacott (1809) shows the Duke with his hand on a plough, with sheep at his feet and four cherubs representing the seasons. 'Winter' is shown well muffled up.

On the north side of Bloomsbury Square is a statue of **Charles James Fox** (1749–1806), third son of the first Lord Holland, ardent Whig, passionate defender of individual liberties, friend of Burke and supporter of the American and French revolutions (he called the fall of the Bastille 'the best news since Saratoga'). The statue by Westmacott (1816) shows Fox with a copy of Magna Carta in his hand. Boswell wrote, 'Fox divided the kingdom with Caesar; so that it was a doubt whether the nation should be ruled by the sceptre of George III or the tongue of Fox'. During his political career he took office briefly, formed coalitions and was dismissed with some frequency. He played a leading role in proceedings against Warren Hastings and constantly opposed Pitt's policies, although after Pitt's death, as Foreign Secretary, he came to appreciate Napoleon's duplicity. Fox's great personal charm, brilliant debating skills, scholarship and love of letters were appreciated but he was an inveterate gambler who lost a fortune at the tables. George Selwyn said his interests were, in order, gambling, women and politics: he was the Prince of Wales's companion in all three pursuits. The King was naturally concerned to see his

The statue to the Duke of Bedford in Russell Square, and one of the plaques on the plinth.

95

heir thus led astray. One day, as Fox and the Prince walked down Bond Street, Fox wagered that he would see more cats on his side of the street than the Prince would on his. Fox won: he knew that cats prefer the sunny side of the street.

Fox attracted various admirers. His election as MP for Westminster in 1784 was aided by an efficient band of Whig ladies, including Georgiana, Duchess of Devonshire, Viscountess Duncannon and the Countess of Carlisle, trading smiles for votes. The landlord of the Intrepid Fox in Wardour Street, Soho, named his tavern after Fox and gave Foxites free beer all day. In the end, despite the uproar he had caused, Fox left little lasting impression. He was deficient in statesmanship and ignorant of the importance of political science. Lecky wrote: 'he failed signally in a long public life in winning the confidence of the nation'.

Congress House, 23–28 Great Russell Street, is the headquarters of the Trades Union Congress. It has an impressive **war memorial** sculpture to trades unionists by Sir Jacob Epstein (1958), cut from a solid 10 ton block of Roman stone and set off by a green Carrara marble background.

The steeple of St George's Church in Bloomsbury Way, by Nicholas Hawksmoor, and based on the King of Caria's tomb at Halicarnassus, one of the wonders of the ancient world, is surmounted by a statue of **George I** (1660–1727), erected by a loyal brewer and described by Horace Walpole as a 'master-stroke of absurdity'. This incongruous figure, in Roman dress, provoked the rhyme:

When Harry the Eighth left the Pope in the lurch,
He ruled over England as head of the church,
But George's good subjects, the Bloomsbury people,
Instead of the church, made him head of the steeple.

Near the junction of Southampton Row and Holborn is a statue of **John**

John Bunyan holds a copy of his 'Pilgrim's Progress'.

Bunyan (1618–88) by Richard Garbe, put up in 1901 on the first floor of the former Baptist Church House. Among Bunyan's many books is *Pilgrim's Progress*, partly written in Bedford gaol, where he was imprisoned for unlawful preaching. The statue bears the first line of the book.

In the wall of the **Bedford Hotel**, Southampton Row, a memorial has this inscription: '24th September 1917. 13 people were killed and 22 injured near this spot on the steps of the Old Bedford Hotel by a 112lb bomb dropped by a Gotha in one of London's first night air raids'. The severity of the raids of 1940–1 in the Second World War has eclipsed those that took place almost twenty-five years earlier.

On the east side of Red Lion Square, among the plane trees, is a bust of **Bertrand Arthur William Russell, third Earl Russell** (1872–1970), by Marcelle Quinton (1980). Russell, the greatest British rationalist philosopher, logician, mathematician and political campaigner of the twentieth century, had a profound influence on modern thought. He wrote widely and vigorously and was honoured with the Order of Merit in 1948 and the Nobel Prize for Literature in 1950. Today he is most generally remembered for his support for the Campaign for Nuclear Disarmament. A sensation was caused by the publication of his three-volume autobiography (1967–9), which threw fresh light on his unhappy childhood, the first of his three marriages and his relationship with Lady Ottoline Morrell. Many stories are told of him. At a rally in Trafalgar Square he was heard to say to a policeman about to arrest him, 'Take me up *very* carefully, I'm *very* old and I *am* an earl'. But it is comforting to find that even this great mind was not equal to every challenge. A cabbie told of picking him up in London one night: 'I sez to 'im, "Well, Lord Russell, what's it all about then?" and d'ye know, he couldn't tell me!' Pointing to his

Below left: *The animated pose of Fenner Brockway's statue reflects the fact that Brockway was still living when it was erected, and he even saw it unveiled.*

Below right: *On the east side of Red Lion Square is this bust of Bertrand Russell.*

Captain Coram's bust in Brunswick Square. He would be happy to know that his Foundation still flourishes in London and Hertfordshire.

bookshelf, Russell used to say, 'There's a Bible on that shelf there. I keep it next to Voltaire. Poison and antidote.'

On the west side of Red Lion Square a statue by Ian Walters of **Archibald Fenner Brockway, Baron Brockway** (1888–1988), was unveiled on 25th July 1985 by Michael Foot, watched by a jubilant Brockway, aged ninety-six, elated to have a statue erected in his lifetime. He celebrated his ninety-ninth birthday by addressing the House of Lords on African affairs. Brockway was a conscientious objector in the First World War, pacifist, pro-disarmament, anti-imperialist, a human rights activist, Labour MP for Eton and Slough, 1950–64 (nicknamed 'MP for Eton and Africa'), and a life peer from 1964. After late sittings the young MP Margaret Thatcher often gave him a lift home to Finchley. One night she asked what he had wanted to be. He said he only wanted to *do*. 'But to *do*, you must *be*,' she replied. It said much about both their temperaments.

Queen Square at the west end of Great Ormond Street has a statue of about 1775, which may be **Charlotte**, **Anne** or **Mary II**. Byron said cattily of these queenly candidates: 'the face is pretty, which should eliminate them all'.

North of Queen Square, Guilford Street runs east to Brunswick Square. At Number 40 are the offices of the Coram Family, formerly the Thomas Coram Foundation, once known as the Foundling Hospital. It was started in 1739 by the compassionate **Captain Thomas Coram** (1668–1751), distressed by the sight of 'deserted infants exposed to the inclemencies of the season' in the streets of London. Outside is Coram's statue by William Macmillan (1963) in a pose taken from Hogarth's portrait.

The Waterbearer in Guilford Place.

Two busts back to back are an unusual feature of Louisa Aldrich-Blake's memorial in Tavistock Square.

In the early days of the hospital Hogarth persuaded fellow artists, including Gainsborough, Kneller and Rysbrack, to present works of art to aid the funds. The resulting art gallery became a fashionable London rendezvous in the reign of George II. In 1749 Handel gave a performance of his own works, which raised 500 guineas for the hospital, and every year his *Messiah* was sung in the chapel there. Over the years the performances raised over £7000 for the furtherance of Coram's work. In addition there is a stone bust of Coram over the door of 40 Brunswick Square by D. Evans (1937).

At the south end of Coram's Fields is Guilford Place. Here stands 'The Waterbearer', a sculpture of a girl with a pitcher. It was placed here about 1870 but the sculptor is unknown. Some call it a memorial to one Francis Whiting.

Frederick Crauford Goodenough (1866–1934), a banker and founder of Barclays Bank, held office with a number of City organisations. He believed in the Empire and particularly admired Oxford University. This led him to found in 1930 the London Goodenough Trust for Overseas Graduates, and London House, a hall of residence for graduate students from the Dominions, enabling them to experience something of the Oxford collegiate atmosphere in London. Overlooking the inner courtyard of London House in Mecklenburg Square is his bronze bust by William Macmillan.

A bronze statue by George Clarke (1831) of **Major John Cartwright** (1740–1824), who lived at Number 37, sits in the gardens named after him, south of Euston Road. A brother of Edmund Cartwright, inventor of the power

Flowers are placed on the statue of Mahatma Gandhi on the anniversary of his death on 30th January 1948.

loom, he helped with the business aspects of the invention but his real interests were his own campaigns for universal suffrage, equal representation, vote by ballot and annual Parliaments modelled on Anglo-Saxon folk-meets, of which causes the inscription describes him as 'The Firm, Consistent, Persevering Advocate'. This was strong medicine and the authorities took fright: at the age of eighty-one Cartwright was arrested for sedition and escaped drastic punishment only by a whisker. Instead of a prison sentence he was heavily fined.

In the courtyard of the British Medical Association building on the east side of Tavistock Square, iron gates commemorate **medical officers who died in the First World War**. Beside them a pool, fountain and statues by James Woodford, representing Sacrifice, Cure, Prevention and Application, form the Second World War memorial, completed in 1954.

In the south-east corner of Tavistock Square is a memorial to **Dame Louisa Brandreth Aldrich-Blake** (1865–1925), the surgeon, by Sir Edwin Lutyens, with a double bust by A. G. Walker. Dame Louisa is described in the *Dictionary of National Biography* as 'distinguished for her skill in boxing and cricket, at that date unusual in a girl'.

In the centre of the square is a statue by Fredda Brilliant of **Mohandas Karamchand Gandhi** (1869–1948), principal creator of India's independence, better known as Mahatma Gandhi. He is depicted in an attitude of prayer.

A model of the first steam locomotive to draw passengers decorates Richard Trevithick's memorial plaque in Gower Street.

General Miranda is at the corner of Fitzroy Street and Grafton Way.

On the north side of the square a rock of Cumbrian slate forms a memorial to **conscientious objectors**, 'to all those who established and are maintaining the right to refuse to kill'.

In 1808 **Richard Trevithick** (1771–1833), a Cornish mining engineer, who in 1801 had designed a steam carriage that reached a speed of 9 mph, stayed in Gower Street and set up an engine called 'Catch Me Who Can', charging the public one shilling for a ride. On the wall of University College in Gower Street, opposite University Street, is a bronze tablet with a medallion portrait by L. S. Merrifield, put up in 1933 by the centenary committee, saying of Trevithick, 'Pioneer of High Pressure Steam. Ran in the year 1808 the first steam locomotive to draw passengers.' A model of the engine is included.

The memorial of the **Second County of London Regiment** (the Rangers) in Chenies Street, off Tottenham Court Road, includes a bronze copy of the regimental badge. In the First World War the Rangers

Robert Stephenson, whose statue stands at Euston station, was Chief Engineer of the London to Birmingham Railway.

This statue of Isaac Newton dominates the forecourt of the British Library.

fought in France; in the Second they fought as part of the King's Royal Rifle Corps, in Greece, Crete and the Western Desert.

At the corner of Fitzroy Street and Grafton Way is a statue of **General Francisco de Miranda** (1750–1816), the 'Precursor of Latin American Independence'. Miranda was born in Venezuela and died a prisoner at Cadiz in Spain on 14th July 1816 after an abortive attempt to free his homeland from Spanish rule. He spent fourteen years in England, the years 1803–10 at 27 Grafton Street (now 58 Grafton Way). In 1978 the house was bought by the Venezuelan government as a museum. Here he planned his campaign and met with Simón Bolívar, Andrés Bello and others, who joined in his work. His statue shows a bareheaded figure in a frockcoat and high boots, with a tasselled sword in his scabbard.

Euston was the London terminus of the London to Birmingham Railway, opened in 1838, and a statue of its chief engineer, **Robert Stephenson** (1803–59), by Marochetti, stands at Euston station today. After working as an engineer in South America Stephenson took part in 1827 in constructing the 'Rocket', the locomotive designed by his father, George Stephenson. He then worked on the London to Birmingham route. A contemporary described him as 'a type and pattern of the onward moving English race, practical, scientific, energetic and in the hour of trial, heroic'. The inventiveness and competence of his work endure. Ox hides laid across marshy ground to sustain the track bed of the London to Birmingham Railway are still in place today and working well. Engineers have seen no reason to remove them. Stephenson's other engineering feats include the Britannia Tubular Bridge across the Menai Straits, the High Level Bridge at Newcastle and the Victoria Bridge over the St Lawrence river in Montreal (1854), at that date the longest bridge in the world. He was also briefly MP for Whitby.

Outside Euston Station a 30 foot high stone obelisk commemorates the employees of the London, Midland and Scottish Railway who died in two world wars. Bronze figures of servicemen stand guard at each corner.

A 12 foot bronze statue by Eduardo Paolozzi of **Sir Isaac Newton** (1642–1727), the physicist and mathematician, shown plotting the immensity of the universe with dividers, based on the image by William Blake, stands in the forecourt of the British Library in St Pancras. Before Einstein, Sir Isaac Newton's discoveries in the fields of optics, mathematics and gravitational

Anne Frank is depicted writing in her diary.

forces held the field. Pope wrote:

Nature and Nature's laws lay
hid in sight:
God said, let Newton be! And
all was light.

Also in the forecourt of the British Library is a life-sized bronze bust of **Anne Frank** (1929–1945) by Doreen Kern, inscribed 'A triumph of the spirit'. It was the gift of Richard and Yvonne Sherrington to mark the 70th anniversary of Anne Frank's birth. A German Jewish girl who died in a German concentration camp, Anne Frank became famous for her *Diary*, published in 1947 and a symbol of Jewish resistance and courage. The statue shows her writing. A few feet away is a tree planted on 12th June 1998 to commemorate Anne Frank and all children killed in wars and conflicts of the twentieth century.

Lady Soane, wife of the architect **Sir John Soane**, died in 1815 and was buried in St Giles's Burial Ground, adjacent to Old St Pancras Church, Pancras Road. Three years later Sir John (1753–1837) designed a mausoleum as a family vault, in which he is buried. A vertical block of inscribed stone stands under a domed canopy on Ionic pillars. The canopy's design is based on that of a Roman ash-chest. The whole is topped by a pineapple, and a balustrade with

Left: *Sir John Soane is buried in this mausoleum, which he designed himself.*

Right: *When the burial ground adjoining Old St Pancras Church became a public garden this decorative memorial was set up to commemorate those buried there.*

Napoleon III was a donor to the Richard Cobden statue fund. The statue stands in Camden High Street.

Soane-style ornaments completes the mausoleum. The monument has been restored.

Nearby, an elaborate **column** commemorates and lists previous occupants of the old St Pancras burial ground when it was converted into a garden.

In Camden High Street is a frock-coated statue of **Richard Cobden** (1804–65), political economist, Liberal MP, a partner in a Lancashire cotton firm, Free Trader and one of the leaders of the Anti-Corn-Law League. The 8 foot statue of Sicilian marble by W. and T. Wills (1868) stands on its original site, now a traffic island. The largest contributor to the statue fund was Napoleon III. Cobden organised the Anti-Corn-Law League of 1839–46 with John Bright. Hundreds of meetings led the agitation for the repeal of the Corn Laws, which placed protective tariffs on imported grain and kept bread prices high. Sir Robert Peel, with appalling misjudgement, supported the repeal. The effect was not felt immediately but by the 1870s American farmers, aided by large-scale production, improved machinery and railways, and a reliable climate, flooded the British market with cheap grain. British prices plummeted. A gradual agricultural decline set in, which, with a few intermissions, has continued to this day. Disraeli attacked Peel and ruined him but it was too late. Cobden, hailed as 'Saviour of the Poor' by Free Traders, was more concerned with cheap food than with national well-being and self-sufficiency. His statue was unveiled to scenes of widespread rejoicing.

In St Martin's Gardens just east of Camden High Street, laid out on the former burial ground of St Martin's-in-the-Fields in Camden Town, a Celtic cross erected by the Kentish Town Musical Society commemorates **Charles Dibdin** (1745–1814), actor, dramatist and prolific writer of patriotic songs, especially about the Royal Navy. His works include such favourites as 'Tom Bowling' (a portrait of his brother, Captain Thomas Dibdin) and 'Saturday Night at Sea', still sung today. At the time of the great naval battles of the eighteenth century, in the age of 'England expects ...', these were seen as valuable aids to naval recruiting, painting a rosy picture of life at sea. So telling was his influence that once, when mutiny threatened the Fleet, Dibdin was sent to sing to the sailors to revive their sense of patriotism.

Still heard on mess nights is Dibdin's toast:

> The wind that blows, the ship that goes
> – and the lass that loves a sailor!

A Celtic cross in St Martin's Gardens, Camden Town, commemorates Charles Dibdin, the renowned composer of naval songs.

This column in Orme Square is said to commemorate the visit of Tsar Alexander I in 1814.

11.
Paddington to Regent's Park

Facing Bayswater Road is Orme Square, built about 1815 and named after Edward Orme, a Bond Street printseller who bought the ground with the proceeds of his Kensington gravel pits. He is said to have sold two shiploads of building gravel to Tsar Alexander I when he visited London in 1814. Here there is a **column surmounted by an eagle**, by an unknown sculptor. It is said to commemorate the triumphal visit of the Tsar and Allied sovereigns to England after Waterloo but the eagle is neither the Orme crest nor the Russian imperial eagle. It remains a mystery.

In Paddington station, the principal terminus for the west of England from the grand days of the Great Western Railway (the GWR or, to its many admirers,

'God's Wonderful Railway'), sits the statue of **Isambard Kingdom Brunel** (1806–59), who is also remembered on the Embankment. The Paddington statue, beneath the clock on Platform 1, is by John Doubleday and was unveiled by the Lord Mayor of Westminster in 1982. Brunel, a brilliant engineer, was also a romantic and arranged the alignment of Box Tunnel, near Bath, the longest in England when it was built, so that the sun shone through it on his birthday, 9th April. On the wall of Platform 1 is a **plaque of Brunel** by E. R. Bevan, showing him with top hat and

Isambard Kingdom Brunel can be found underneath the clock on Platform 1 on Paddington station.

Paddington Bear, with his label and luggage at Paddington station.

cigar, put up to commemorate the station's centenary in 1954.

Also on Platform 1 stands an impressive **war memorial**, commemorating 3312 men and women of the GWR who died. It is in the form of a soldier of the First World War. The sculptor was C. Sargeant Jagger, whose other work included the Royal Artillery memorial in Hyde Park.

A statue of **Paddington Bear**, a marmalade-loving Andean forest bear, who arrived 'from darkest Peru', and was one of Paddington's most famous passengers, stands at the foot of the escalator in a glassed-in shopping and eating complex. The public can use the plinth as a seat. The Paddington Bear stories, by Michael Bond, enjoy enduring popularity. Sadly, Andean bears are now an endangered species, victims of deforestation and hunting.

On Paddington Green is a white marble statue of **Mrs Sarah Siddons** (1755–1831), the actress, by Léon-Joseph Chavalliaud, inspired by Sir Joshua Reynolds's painting *The Tragic Muse*. It was erected in 1897 and was unveiled by Sir Henry Irving. Sarah Siddons came to London in 1782, where she drew crowds until her retirement in 1812. She failed in comedy but was a brilliant tragedian. The statue (illustrated on the cover of this book) shows her in a characteristic pose. She was painted by all the leading portraitists of the day but Thomas Gainsborough, at least, had difficulty with her likeness. He is said to have thrown down his brush with an exasperated retort, 'Dammit, Madam, there is no end to your nose!' Her funeral, the most spectacular ever seen in Paddington, was attended by five thousand mourners.

In Chapel Street, by Edgware Road underground station, is Alan Sly's bronze **The Window Cleaner**.

South of the open space of Wormwood Scrubs and off Du Cane Road is Wormwood Scrubs prison, built 1874–90 as a model prison, with sunlight in every cell. On either side of the entrance gate are stone medallions of **Elizabeth Fry** (1780–1845) and **John Howard** (1726–90) by an unknown sculptor. Elizabeth, daughter of John Gurney, a wealthy Norfolk

The GWR war memorial.

Quaker, married a London merchant, also a Quaker. Following a visit to Newgate prison in 1813, she devoted her life to prison reform and to such matters as the improvement of conditions for convicts en route to Australia and vagrants in London and Brighton. John Howard's is perhaps the greatest name among prison reformers. As High Sheriff of Bedfordshire he toured country prisons and laid information before Parliament that led to such changes as enforced cleanliness in gaols and to the payment, rather than the bribing, of gaolers. The Howard League for Penal Reform (established 1866) flourishes, with a powerful voice on prison administration.

At Lord's Cricket Ground, St John's Wood, headquarters of Middlesex County Cricket Club (MCC), the main entrance gates, designed by Sir Herbert Baker (1923), are a memorial to the legendary player **W. G. Grace** (1848–1915). Grace played forty-four seasons of first-class cricket, made 54,896 runs, took 2876 wickets and made 126 centuries, at the same time running a medical practice. His record stood until broken by Jack Hobbs. On the gates' central pillar are the initials WGG, above them a set of stumps and bails with a ball below and a bat on either side. A lion supervises these items. This is the place to remember WGG's imperturbability under fire. In 1896 Ernest Jones, the Australian fast bowler, bowled straight through Grace's magnificent beard. The Master was unshaken, merely enquiring mildly, 'Whatever are you at?' Grace went to the wicket for the last time at Grove Park on 14th July 1914 and, aged sixty-six, made sixty-nine not out.

On an island at the Lord's end of Prince Albert Road a St George and Dragon group presented in 1907 by Sigismund Goetze (donor of decorations to Regent's Park) later became a **war memorial,** inscribed: 'To the men and women of St Mary-le-Bone who by their service and sacrifice for King and Country freely played their part in both world wars'. The sculptor was C. L. Hartwell.

At the junction of Abbey Road and Grove End Road, just north of the cricket ground, is a bust by A. C. Lacchesi of **Edward Onslow Ford** (1852–1901), the

Edward Onslow Ford's memorial overlooks the Abbey Road pedestrian crossing made famous by the Beatles.

sculptor. A copy of the Muse which the sculptor himself designed for the Shelley monument in University College chapel, Oxford, also forms part of the monument. The Muse holds a broken-stringed lyre, and the inscription reads 'To thine own self be true', from *Hamlet*. The monument was erected in 1903 by friends and admirers.

Sigmund Freud (1856–1939), the eminent psychoanalyst and founder of his subject, lived at 20 Maresfield Gardens, Hampstead, his home after he fled from Nazi Austria in 1938 (and now the Freud Museum). Despite the pressures of flight, he brought with him furniture (including the famous couch), books and financial resources, and reconstructed his Vienna study in London, where it became a meeting place for psychoanalysts. He retained a certain dry humour about his expulsion: 'What progress we are making! In the Middle Ages they would have burned me. Now they are content with burning my books.' Freud died on 23rd September 1939. He was seeing patients only weeks before his death. His statue, by Oscar Nemon, now stands just north of Swiss Cottage underground station, outside the Tavistock Clinic in Belsize Lane and Fitzjohn's Avenue, a world-famous centre for psychotherapy established in 1920. The statue had for years been largely unseen behind Swiss Cottage Library, where it was unveiled on 2nd October 1970 by three of Freud's great-grandchildren. It was moved to its new site on 14th September 1997 in the presence of George Freud, aged two, a great-great-grandson.

At the Zoo end of the Broad Walk, Regent's Park, stands the 6 foot **Parsee Fountain** (1869), of granite and marble with a marble head of Queen Victoria. It was the gift of a wealthy Parsee of Bombay, Sir Cowasjeen Jehangir, 'a token of gratitude to the people of England for the protections enjoyed by him and his Parsee fellow countrymen under British rule in India'. This gratitude had its roots in the history of Sir Cowasjeen's people. They were disciples of Zoraster, paying homage to the sun and fire, and were descendants of those who had fled

Above: *Sigmund Freud was moved to a better site in 1997.*

Left: *The Parsee Fountain in Regent's Park, a token of gratitude from Sir Cowasjeen Jehangir.*

Sigismund Goetze, a benefactor to Regent's Park, is commemorated by a pool with merfolk.

The Goetze Memorial Gates on the east side of Regent's Park.

from Persia to India to escape Moslem persecution. By the nineteenth century they formed a small, wealthy group of merchants, largely in Bombay. Today there are some 76,000 Parsees in India, still centred in Bombay.

The painter and sculptor Sigismund Christian Hubert Goetze (1866–1939) did much to adorn Regent's Park. The **Goetze Memorial Fountain** in Queen Mary's Garden by William Macmillan, with bronzes of a merman and two mermaids, commemorates him. He is also remembered by the magnificent gilded **Goetze Memorial Gates**. Goetze was also a benefactor of the Zoo and is commemorated at the entrance to the Children's Zoo by a bronze statue of a **child riding upon a bear** set on a brick base. The inscription reads: 'In memory of Sigismund Goetze, presented by his widow'. In 1944 Mrs Constance Goetze founded the Constance Fund in memory of her husband. (The fund paid for the Joy of Life Fountain in Hyde Park and the Diana Fountain in Green Park.)

Winnie-the-Pooh, a seemingly very British bear, was Canadian by birth. The statue by Lorne McKean in the Children's Zoo depicts Winnie, the black bear mascot of Canadian troops in England, and commemorates her residence at the Zoo; the bear was given to the Zoo when they were sent to France in December 1914. Winnie had been rescued as a cub by Captain Harry Colebourn, veterinary officer of the Second Canadian Brigade, who bought her for $20 when her mother was killed by a hunter. The City of Winnipeg, after which Winnie is named, later erected a statue of Pooh and gave a replica to the Zoo. Captain Colebourn, in uniform, is shown holding Winnie's paws. The real-life Winnie was the inspiration for A. A. Milne's character. Milne's son, Christopher Robin, who unveiled the statue, remembered visiting the bear with gifts of condensed milk, rather than the honey for which Pooh expressed a liking. A painting of Pooh (the only one known) by E. H. Shepard, who illustrated Milne's work, was auctioned in November 2000 and was bought by the City of Winnipeg, where a 'Winnie-the-Pooh Day' is held every August. The painting will hang in a museum to be built in Pooh's honour.

In the centre of the Zoological Gardens the **Ambika Fountain** commemorates Ambika Paul (12th November 1963 to 19th April 1968). The plaque was unveiled by Swraj Paul, the Labour peer and Chairman of the Caparo Group, and his family on 12th November 1994. In 1992 they donated

Winnie-the-Pooh in the Children's Zoo, Regent's Park.

£1 million to build a new children's zoo and the Ambika Paul Memorial Gardens in memory of their daughter's pleasure in visiting the Zoo. The fountain, sculpted by Shenda Amery, depicts a small girl kneeling down, with a dove perched on her outstretched palm.

'A famous inhabitant of London Zoo 1947–1978. Presented by the sculptor William Timyn in 1982,' is the inscription on a statue of **Guy the Gorilla**. Like a number of other London statues this was cast by the Morris Singer Foundry. Guy originally travelled from the French Cameroons to Paris before his transfer to the Zoo when he was about eighteen months old. He died at the age of about thirty-two.

The **war memorial** to employees of the Zoo who lost their lives in both world wars takes the unusual form of a tall obelisk with minaret-like piercings near the top.

The Regent's Park terraces and the now sadly debased Regent Street were the creation of **John Nash** (1752–1835). In 1930 Lord Gerald Wellesley, later the seventh Duke of Wellington, had a cast taken from a marble head of Nash by William Behnes (1831) and set it between the first-floor windows of his house at 3 Chester Terrace on the eastern edge of the park.

The fountain commemorating Ambika Paul.

Guy the Gorilla, one of the Zoo's most famous inhabitants.

12.
STRAND TO FLEET STREET

David Garrick (1717–79), the actor and theatre manager, lived at 27 Southampton Street, which runs north from the Strand. It overlooked Covent Garden and was convenient for Drury Lane Theatre, which he managed from 1747 until his death. Over the door of the house is a bronze medallion of Garrick, set in a terracotta surround, with figures of Comedy and Tragedy, surmounted by a lyre. Garrick's famous song 'Heart of Oak' is still an inseparable part of naval parades. Johnson found Garrick's productions alluring, saying, but not meaning: 'I'll come no more behind your scenes, David, for the silk stockings and white bosoms of your actresses excite my amorous propensities'. When Garrick died Johnson wrote sadly of 'That stroke of death, which has eclipsed the gaiety of nations, and impoverished the public stock of harmless pleasure'. Garrick's memorial, set up by the trustees of the eleventh Duke of Bedford, is by H. C. Fehr, after a sketch by C. Fitzroy (1901).

Drury Lane Theatre has played a distinguished part in London's theatrical life for centuries. Beside the theatre's main portico is a memorial to **Sir Augustus Harris**, who ran the theatre from 1879 to 1897, became a sheriff of London and was knighted. The elaborate memorial has a fountain, putti and columns surmounted by a lyre. In the centre is a bronze bust of Harris by Sir Thomas Brock.

In the foyer of the theatre, near the ticket office, is a statue of **Sir Noël Coward** (1899–1973), actor and playwright, perhaps best known for his songs 'Mad Dogs and Englishmen' and 'The Stately Homes of England', and for his plays, which include *Bitter Sweet* (1929), *Private Lives* (1930), *Cavalcade* (1931), *Blithe Spirit* (1941) and *This Happy Breed* (1943). He also produced enduringly popular films, such as *In Which We Serve* and *Brief Encounter*. The statue was unveiled by Queen Elizabeth the Queen Mother, a long-time friend of Sir Noël, on 9th December 1998 and marked the launch of a number of

Count Peter of Savoy stands over the entrance to the Savoy Hotel.

The bronze relief of Andrew Young on Bush House.

IN MEMORY OF
ANDREW YOUNG FS1
FIRST VALUER TO THE LONDON COUNTY COUNCIL
1889 – 1914
HE LABOURED TO BEAUTIFY
THE LONDON HE LOVED

events to celebrate the centenary of his birth.

Over the Strand entrance of the Savoy Hotel stands the gilt bronze figure by Frank Lynn Jenkins of **Count Peter of Savoy** (1203–68) in medieval dress with a shield and a 14 foot spear, erected in 1904. Henry III gave the site to Peter, Earl of Savoy and Richmond, uncle of Henry's wife, Eleanor of Provence, and brother of Boniface, Archbishop of Canterbury, for an annual rent of three barbed arrows. Here in 1246 he built the Savoy Palace. When Peter died he left the property to the Great St Bernard Hospice in Savoy but Eleanor bought it back two years later. Much later the Savoy Hotel, which dates from 1903–10, was built on the site.

On the south side of Bush House, Aldwych, is a bronze relief of **Andrew Young**, first valuer to the London County Council, 1889–1914, with the inscription: 'He laboured to beautify the London he loved'.

Also on Bush House, on the north side, are **two 12 foot figures**, 'England' and 'America', representing 'Youth' by Malvina Hoffman (1926), symbolising Anglo-American friendship. The building was named after Irving T. Bush, an American business executive.

The building at the junction of Aldwych and Kingsway is the **former main headquarters of the Royal Air Force**. It bears a bronze plaque with an inscription. As Adastral House it was occupied by the Air Ministry from 1919 to 1955.

Between the Strand and Aldwych in India Place, as the north end of Montreal Place was renamed in 1996, is a bust commemorating **Jawaharlal Nehru** (1889–1964), statesman and first Prime Minister of India after independence.

Also here is a memorial to **Detective Constable Jim Morrison**, one of a number of memorials erected in London by the Police Memorial Trust to police officers who have lost their lives in the course of duty.

The façade of the newly refurbished Somerset House bears stone medallions by

Nehru, India's first Prime Minister, in the renamed India Place.

Joseph Wilton (1780) of **George III**, **Queen Charlotte** and the **Prince of Wales** (later George IV). In the quadrangle is a bronze group by John Bacon senior (1788) of Neptune and **George III**, in Roman costume, leaning on a ship's rudder with lion couchant and a ship's prow. Queen Charlotte did not care for it. She asked the sculptor, 'Why did you make so *frightful* a figure?' Bowing, Bacon came back smoothly, 'Art cannot always effect what is ever within reach of Nature – the union of Beauty and Majesty'.

Here, too, is the memorial of the **15th County of London Battalion, the London Regiment, the Prince of Wales's Own Civil Service Rifles**, erected in 1919. A tall column surmounted by an urn with the regimental colours commemorates the 1240 members of the regiment who fell in the First World War. The memorial overlooks the new Riverside Terrace.

Outside St Clement Danes, the RAF's church, at the east end of the Strand stands a statue of **Air Chief Marshal Hugh Dowding, first Baron Dowding** (1882–1970), to whom Britain owed her victory in the Battle of Britain of 1940. 'Stuffy' Dowding began service life in the Army, then joined the Royal Flying Corps and in 1918 the new Royal Air Force. From 1930 to 1935 he served on the Air Council as member for Supply, Research and Development. In 1936 Dowding was appointed to the post of Commander-in-Chief of Fighter Command, which was to win him and his pilots the admiration of the nation. He began to build up a force of fast, manoeuvrable Hurricane and Spitfire fighter aircraft. In May 1940, when France was crumbling, the government was pressed to send RAF squadrons to France to stiffen a failing defence. Dowding, aware like Churchill that the Battle of France was over and that the Battle of Britain was about to begin, refused. His slim resources had to be preserved for the island's defence. The refusal did much to ensure British victory in July to October 1940. Dowding's larger-than-life bronze statue by Faith Winter was unveiled on 31st October 1988 by Queen Elizabeth the Queen Mother (who was

Above left: The 9 foot bronze statue of 'Bomber' Harris by Faith Winter.
Above right: William Ewart Gladstone, four times British Prime Minister.

herself resident in London during the battle) at 10.45 a.m. and, exactly on time, a solitary Spitfire flew in salute overhead. Dowding is shown in uniform in a characteristic pose, thumbs hooked into breast pockets. His son Derek, himself a Battle of Britain pilot, described the statue as 'an uncanny likeness'. It was long overdue; as the statue was craned into place a veteran in the crowd was heard to growl, 'And about bloody time too!'

Also by Faith Winter, a 9 foot bronze statue of **Marshal of the Royal Air Force Sir Arthur Travers Harris** (1892–1984), who was called upon by Portal in 1942 to be Commander-in-Chief of Bomber Command, was unveiled by Queen Elizabeth the Queen Mother on 31st May 1992. It shows Harris in uniform, in contemplative pose, his hands linked behind him. 'Bomber' Harris is remembered for the great raids on German cities such as Hamburg. There is no question that his steadfastness and the great gallantry of his bomber crews had a decisive effect on the outcome of the Second World War and made an outstanding contribution to Allied victory.

Also near the west front of St Clement Danes is a memorial to **William Ewart Gladstone** (1809–98) by Sir William Hamo Thornycroft, showing the statesman in the robes of Chancellor of the Exchequer with groups expressing Brotherhood, Education, Aspiration and Courage. The statue of this dour statesman and Prime Minister (not a favourite of Queen Victoria, who complained, 'He speaks to me as if I were a public meeting,') was unveiled in 1905 by Lord Morley. Gladstone, eventually nicknamed 'The Grand Old Man' of British politics, started life as a Conservative but moved to the Liberal Party. Few statesmen could boast a greater volume of successful legislation; his only real failure was Irish Home Rule. A fluent writer, he is little read today. His oratory is better remembered. There is timeless common sense in his famous words, 'All the world over, I will back the masses against the classes'.

Samuel Johnson's statue faces down Fleet Street.

At the other end of St Clement Danes church, facing Fleet Street, is a bronze statue by Percy Fitzgerald (1910) of **Dr Samuel Johnson** (1709–84), 'Critic, Essayist, Philologist, Biographer, Wit, Poet, Moralist, Dramatist, Political Writer, Talker'. He lived for a time in Gough Square and was a regular worshipper at the church. His house, open to the public, has Johnsonian relics and the attic where he and six indefatigable assistants worked on the *Dictionary*, published in 1755. Boswell's *Life of Johnson* describes the final day's work; Mr Millar, bookseller, undertook publication of the work. When the messenger who carried the last sheet to Millar returned, Johnson asked, 'Well, what did he say?' 'Sir,' (answered the messenger) 'He said, "Thank God I have done with him" '. 'I am glad,' replied Johnson with a smile, 'that he thanks God for anything.' The Doctor was a robust conversationalist. Goldsmith said: '... there was no arguing with Johnson, for when his pistol misses, he knocks you down with the butt end of it.' And Boswell remembered another spirited exchange; 'Johnson: "Well, we had a good talk"; Boswell: "Yes, Sir, you tossed and gored several persons".' Johnson, to an awestruck Boswell, 'Stupendous Johnson', and to Smollett, 'The Great Cham of Literature', is shown reading a book, with other books at his feet, recalling his words: 'A man will turn over half a library to make one book.' The bronze book Dr Johnson holds was stolen. Faith Winter replaced it in return for help she received in planning her statue of Sir Arthur Harris, and Burghfield Arts Foundry cast the book free of charge, perhaps a measure of the affection still felt for the greatest Londoner of all time, if by adoption, rather than birth.

Johnson's bulky figure, in bushy full-bottomed wig, vividly reflects his appearance in life. He was irredeemably untidy, with sagging stockings and an old wig burned to the network by reckless encounters with bedside candles; his only concession to fashion was to appear at the opening of his play *Irene* at Drury Lane in a scarlet waistcoat with gold braid and a gold-laced hat. It did not help. The piece failed. Asked how he felt, Johnson replied gloomily 'Like the Monument!'

Commemorated by bronze medallions on the statue's base are **James Boswell** (1740–95), Johnson's brilliant biographer,

Dr Johnson and his biographer Boswell feature on the statue's plinth.

Robert Devereux, third Earl of Essex, overlooks the Devereux Inn off the Strand.

and his close friend **Mrs Hester Lynch Thrale** (1741–1821), 'short, brisk and plump', wife of the wealthy brewer Henry Thrale, who owned the Anchor brewery on Bankside and Streatham Park, where Johnson spent much time after their meeting in 1765.

On the south side of the Strand, Essex Street runs down to the Embankment. On the second floor of the Devereux Inn in Devereux Court is a wigged, painted bust of **Robert Devereux, third Earl of Essex** (1591–1646). The bust is dated 1676. An inn has existed here since the reign of Edward II and the Devereux family had a house near its site. Robert Devereux was the grandson of the Earl of Essex, Elizabeth's favourite, beheaded in 1601. The earldom was restored by James I in 1604, and Robert became a courageous but disastrous Parliamentary general, leading a failed march into Cornwall. He fled abroad.

Near the Law Courts (the Royal Courts of Justice) is the **Temple Bar Memorial** (1880), surmounted by a griffin, the unofficial badge of the City of London. It stands in the middle of Fleet Street on the site of old Temple Bar, one of the gateways into the City. The memorial has statues of Victoria and Edward VII (as Prince of Wales) by Boehm, sculptor to the Queen. The griffin, by Charles Birch, stands on a plinth with bronze reliefs of the last occasion when royalty passed through the old gate in 1872, on their way to give thanks at St Paul's for the Prince's recovery from typhoid. Until 1772 heads of executed criminals were displayed on the iron spikes of the gate. Interested visitors hired telescopes for a halfpenny for a better view. When the sovereign visits the City she receives here the symbolic sword from the Lord Mayor. The old gateway, too narrow for modern traffic, was sent to Theobald's Park, Hertfordshire, in 1878.

Chancery Lane leads north from Fleet Street to Lincoln's Inn, where are intricate wrought-iron gates that date from 1872 and commemorate **Lieutenant Colonel W. B. Brewster**, the first commanding officer of the Inns of Court Volunteer Rifle Corps. Nearby is the Inn's **war memorial** in the form of seating flanking an inscribed stone.

In the north-east corner of Lincoln's Inn Fields is

The Temple Bar Memorial.

The Brewster gates at Lincoln's Inn.

a stone plinth and seat to **William Frederick Danvers Smith, second Viscount Hambleden** (1868–1928), head of W. H. Smith, the stationers and booksellers. The surmounting bust has gone.

Canada Walk, the north walk of Lincoln's Inn Fields, was the wartime headquarters of the **Royal Canadian Air Force**. A memorial plinth, with a red maple-leaf design, bears this inscription in English and French, Canada's two official languages:

Here in a building opposite at 20 Lincoln's Inn Fields was the headquarters of the Royal Canadian Air Force in Great Britain during the Second World War. This Headquarters provided central support to some 85,000 Canadian personnel who served in 48 RCAF squadrons and with numerous RAF units. In all 14,455 Canadian airmen made the supreme sacrifice while serving overseas.

Further west is the memorial seat by R. R. Goulden to **Margaret Ethel MacDonald**, the wife of James Ramsay MacDonald, Prime Minister in the first Labour government. She died at their home at 3 Lincoln's Inn Fields in 1911. She is shown with a group of children, with the inscription: 'She brought joy to those with whom and for whom she lived'.

In the south-west corner is N. F. Boonham's bust of **John Hunter** (1728–93), founder of scientific surgery, erected in 1977 by the President and Council of the Royal College of Surgeons to mark the Silver Jubilee of Queen Elizabeth II and the College's long association with Lincoln's Inn.

In the south-east corner of the Fields is a 12 foot high drinking fountain inscribed 'In memory of **Philip Twells**, Barrister at Law of Lincoln's Inn and sometime Member of Parliament for the City of London. 8th May AD 1880'. It bears a monogram composed of Twells's initials.

South of Lincoln's Inn, at the corner of Carey Street and Serle Street, behind the Law Courts, is a stone statue at first-floor level of **Sir Thomas More (**1478–1535) by Robert Smith (1886). It is inscribed 'The faithful servant of both God and King. Martyred 6th July 1535.'

Over the door of St Dunstan-in-the-West, on the north side of Fleet Street, is **Queen Elizabeth I** (1533–1603) by William Kerwin (1586). This statue and those of **King Lud and his two sons**, within the porch, came from Ludgate, which stood on Ludgate Hill until demolished in 1760–1.

The Royal Canadian Air Force memorial.

The memorial seat to Margaret MacDonald.

On the east side of the porch is the sculpted head of **John Donne** (1571?–1631), who held the living until his death, and to the west, **William Tyndale** (died 1536), translator of the Bible.

Also on the outside of the church is a memorial to **Izaak Walton** (1593–1683), an angler and the author of the most famous of all fishing treatises, *The Compleat Angler* (1653), which was published in St Dunstan's churchyard. His view: 'We may say of angling as Dr Boteler said of strawberries, "Doubtless God could have made a better berry, but doubtless God never did".' The

Left: *The drinking fountain in memory of Philip Twells.*

Below: *Queen Elizabeth I in Fleet Street and Sir Thomas More in Carey Street.*

William Tyndale who translated the Bible into English, fled to Antwerp where he was captured and executed.

memorial, with a stained-glass window, was set up in 1895 by 'some Anglers and other admirers'.

There is also here a bronze bust by Lady Scott of **Alfred Charles William Harmsworth, Viscount Northcliffe** (1865–1922), the newspaper proprietor, who, with his brother, later Lord Rothermere, bought the *Evening News* in 1894, founded the *Daily Mail* and the *Daily Mirror* and acquired control of *The Times*. A realist, he famously sent his staff a memo reminding them of the mental age of their readers: 'They are only 10'.

Opposite St Dunstan-in-the-West, behind the south side of Fleet Street, stands the Temple Church, one of England's rare 'round' churches. Severely damaged in an air raid of 10th May 1941, it has been skilfully repaired and enhanced. A service marked the sixtieth anniversary of the raid and four commemorative **stone benches** are under construction (March 2002) and will be set in niches outside the church.

Nine French knights, the original Knights Templar, in 1119 pledged to protect pilgrims to the Holy Land. Their white habits carried a red cross on the left shoulder (proclaiming their immunity from any jurisdiction save the Pope's); their warcry was *Bauseant*, Old French for 'piebald horse', a reference to their black and white striped banner. Their seal was formed of two knights riding on one horse, emblematic of the order's poverty; the first Master was said to be so poor he shared a horse with a follower. First installed in London in 1121 near present-day High Holborn, the Templars later moved nearer the Thames and built their second round church, its shape based, it was said, on the Holy Sepulchre in Jerusalem or the Dome of the Rock. The order, discredited by Edward II, lost its property to the Knights Hospitaller, who later leased it to 'students of the law'. The lawyers have remained to this day.

In Temple Court by the Temple Church stands a **column** in Gothic style erected in 2000 and surmounted by a bronze equestrian sculpture of two knights on one horse, the Templars' seal. The column's shaft is of Ketton stone and its octagonal base is of white Purbeck stone. The inscription reads: NE TEMPLO DEESSET MONUMENTUM TERTII MILLENNII INCIPIENTIS HOC SIGNUM ERIGENDUM CURAVIT HON SOC INT TEMPLI

Lord Harmsworth, founder of the 'Daily Mail' and the 'Daily Mirror'.

The 'Millennium Column' erected in 2000, stands in Temple Court.

('Lest the Temple should be without a memorial of the start of the third millennium the Hon. Society of the Inner Temple caused this monument to be erected'). Details of the project appear on a plaque opposite the column.

On 2nd April 2000 a ceremony of dedication conducted by the Master of the Temple, the Reverend Robin Griffiths-Jones, was followed by luncheon in the Inner Temple Hall, hosted by the Right Honourable Lord Lloyd of Berwick, at which all those who had contributed were saluted and thanked.

The column stands in the centre of what was formerly the cloister courtyard of the monastery of the Knights Templar, and also marks the point at which the Great Fire of 1666 was extinguished, thus saving the church. Its overall design was by Tom Stuart-Smith; Ptolemy Dean designed the column and Nicola Hicks the sculpture. James Honeywood carved the inscription. The London plane trees were presented by Christian Bevington, a Bencher of the Inner Temple, in memory of Canon Joseph Robinson, Master of the Temple 1980–99, and the column and sculpture were the gift of Lord Lloyd of Berwick, Treasurer (Inner Temple) 1999.

Leading north from Fleet Street is Fetter Lane, in which a statue of **John Wilkes** (1727–97) proclaims him 'A champion of English freedom'. He founded the weekly periodical *North Briton* in 1762 to attack Lord Bute's government. It was so named because Smollett conducted *The Briton* on behalf of Bute. After one violent outburst Wilkes was imprisoned in the Tower of London under a general warrant but was released in 1763. Such was the outcry that such warrants were ruled illegal two years later. Wilkes's outspoken defence of freedom secured valuable political rights. Newspapers might publish full proceedings of both Houses and legally elected MPs could not be kept from the House for their political views. Three times the electors of Middlesex returned Wilkes; three times he was denied his seat before this right was established. Finally, in 1774, he took his seat and in the same year was elected Lord Mayor of London. Wilkes was an active upholder of law and order. In 1780, when the Bank of England was attacked by the Gordon Rioters, they were forced back by militia and volunteers, including John Wilkes. It is said that the defenders fired bullets made from the melted-down lead inkwells from the Bank. Wilkes married an heiress much his senior. A member of the Hellfire Club, his mixture of dissipation, low morals, ability and wit made him the darling of the mob. He had a knack with the riposte. To Lord Sandwich, who had told him he would die either on the gallows or of the pox, he replied, 'That must depend on whether I embrace your lordship's principles or your mistress'. In the streets 'Wilkes for Liberty!' was the cry. He might have led a revolution:

in fact he was a thoughtful and fair-minded alderman and magistrate. His statue by James Butler, unveiled on 31st October 1988, clearly shows Wilkes's famous squint.

On a plinth facing Dr Samuel Johnson's house in Gough Square, a life-sized bronze set up in 1997 of his much-loved cat **Hodge** sits on a copy of the famous *Dictionary of the English Language*, with oyster shells at his feet. (Hodge was fond of oysters provided by an indulgent owner.) The inscription reads 'A very fine cat indeed', an allusion to Boswell's story of 1783: 'When I observed he was a fine cat, Johnson replied "Why yes, Sir, but I have had cats whom I liked better than this"; and then, as if perceiving Hodge to be out of countenance, adding, "but he is a *very* fine cat, *a very fine cat indeed*".' It was generous of Boswell to admire Hodge: he was uncomfortable in the presence of cats and perhaps feared a rival. He reflected moodily, 'I frequently suffered a good deal from the presence of this same Hodge'. On the reverse of the Portland stone plinth, which was carved by stonemasons at St Paul's Cathedral, is the inscription: *Castigavit et Emendavit* ('he refined and corrected'). This is H. W. Fowler's tribute to the work of Major Byron F. Caws in the preparation of the *Concise Oxford Dictionary*, 'Erected by his grandson Richard Byron F. Caws September 1997'. The statue, by Jon Bickley, commemorates both Dr Johnson and Major Caws, who had been closely involved in corrections to the *Oxford English Dictionary* on a regular basis. The figure of Hodge was felt to be of a more suitable scale for Gough Square than a full-length statue of Dr Johnson and was accepted by the Trustees of Dr Johnson's House. Both memorials were thus combined in a single statue, which now belongs to the Corporation of the City of London.

Hodge sits on a copy of Dr Johnson's 'Dictionary' in Gough Square.

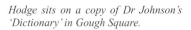

Mary, Queen of Scots has a statue at 147 Fleet Street, even though she never came to London.

An incongruous statue of **Mary, Queen of Scots** (1542–87), stands in a niche on the first floor of 147 Fleet Street, a Gothic building of 1880 on the north side of the street. The Queen never set foot in London but a Scottish admirer, Sir John George Tollemache Sinclair (1825–59), set her statue here.

On the south side of Fleet Street, on the old *News Chronicle* building, is a bronze bust by F. Doyle-Jones of the Irish journalist and politician **Thomas Power O'Connor** (1848–1929), nicknamed 'TP', who entered Parliament for Galway in 1880 and became prominent in the Parnell party. The inscription reads: 'His pen could lay bare the bones of a book or the soul of a statesman in a few vivid lines'.

Salisbury Square, reached via Salisbury Court on the south side of Fleet Street, is dominated by an obelisk to **Robert Waithman**, Lord Mayor in 1823, MP and 'the Friend of Liberty'. The redeveloped square was dedicated in 1990 by Lord Mayor Sir Hugh Bidwell to mark the eight hundredth anniversary of the mayoralty of the City of London in 1989.

Off Salisbury Square, on the arch of Warwick House, Dorset Rise, stood the stone carved head of **Samuel Richardson** (1689–1761), novelist and master printer, whose printing works was in Salisbury Square for thirty-five years. Richardson, Master of the Stationers' Company, was author of *Pamela, or Virtue Rewarded* (the first modern English novel), *Clarissa Harlowe* and *Sir Charles Grandison*, novels which were to influence the future course of fiction in England and abroad. He had a wide and appreciative readership. When Pamela was married and virtue *was* indeed

The Irish Nationalist T. P. O'Connor was a member of Parliament for so long that he became 'Father of the House of Commons'.

123

The Waithman obelisk in Salisbury Square.

rewarded, one delighted village rang its church bells. Dr Johnson said 'If you were to read Richardson for the story your impatience would be so much fretted that you would *hang* yourself. But you must read them for the sentiment' – and there was an abundance of that. Richardson set up in the square about 1724, built a range of printing works and warehouses and employed Oliver Goldsmith as proofreader. As an employer Richardson was no mean psychologist; it is said that he hid halfcrowns in the trays of type to be found by early birds among his pressmen. Redevelopment has changed this area a great deal but Richardson's head has been saved and will be placed on one of the new buildings later.

On the north-west side of Ludgate Circus, where as a boy he had sold newspapers, a tablet with a relief portrait commemorates **Edgar Wallace** (1875–1932), crime novelist and journalist, best known for his novels *Four Just Men* and *Sanders of the River.* The memorial, by F. Doyle-Jones, erected in 1934, bears the words: 'He knew wealth and poverty yet had walked with kings and kept his bearing. Of his talents he gave lavishly to authorship – but to Fleet Street he gave his heart.' Wallace wrote novels at a prodigious rate. *Punch* had a joke of a bookseller asking a customer: 'Have you read the midday Wallace, Sir?'

Edgar Wallace wrote over 150 books, some of which he dictated without notes to his secretary.

Queen Boadicea in her chariot stands at the corner of Westminster Bridge.

13.

VICTORIA EMBANKMENT:
WESTMINSTER TO BLACKFRIARS

The embankment of the Thames in central London was the crowning achievement in 1864–70 of the engineer Sir Joseph Bazalgette (1819–91). The heavy cost was met by a levy on all coal sold in the metropolitan area. The work entailed reclaiming land that was daily covered by tides and building a river wall 8 feet thick. The official opening by the Prince of Wales and Princess Louise took place on 13th July 1870. It is one of the finest riverside walks in the world.

At the corner of Westminster Bridge is a statue by Thomas Thornycroft (unveiled 1902) of the British **Queen Boadicea**, or Boudicca (died AD 62), in her chariot. Boadicea was described by the Greek historian Dio Cassius as 'tall, fine-eyed and tawny-haired'. By her dying husband Prasutagus she was made joint heir in AD 61 with the Emperor Nero to the East Anglian kingdom of the Iceni. The Romans treacherously seized the kingdom, assaulted Boadicea and raped her daughters. While Governor Suetonius Paulinus was away, the Iceni rebelled. Paulinus returned and roundly

Shaw's medallion faces the Thames.

125

This memorial (left) commemorates the Chindit Special Force which fought behind Japanese lines. A plaque (below) on the side of the monument depicts Orde Wingate, the force's commander.

defeated the Iceni, and Boadicea committed suicide. On the plinth are Cowper's lines: 'Regions Caesar never knew, Thy posterity shall sway'.

Richard Norman Shaw (1831–1912) was one of the most original architects of his day. A few of his London buildings survive, among them the former Scotland Yard building (1888–90) at the Big Ben end of the Embankment, now Norman Shaw House. Perhaps appropriately, the granite facings were quarried by convicts on Dartmoor. On the second-floor frontage facing the Thames is a stone medallion of Shaw by Sir William Hamo Thornycroft (1914).

Further along the Embankment, on the lawns next to the former Cannon Row police station is the memorial to those who fought against the Japanese in Burma in 1943–4 with Major-General Orde Wingate's **Chindit Special Force**, operating in the most dangerous conditions behind Japanese lines. Four of the Force won the Victoria Cross. The monument is in the form of a bronze *chinthe* – the lion-like guardian of Burmese temples from which the

Hugh Montague Trenchard, the 'Father of the Royal Air Force'.

Viscount Portal of Hungerford, of whom Sir Arthur Harris said: 'Anything you could do, Peter Portal could do better.'

Chindits took their name and insignia. Wingate was killed in an air crash before the end of the war; Churchill described him as 'a man of genius who might well also have become a man of destiny'. The memorial, by David Price and Frank Foster, was unveiled by the Duke of Edinburgh on 10th October 1990.

In front of the former Air Ministry is the statue of **Hugh Montague Trenchard** (1873–1956), the 'Father of the Royal Air Force' or, more familiarly, 'Boom' because of his forceful speech. He started service life in the Army but learned to fly in 1913 and rose to command the Royal Flying Corps in the First World War. His was the inspiration for innovative reconnaissance and bombing sorties. On 1st April 1918 the Royal Air Force was formed. Trenchard was the first Chief of the Air Staff in 1919 and built the new service, not without opposition from the Army and Royal Navy. He knew he was dealing with 'a new breed of fighting men grappling with unknown forces in the loneliest element of all'. After retirement he began a third successful career as Commissioner of the Metropolitan Police (1931–5) and founded the Hendon Police College. His statue, by William Macmillan, shows him in uniform.

As Chief of Air Staff from 1940 **Charles Frederick Algernon Portal, Viscount Portal of Hungerford** (1893–1971), Marshal of the Royal Air Force, fought his war at the great Anglo-American conferences and in Whitehall, where his statue by Oscar Nemon (1975) was unveiled by Harold Macmillan on the lawns of the Ministry of Defence. Not only did the day-to-day supervision of the RAF fall to Portal but also decisions on strategic plans, priorities and allocations. Portal reckoned he attended nearly two thousand chiefs of staff meetings, 'each taking one and a half to two hours, or more and needing three or four hours of reading beforehand'. His stature is confirmed by the judgements of wartime colleagues: 'Bomber' Harris said, 'Anything you could do, Peter Portal could do better'; Eisenhower, 'Greater even than Churchill'; and Churchill, 'Portal had everything'.

Nearby is the long-overdue memorial to those who served and lost their lives in the **Fleet Air Arm**. Naval aviation in Britain dates from 1912. At first controlled by the Royal Air Force, it was given the name Fleet Air Arm in 1924 and in 1937 passed under Admiralty control. Its distinguished service in the Second World War is well known, exemplified by its surprise attack on

The Fleet Air Arm figure wears a pilot's helmet.

Above: *The RFC and RAF Memorial now has a backdrop of the London Eye.*

Left: *In the Victoria Embankment Gardens stands Gordon of Khartoum, holding the cane with which he led his troops against the Taiping rebels.*

the Italian fleet at Taranto. So successful was this that the Japanese used it as their model for the attack on Pearl Harbor. The memorial, in the form of the figure of Daedalus, the Athenian inventor and aviator, with outstretched wings and wearing a pilot's helmet, is from a design by the architect Tim Kempster and was sculpted by James Butler. It was unveiled by the Prince of Wales on 1st June 2000. *Daedalus* is a name of significance for the Royal Navy: since the eighteenth century five of its ships have borne this name.

Next, cane under arm and Bible in hand, is **General Charles George Gordon** (1833–85) by Sir William Hamo Thornycroft. 'Chinese' Gordon was put in command of the 'Ever-Victorious Army' of Chinese troops, officered by Britons and Americans. It put down the Taiping Rebellion in 1863–4. When the Mahdi's rebellion broke out in the Sudan, Gordon was sent to assist the Egyptian army. He defended Khartoum for nearly a year; Wolseley was sent to relieve him, but arrived three days too late. Gordon had been killed on 26th January 1885. Gladstone's government was severely criticised for its dilatory response to Gordon's situation and Gordon became a martyr.

At Whitehall Stairs by the Thames is the **Royal Flying Corps and Royal Air Force Memorial**, a stone pedestal designed by Sir Reginald Blomfield surmounted by a gilt eagle on a globe by Sir William Reid Dick. It was unveiled on 23rd July 1923 by the Prince of Wales, with an addition for the Second World War unveiled by Lord Trenchard on 15th May 1946.

In the gardens beyond Horse Guards' Avenue is a statue by Boehm (1884) of

Set into the wall of the Embankment he created is Sir Joseph W. Bazalgette.

William Tyndale (*c.*1484–1536), a leading figure in the Reformation and translator of the New Testament. After work in England persecution drove him to Germany, where the translation was completed in 1525. Later in Antwerp he was working on the Old Testament. His translation was widely popular but Tyndale was eventually seized by church authorities and was burned as a heretic at Vilvorde in the Netherlands. His last words were 'Lord, open Thou the King of England's eyes'. Within a year of his death a Bible was placed in every parish church in England, by the King's command.

Sir Henry Edward Bartle Frere (1815–84), the statesman, spent thirty-three years in India. He made Bombay a healthier city than London, did good work in the Indian Mutiny and later became Governor of Cape Colony and High Commissioner of South Africa. His statue is by Sir Thomas Brock (1888).

Here too is **General Sir James Outram** (1803–63), who joined Havelock in the relief of Lucknow. Napier called him the 'Bayard of India', Bayard being the knight *sans peur et sans reproche* ('without fear and reproach'). His statue by Matthew Noble shows him wearing the Star of India.

Outside the gardens by the road facing the Thames is **Samuel Plimsoll** (1824–98) by Ferdinand V. Blundstone. Plimsoll, 'the Sailors' Friend', became an MP in 1868 and tackled the problem of so-called 'coffin ships' – old, neglected, over-insured, unseaworthy ships sent out in the hope of a wreck and an insurance claim. Plimsoll's vehement campaigning caused his suspension from the House of Commons. Later the Merchant Shipping Act (1876) was passed. The line painted round British ships indicating the freeboard required for safety is still called the Plimsoll Line. Plimsoll became first President of the Seamen's and Firemen's Union. The National Union of Seamen erected the memorial in 1929. It includes a bronze bust, a ship, sailors and a plaque showing the famous Line.

Set into the Embankment wall at the foot of Northumberland Avenue is a bronze monument by George Simonds (1899) to **Sir Joseph W. Bazalgette** (1819–91), with the inscription 'Engineer of the London Main Drainage System and of this Embankment', and the words *FLVMINI VINCVLA POSVIT* ('He put the river in chains'). Following the year of the 'Great Stink' (1858), when sheets soaked in chloride of lime were hung at the windows of the House of Commons to counter the stench, cholera broke out and there was a boycott on river excursions, an Act empowering the Metropolian Board of Works to

The statue of Robert Burns and the Imperial Camel Corps memorial in Embankment Gardens. Burns's statue was the gift of a fellow Scot, John Gordon Crawford. Rossetti said: 'Burns of all poets is the most a man.'

embank the Thames was passed in 1862. Bazalgette was knighted for his work. The camel and sphinx seats and lamp standards date from this period. The position of the **York Water Gate**, overlooking the gardens beyond Embankment underground station, shows how wide the Thames had been.

Near Charing Cross Pier is a bronze medallion of **William Schwenck Gilbert** (1836–1911) by Sir George Frampton. With Sir Arthur Sullivan, Gilbert produced the immortal operas at the Savoy Theatre. 'His foe was folly and his weapon wit', as the inscription accurately states.

A further section of Embankment Gardens contains a memorial to **Robert Burns** (1759–96), the Scottish poet, whose bronze is by Sir John Steell (1884). He would have had little in common with his neighbour, **Sir Wilfrid Lawson** (1829–1906), the Liberal MP and temperance advocate, nicknamed 'Dry Wilf'. His monument by David McGill had figures of Temperance, Peace, Fortitude and Charity; they were stolen in 1979. Lawson was by no means the dull dog suggested by his austere views. He pointed out that alcohol had raised £3 million in taxes and that the same sum had been expended on gunpowder to kill people: 'These sums balance very nicely, *that* is the beauty of the system'.

The memorial to the **Imperial Camel Corps** of the First World War (1920) is in the form of a soldier riding a camel, with campaign scenes on the plinth. The sculptor, Major Cecil Brown, was himself a Corps member. The ICC's task was to patrol the Western Desert

W. S. Gilbert, whose witticisms sometimes offended Queen Victoria, had to wait to receive his knighthood from Edward VII.

Above left: *Gloucester newspaper proprietor Robert Raikes started a local Sunday school that was widely copied.*

Above right: *The blinded Henry Fawcett became Postmaster General and introduced postal orders and telegrams.*

and Northern Sudan in the campaign against the Ottoman Empire and to maintain contact with the friendly tribes of Senussis. Originally there were thirty officers, eight hundred NCOs and men and a thousand camels. Seventeen companies were of bull camels; the eighteenth, the Cow Camel Company, was held at a discreet distance. Personnel included Australians, New Zealanders, Sikhs from Singapore and Hong Kong, volunteers from the Rhodesian Mounted Police, a South African mine prospector who had fought the British in the Boer War, a Canadian cowboy, an Argentinian polo-player and one American. Camels were more effective for desert patrols than horses and T. E. Lawrence ('Lawrence of Arabia') used the Corps against the Turks. The regimental sports day was a dignified affair, with judges, stewards and such esoterica as the 'Camel scurry egg and spoon race'. The regimental newspaper, *Barrak: the Irregular News-Letter of the Old Boys of the Imperial Camel Corps*, was first published in Beersheba in 1917 (*barrak* is the command given to a camel to indicate that it is to kneel to be hobbled).

Henry Fawcett (1833–84), the economist and politician, was blinded in a shooting accident as a young man but rose to be Postmaster General, with the introduction of postal orders to his credit. His bronze medallion and wall fountain are by Mary Grant and Basil Champneys (1886).

Robert Raikes (1735–1811) of Gloucester promoted and perhaps founded Sunday schools. His monument is by Brock. Two replicas were made, one for Gloucester, the other for Toronto, Canada.

Sir Arthur Seymour Sullivan (1842–1900), who with William Schwenck Gilbert wrote the Savoy operas, has a memorial bust here by Sir William

Appropriately facing the Savoy in Embankment Gardens is this poignant memorial to Sir Arthur Sullivan, composer of the Savoy operas.

Goscombe John (1903). Sullivan composed 'Onward Christian Soldiers' in 1873 and 'The Lost Chord' (to be the first phonograph record made in England). In 1871 he began his eighteen-year partnership with W. S. Gilbert, from which emerged *The Mikado, The Gondoliers, The Pirates of Penzance* and other operas. A weeping girl embraces the pillar on which Sullivan's bust stands. The inscription is from Colonel Fairfax's song in *The Yeoman of the Guard*:

Is life a boon?
If so it must befall
That death whene'er he call
Must call too soon.

The nymph, modelled in Paris about 1899, was added as an afterthought. This has been called 'the most erotic statue in London' and gave rise to the rhyme:

Why, O nymph, O why display
Your beauty in such disarray?
Is it decent, is it just?
To so conventional a bust?

A monument by Lutyens commemorates **Herbert Francis Eaton, Baron Cheylesmore** (1848–1925), a Grenadier, Chairman of the National Rifle Association and of London County Council (1912–13). During the First World War he presided over several courts-martial, including that which condemned the spy Loder to death.

Near here and by the river is **Cleopatra's Needle**, a pink granite monolith 68¹/₂ feet high and weighing 186 tons, erected here in 1878. Mohammed Ali, Viceroy of Egypt, presented it to Britain in 1819 but it was not brought over until many years later when it was encased in a metal hull and, in 1877, towed towards England by the tug *Olga*. Twice the tow had to be abandoned in storms in the Bay of Biscay. The six sailors who died trying to save it have a memorial on the base of the Needle. The obelisk, retrieved by SS *Frogmaurice*, was finally erected on the Embankment. The following morning this rhyme was found pinned to it:

This monument, as some supposes,
Was looked on in old days by Moses.
It passed in time to Greeks and Turks,
And was stuck up here by the Board of Works.

This exedra and pond by Lutyens commemorate Baron Cheylesmore.

In fact the column has no connection with Cleopatra. It was erected at Heliopolis by Tethmosis III of the Eighteenth Dynasty, and dedicated to Tum. Companion obelisks stand in New York and Paris. The bronze sphinxes at the base, by G. J. Vulliamy, still bear bomb scars from the First World War. In 1979 the Needle was cleaned (with financial aid from an anonymous Arab donor) and resumed its original pink colour. Under the pedestal were placed in 1878 earthenware jars with a collection of objects certain to puzzle future archaeologists: a baby's feeding bottle, hairpins, a case of cigars, coins, *Bradshaw's Railway Guide*, a razor, an hydraulic jack, a copy of *The Times* for the day of unveiling, and photographs of beautiful women of the Victorian age.

Opposite the Needle is the monument to **Belgium's Gratitude for British Aid in 1914–18**, designed by Sir Reginald Blomfield (1920) with sculpture by Victor Rousseau. Over 250,000 Belgian refugees fled to England in 1914.

A **sundial** in a lead tub in Savoy Gardens (1989), between the hotel and the river, commemorates the centenary of the Savoy Theatre, home of the Gilbert and Sullivan operas, and the D'Oyly Carte family. It is inscribed:

> Every season has its cheer,
> Life is lovely all the year.

At the corner of Savoy Street and Savoy Place, outside the Institute of Electrical Engineers, is a bronze copy (1988) of John Foley's marble statue held by the Royal Institution of Great Britain of **Michael Faraday** (1791–1867), the experimental physicist who discovered the induction of electric current and in 1812 made the first electric cell. A brilliant experimenter, Faraday

One of the two sphinxes flanking Cleopatra's Needle.

In September 1878 Cleopatra's Needle was set up on Victoria Embankment.

examined the connections between light, heat, electricity and magnetism, and his findings formed the basis of the modern electrical industry. Some were puzzled by these mysteries. Gladstone asked Faraday of what use electricity would be; Faraday answered soothingly, 'One day you'll be able to tax it, Sir'.

Notable as the first memorial in London with spectacles is that of **Sir Walter Besant** (1836–1901), novelist, man of letters, social commentator and historian of London, who, with a dozen others, founded the Society of Authors in 1884, with Alfred, Lord Tennyson, as President. The bronze bust on the Embankment opposite Savoy Street, by Sir George Frampton (1904), is inscribed: 'Erected by his grateful brethren in Literature'.

Beyond Waterloo Bridge, at the corner of Temple Place, is a statue by Marochetti (1877) of **Isambard Kingdom Brunel** (1806–59), holding quill pen and dividers. An outstanding engineer, who assisted his equally famous father, Marc Isambard Brunel, in the construction of Wapping Tunnel under the Thames, he was Chief Engineer to the Great Western Railway in 1833. He later

became interested in shipbuilding and his *Great Western* (1838) was the first steamship to sail the Atlantic regularly. His *Great Britain* (1845), the world's first large iron steamship and the first with a screw propeller, was used extensively on the Australian run. After some forty years' service it was damaged in a storm off Cape Horn and became a coal hulk in the Falkland Islands. In an epic of towage, in 1970 the *Great Britain* was brought back to Bristol, to the very dock in which she had been built, and was refurbished as a national engineering monument to Brunel's genius. His third ship, the *Great Eastern* (1858), at the time

The Sundial in Savoy Gardens.

Michael Faraday stands outside the Institute of Electrical Engineers.

the largest ship ever built, weighed 18,915 tons and could carry four thousand passengers to Australia non-stop. But two days before the *Great Eastern*'s maiden voyage Brunel suffered a severe stroke and died on 7th September 1859.

In the gardens to the east of Temple station is a statue of **W. E. Forster** (1818–86) by H. R. Pink (1890). Forster, statesman and pioneer of mass education, carried through the Elementary Education Bill of 1870.

The figure of a young girl crowns a drinking-fountain and bird-bath, which commemorates **Lady Henry Somerset**, President of the National British Women's Temperance Association (1897).

The statue by Thomas Woolner of **John Stuart Mill** (1806–73), philosopher and economist, was unveiled by his admirer, Professor Fawcett.

On the river parapet is a memorial by Sir George Frampton to **W. T. Stead** (1849–1912), journalist and spiritualist, who was lost in the *Titanic.*

On the twenty-fifth anniversary of the accession of George V, the Port of London Authority, with the King's permission, named the reach of the Thames between London Bridge and Westminster Bridge **King's Reach**. A brass tablet under an arch records this (1935).

Either side of the roadway by Temple Gardens are **cast-iron dragons** of 1849, from the City's Coal Exchange, demolished in 1963.

Alongside the dragons is a plaque commemorating the **last visit of Queen Victoria** to the City of London in 1900.

Plaques decorating the memorial on the Embankment opposite Temple Gardens commemorate those **lost at sea in submarines** in the two world wars. One shows the control room of a First World War submarine, with floating ethereal figures. There are lists of boats lost in each war, with figures of Truth and Justice and, underneath, a depiction of a submarine on the surface. The design (1922) was by F. Brook Hatch and A. H. Ryan Tenison. Additions were made after the Second World War. The Portsmouth Division of the Submarine Service sent a wreath of flowers in the shape of a submarine for the unveiling.

At the river end of Inner Temple Gardens is a fountain with the figure of a youth holding a book inscribed with the words of **Charles Lamb** (1775–1834), the essayist: 'Lawyers, I suppose, were children once'. It is a fibreglass copy by Margaret Wrightson of the original set in the gardens in 1928 and stolen in 1970. Lamb was born in Crown Office Row and lived in the Temple until 1817.

Here too is the kneeling figure of a **Moor with a sundial**, said to be by John van Nost and given to Clement's Inn by Holles, Earl of Clare, in 1705, supposedly in atonement for the murder of two of the Inn's students by the Earl's servant. It was brought here in 1884. The following lines were once found attached to it:

Lady Henry Somerset, the temperance campaigner, is commemorated by this drinking-fountain in the gardens to the east of Temple station.

The Submarine Memorial on the Embankment has hooks on which poppy wreaths are placed.

Right: *The dragons from the City of London's Coal Exchange.*

Façade figures on the old City of London School, Blackfriars, include William Shakespeare and John Milton.

A statue of Queen Victoria can be found on the north side of Blackfriars Bridge.

In vain, poor sable son of woe,
Thou seek'st the tender tear,
From thee in vain with pangs they flow,
For mercy dwells not here.
From cannibals thou fled'st in vain;
Lawyers less quarter give;
The first won't eat you till you're slain,
The last do it alive.

On the second floor of the old City of London School by Blackfriars Bridge are façade figures of, from left to right, **Francis Bacon**, **William Shakespeare**, **John Milton** and **Isaac Newton**. These stone figures are the work of J. Daymond & Son (1882).

On the north side of Blackfriars Bridge is an ugly statue of **Queen Victoria** by John Bell Birch, unveiled on 21st July 1896. There are said to be some 150 statues of Victoria in the world, forty of them in India.

14.
Holborn to St Paul's

Yet another statue of **Edward VII** is to be found on the top floor of 114 High Holborn, a companion to a far less commonly commemorated **Edward I**. Both are by Richard Garbe (1902). Edward I (1239–1307) was on the last Crusade when his father, Henry III, died. He was not crowned until his return two years later. Edward I is remembered as a lawgiver who extended the franchise. But he also expelled 16,000 Jews from England, subdued Wales and partially subdued Scotland. He removed the Coronation Stone (Stone of Destiny) from Scone to Westminster Abbey. It was not returned to Scotland until 1996.

The alleviation of poverty and the care of crippled children was the life's work of **Sir John Kirk JP** (1847–1922). On the façade of John Kirk House, 31–2 John Street, on the north side of Theobald's Road, is a bronze medallion portrait of him by an unknown sculptor, erected in 1925, with the inscription: 'Christian Philanthropist. The Children's Friend.' Kirk was secretary of the Open Air Mission and a director of the Shaftesbury Society and the Ragged School Union (whose headquarters were here from 1914). He was knighted in 1907.

In the south square of Gray's Inn (one of the four remaining Inns of Court) is a statue of **Francis Bacon, Baron Verulam and Viscount St Albans** (1561–1626), who became Lord Chancellor and Treasurer of the Inn, retaining his rooms here until his death. His statue is by F. W. Pomeroy and was erected to mark the tercentenary of Bacon's election as Treasurer in 1608. The catalpa tree in the garden, by tradition planted by Bacon, is said to have been brought from America by Raleigh. Bacon was a keen gardener. His statue carries a quotation from his essay *Of Gardens*: 'God Almighty first planted a garden and

Sir John Kirk's work for children earned him the title 'The Children's Friend'. This medallion is at 31-2 John Street.

Francis Bacon's statue in Gray's Inn marked the tercentenary of his election as treasurer of the Inn.

indeed it is the purest of human pleasures'. The gardens he laid out at the Inn were described by Charles Lamb as 'the best gardens of the Inns of Court, my beloved Temple not forgotten'.

A little to the south-west of Gray's Inn, in a house on the site of 4 Warwick Court, lived the Chinese revolutionary leader **Sun Yat Sen** (1866–1925) while in exile. It is marked by a bronze relief portrait, inscribed 'Father of the Chinese Republic'.

North-east of Gray's Inn, at the junction of Clerkenwell Road and Rosebery Avenue, is 10 Laystall Street, where **Giuseppe Mazzini** (1805–72), the Italian nationalist and a key figure in the *Risorgimento* (resurgence) movement as leader of the anticlerical, republican group, lived for a time while resident in London. He is remembered by a decorative bronze plaque, inscribed: '*Dio Popolo Pensiero* … the apostle of modern democracy. Inspired Young Italy with the ideal of the independence, unity and regeneration of his country.' The plaque carries a sculpted relief bust of Mazzini with a laurel wreath and the symbolic device of clasped hands. After expulsion from Italy in 1831, Mazzini organised the secret society Young Italy. When revolution broke out in 1848 he returned to Italy. The plaque was set up in 1922.

In the Holborn roadway, close to Gray's Inn Road, stands the bronze memorial to **The Royal Fusiliers, (City of London Regiment)** by Alfred Toft (1922). It is in the form of a Royal Fusilier with rifle and bayonet. A sergeant of the regiment acted as the sculptor's model.

At the foot of Gray's Inn Road, opposite Staple Inn, are the **Holborn Bars**, marking the entrance to the City of London. At these stone obelisks, topped by griffins, first set up in 1130, tolls were exacted and guards prevented lepers, rogues and vagabonds from entering.

On the left, the red brick Gothic building of the Prudential Assurance Company is on the site of Furnival's Inn,

The Royal Fusiliers' memorial divides the traffic in Holborn.

where **Charles Dickens** (1812–70) lodged in 1836, while writing the first part of *Pickwick Papers*. A memorial tablet and bust by Percy Fitzgerald (1907) in the entrance archway recall this. *The Dickensian* called it a 'recognisable likeness'.

The statue of **Prince Albert** (1819–61) in Holborn Circus is by Charles Bacon. The Prince is politely raising his hat. Plaques show Albert laying the foundation stone of the Royal Exchange, and Britannia distributing 1851 Exhibition awards.

On the wall of 5 Hatton Garden another tablet with a device of clasped hands and a bas-relief portrait of **Giuseppe Mazzini** commemorates the Italian patriot who inspired Italy's struggle for freedom. He resided here from 1836.

At the junction of Hatton Garden and Cross Street, on the Hatton Garden frontage of a former **charity school**, bombed and rebuilt, are figures of two schoolchildren; the boy holds a book bearing a cross on its cover.

In financial circles it is a rare week that passes without someone quoting Gresham's Law – 'Bad money drives out good money'. A statue of **Sir Thomas Gresham** (1519–79) by J. Bursill (1868) stands on the first floor of Gresham House, 24 Holborn Viaduct. Gresham, an astute merchant and financier of the City of London, founded the Royal Exchange, advised four sovereigns including Elizabeth I (whose 'royal merchant' he was) on financial matters and was knighted in 1559.

At 25 Holborn Viaduct is a statue by H. Bursill (1868) of **Henry FitzAilwin** or FitzEylwin (died 1212), first Mayor of the City of London. He first appeared as Mayor in 1193 (the plinth gives the date as 1189) and held the office until his death. The title was not officially recorded until 1545.

Above: *Prince Albert acknowledges the crowds in Holborn Circus.*

Sir Thomas Gresham on the first floor of Gresham House in Holborn Viaduct.

Henry FitzEylwin, mayor of London from 1193, on FitzEylwin House, Holborn Viaduct. The date on the plinth is incorrect.

Also commemorated here with a statue is **Sir William Walworth**, Lord Mayor of London and Master of the Fishmongers' Company, who in 1381 stabbed to death Wat Tyler, the leader of the Kentish rebels, whose mob was burning and plundering London during the Peasants' Revolt. The dagger used for the deed is a cherished relic of the Company. There is also a statue of **Sir Hugh Myddleton**, who is also commemorated on Islington Green.

The site of the palace of **Guy of Warwick**, a hero of fifteenth-century romance, lay between Newgate Street and Warwick Lane. On a modern building at the corner is a 2¹/₂ foot stone statue of Guy. The statue, dated 1668, was restored in 1814. Guy won the hand of Felice, daughter of the Earl of Warwick, by feats of valour, including killing the Dun Cow of Dunsmore and Giant Colbrand. Repenting of slaughter, he made a pilgrimage to the Holy Land, returned in disguise to his wife and retired to a hermitage. On his deathbed he sent her a ring, which she recognised and so came to bury him. She herself soon died and was buried at his side.

The **Pie Corner Cherub**, a fat gilded boy, stands on the corner house at the junction of Cock Lane and Giltspur Street, marking Pie Corner, where the Great Fire of 1666 stopped. As it began in Pudding Lane, the Puritans were quick to blame gluttony for the catastrophe. The figure was placed here in 1910. The previous building on the site was The Fortunes of War inn, a meeting place for resurrectionists – body snatchers who provided corpses for apprentice surgeons at St Bartholomew's Hospital.

In Giltspur Street is the bust by Sir William Reynolds Stephens of **Charles Lamb** (1775–1834), the essayist, a Bluecoat boy for seven years at Christ's

This statue of Guy of Warwick is on a building near to where his palace once was.

Hospital in Newgate Street and, as the plinth suggests, 'Perhaps the most beloved name in literature'. When the school moved out of London the bust was placed here.

At the east end of St Sepulchre's Church, Holborn Viaduct, is **London's first drinking-fountain**. It was opened on 21st April 1859 by Mrs Wilson, daughter of the Archbishop of Canterbury. She was handed a handsome silver cup, which she filled from the fountain before taking the first drink. Many followed: eight users per minute were reported on opening day. Captain John Smith, Governor of Virginia, is buried here. In May 2001 Patricia Cornwell, the American novelist, offered to the church seven stained-glass windows depicting Captain Smith, Pocahontas and the departure of the Virginia Settlers from the Thames.

Nearer St Paul's, on the left, are the buildings of the General Post Office. The King Edward Building has a statue outside to **Sir Rowland Hill** (1795–1879), who introduced the revolutionary penny postage in 1840, with the world's first adhesive postage stamp, the Penny Black. The way had been paved by his pamphlet *Post Office Reform* (1837). The statue, by Onslow Ford, was moved here in 1923.

Some of the most appealing memorials in London are at **Postman's Park** next to the GPO, made up of the churchyards of St Botolph's; Christchurch, Newgate; and St Leonard's, Foster Lane. Here is a wall with decorative plaques to everyday heroes such as **Joseph Onslow**, a lighterman who tried to save a boy from drowning in 1885; **Mary Rogers**, stewardess of the *Stella*, who gave up her life-jacket to a passenger when the ship sank and thereby drowned; **William Donald**, aged nineteen, a railway clerk of Bayswater, who was drowned trying to save a boy entangled in water-weed; and **George Stephen**

Funnell, a police constable who died trying to rescue those trapped in a fire at the Elephant and Castle.

The Park was the idea of **George Frederick Watts** (1817–1904) and was intended to commemorate the 1887 Jubilee. Watts searched newspaper files for his first twenty-four heroes. After his death his widow added to the plaques; the last, set up in 1928, included one to a Metropolitan policeman and four employees of East Ham sewage works who died trying to rescue colleagues overcome by gas. Fixed to the plaque wall is a wooden statue by T. H. Wren of Watts himself. Only 11 inches high, the statue bears this inscription: 'G. F.

In between two post boxes is the statue of Sir Rowland Hill, creator of the postage stamp.

Watts, who desiring to honour the heroic self-sacrifice placed these records here'. Watts was one of the most popular Victorian painters although his works such as *Sir Galahad* and *Love Triumphant* are perhaps too sentimental for modern taste.

On the wall of St Bartholomew's Hospital is a memorial to **Sir William Wallace**, hanged, drawn and quartered near this spot on 23rd August 1305. The parts of his body were sent to Perth, Stirling, Berwick and Newcastle, and his head spiked on London Bridge, the first recorded instance of this practice. Wallace was a thorn in the side of the English, whom he defeated at Stirling Bridge in 1297. The memorial bears the lion of Scotland, two St Andrew's crosses and the Gaelic words *Bas Agus Buaidh* ('Death and Victory'). It was set up in 1956 and wreaths are laid here on the anniversary of the execution. One wreath bore the terse message 'Wallace was right'. In October 2000 the Scottish Roman Catholic Church proposed that Wallace be made a saint.

Also remembered here are **Protestant martyrs** of the reign of Mary I. Seven were burned on 27th June 1558. Bartholomew Legate, who died here in 1611, is described as 'very unblameable'. In 1849, during sewerage excavations, blackened stones, bones and the remains of posts and rings were found – sad relics of these executions.

On the hospital gateway, dating from 1702, is a statue by Francis Bird of **Henry VIII** (1491–1547), who founded the hospital.

15.
St Paul's

Before the west front of St Paul's Cathedral is a statue of **Queen Anne** (1665–1714), in whose reign the rebuilding after the Great Fire of 1666 was completed. The present statue is a replica by R. Belt (1886) of the original by Francis Bird (1712), removed when it deteriorated. The Queen, who was supposed to be fond of spirits, has her back to St Paul's; a gin shop stood opposite, provoking a ribald rhyme:

> Brandy Nan, Brandy Nan, you're left in the lurch,
> Your face to the gin shop, your back to the church.

When Queen Victoria's Diamond Jubilee service was to be held at the cathedral in 1897 it was found that the statue blocked the way and its temporary

The statue of Queen Anne by Francis Bird erected in 1712 in front of St Paul's has been replaced by this accurate replica.

145

removal was proposed. Victoria famously responded: 'What a ridiculous idea! Move Queen Anne? Most certainly not! Why, it might some day be suggested that *Our* statue should be moved, and that We should very much dislike!' Accompanying figures represent North America (with Indian bow and arrows), France (of which Anne was still notionally Queen) and Ireland (with a harp). In 1710 four Indian chiefs had visited Anne's court offering assistance against the French in Canada. The Indian figure may be a compliment to them.

On the south front tympanum is a **phoenix** by Caius Gabriel Cibber, symbolising the rise of the new St Paul's after the Great Fire. Francis Bird made the bas-relief of the **Conversion of St Paul** and decorations on the west and north pediments.

A statue of **John Wesley** (1703–91), founder of Methodism, stands on the north side of St Paul's churchyard. It was erected by the Aldersgate Trustees of the Methodist Church in 1988. Wesley's statue, 5 feet 1 inch, his height in life, is shown preaching. It was cast from an original by Samuel Manning and his son (1839).

Near the Wesley statue is a memorial to the **people of London** in the form of a low dome with the inscription: 'Remember before God the people of London 1939–1945'.

To the north-east of the cathedral the foundations of **Old St Paul's Cross**, where sermons were preached and heretics recanted, were found in 1879. Nearby, a column with St Paul commemorates the **Richards family**, benefactors of the cathedral in the nineteenth and early twentieth centuries.

On 29th December 1170, heeding Henry II's angry words, 'Will no one rid me of this turbulent priest?' four of Henry's knights murdered Thomas à Becket, Archbishop of Canterbury, at the high altar of Canterbury Cathedral. It had been a stormy relationship. Henry, a proud, wilful man, realised that to avoid offending the papacy he needed an ally in the post of Archbishop of Canterbury and in 1162 appointed his Chancellor **Thomas à Becket** (1118–70) to the post, against Becket's will. Arguments intensified, Becket fled to France and returned for a brief reconciliation with the King. Finally the fateful words were uttered and the deed was done. E. Bainbridge Copnall's bronze statue of Becket on the south side of the cathedral shows the Archbishop fallen and at the point of death. The siting is apposite: Becket was born in nearby Cheapside, east of St Paul's.

In his 12 foot composition **Blitz** John W. Mills commemorates in bronze the 1002 fire-fighters who died fighting fires in Britain during the Second World War. Late in appearing, it was unveiled in Old Change Court (opposite the south side of St Paul's) on 4th May 1991 by Queen Elizabeth the Queen Mother. The cathedral itself was saved only by the devotion of the cathedral staff and the firemen, fighting a massive battle in the surrounding streets. The

An engraving of the monument to the Panyer Boy in Panyer Alley.

WHEN Y HAVE SOUGH
THE CITTY ROVND
YET STILL TH'S IS
THE HIGHST GROVND
AVGVST THE 27
⌘ 1688 ⌘

photograph of the dome and its gleaming cross silhouetted against the flames and smoke became a worldwide symbol of London's defiance of the German air attacks of 1940–1.

North of St Paul's, Paternoster Square is being rebuilt and is still a building site (January 2002) but the ornate gold central **column** has already been set in place. It is based on the fragmentary remains of Inigo Jones's original colonnade for Old St Paul's, which he designed after his appointment as King's Surveyor in 1637. The old cathedral was destroyed in the Great Fire of 1666. Not only does the column provide a visual focal point but it also provides ventilation for the passage that runs beneath it.

In Panyer Alley, off Paternoster Row, to the north of St Paul's Churchyard, one of London's most endearing monuments, the **Panyer Boy**, a relief of a small boy seated upon a pannier or bread basket, was a reminder that, as Stow suggests in his *Survey*, bakers and a corn market were once nearby. In his *Every-day Book* (1827) William Hone said that some called it, inelegantly, 'Pick-my-Toe'. The boy seems to be pressing grapes between his hand and foot. (An old inn in the borough, the Pick-my-Toe, had a sign of a Roman slave removing a thorn from his toe.) The plinth bears this rhyme and date:

> When ye have sought the City round,
> Yet still this is the highest ground. August the 27th 1688.

This is not quite correct: Panyer Alley is 58 and Cornhill 60 feet above sea level. Since John Stow in his *Survey of London* (1598 and 1603) mentions the boy, the date must refer to the figure's repair or to its erection here. The Panyer Boy is the property of the Vintners' Company and spent the war in the safety of the vaults of the Central Criminal Court. It has again been removed, during re-development, but will be returned to this site or one nearby subsequently.

On a new site enclosed by New Change, Bread and Watling Streets is a memorial to **Vice-Admiral Arthur Phillip** (1738–1814), who commanded the First Fleet carrying 1030 convicts and settlers to Australia in 1787. His fleet was made up of the frigate *Sirius*, the tender *Supply*, six transports and three store ships. He reached Botany Bay on 18th January 1788 but disliked the anchorage and moved on to hoist the British flag at Sydney and found the settlement. He stayed there until ill health forced his return in 1792. In a letter

Arthur Phillip transported the first convicts to Australia and settled them at Sydney. A plaque on his monument shows the British flag being hoisted.

to Lord Sydney, Under Secretary of State for Home Affairs, he wrote: 'Nor do I doubt but this country will prove the most valuable acquisition Great Britain ever made.' It was said that 'His firmness and sense of justice helped the settlement to prosper'. The memorial describes Phillip as 'Founder and Governor of Australia'. On either side of the bust by Charles Hartwell are bronze plaques depicting Phillip being rowed ashore with his ship at anchor, sails furled, and on land, having claimed the territory. Phillip was born in the Bread Street Ward of the City of London and the monument, given in 1932 by Viscount Wakefield of Hythe, originally stood outside St Mildred's, Bread Street, a church destroyed in the Blitz. Happily, the monument survived, was set up first in Cannon Street in 1968 and subsequently relocated here. Phillip is buried at Bathampton, Somerset, with a shrine erected by the Fellowship of the First Fleeters, descendants of those who made the first voyage.

A seafarer, adventurer and member of an expedition to Virginia in 1607, **Captain John Smith** (1580–1631) became 'First among the Leaders of the Settlement of Jamestown, Virginia, from which began the overseas expansion of the English Speaking Peoples'. A romantic story tells that Smith was rescued by the eleven-year-old Princess Pocahontas from death by crushing after he had been captured by the Powhatan Indians. He was

John Smith, leader of the Jamestown settlers, was saved from death by Princess Pocahontas.

On the north side of St Paul's Churchyard are the column dedicated to the Richards family (above) and the statue of John Wesley, founder of Methodism (right).

Far left: *'Blitz' is a memorial to 1002 fire-fighters who died during the Second World War.*

Left: *The new Paternoster column north of St Paul's.*

eventually elected the colony's Governor in 1608. He returned to England to promote more expeditions and mapped the North American coast from Nova Scotia to Rhode Island. As Admiral of New England he advised the Pilgrim Fathers but because of a clash of personalities did not sail with them. He continued to write and publish widely: his works, such as *The General History of New England and the Summer Isles* (1624), are of great historical value. Smith's statue, unveiled by Queen Elizabeth the Queen Mother on 31st October 1960, is a replica by Charles Rennick of one in Virginia by William Couper. It stands beside St Mary-le-Bow, Cheapside, and was presented by the Jamestown Foundation of the Commonwealth of Virginia to commemorate Smith's return to England. He appears in Elizabethan dress with a book in his right hand and a sword in his left – a telling combination for an enterprising pioneer.

John Milton (1608–74), born in Bread Street, which runs south from Cheapside, is commemorated by a tablet on the exterior of St-Mary-le-Bow and by a stained glass window within. It was brought here from All Hallows, Bread Street, when in 1876 the parishes were amalgamated and All Hallows was demolished.

Over the entrance to Bracken House, 10 Cannon Street (the old *Financial Times* building), is an astronomical clock with signs of the Zodiac and, in the centre, a bronze mask of **Winston Churchill** by Frank Dobson (1959). Brendan Bracken, Chairman of the *Financial Times*, was a great friend of Churchill.

Near the Barbican a **stone tablet** in the wall of Fore Street, round the corner from Wood Street, records: 'On this site at 12.14 a.m. on 25th August 1940, fell

the first bomb in the City of London in the Second World War'. It was the first of many.

In Nettleton Court next to the Museum of London, 150 London Wall, is a memorial (1981) to **John Wesley**, marking the spot of his conversion in 1738. It is in the form of a leaf from his *Journal*, a remarkable record of spiritual life and tireless activity.

The John Wesley conversion memorial.

16.
THE BANK AND ROYAL EXCHANGE

A statue by Sir William Reid Dick of **Sir John Soane**, architect to the Bank of England from 1788 to 1833, is on the north side of the Bank building at the corner of Lothbury. The Bank was named the 'Old Lady' in the eighteenth century. A James Gillray cartoon dated 22nd May 1797 refers to the temporary stoppage of payments on 26th February and the issue of £1 notes on 4th March. It was entitled 'Political Ravishment, or the Old Lady of Threadneedle Street in Danger'. William Cobbett likened the Bank's directors to the 'Old Ladies of Threadneedle Street', attempting to hold back the tide of national progress. Round the Bank are sculptures by Sir Charles Wheeler, including, on the pediment, the **Old Lady of Threadneedle Street** holding a model of the old Bank on her knees, with a pile of coins at her side. The present building by Sir Herbert Baker (1925) lies within Soane's external walls.

Above the Corinthian portico of the Royal Exchange, a group represents **Commerce** holding the charter of the Exchange, attended by the Lord Mayor, British merchants and foreign representatives. The 177 foot high campanile has a statue by William Behnes (1845) of **Sir Thomas Gresham** (1519–79), founder of the Exchange. The grasshopper weathervane recalls a story that young Gresham, lost in a field, was found through the chirping of grasshoppers. The grasshopper became the Gresham crest.

In front of the Exchange, an equestrian statue of the **Duke of Wellington** (1769–1852) by Sir Francis Chantrey, showing the Duke riding stirrupless, was unveiled in the Duke's presence. Afterwards the Duke made for the great door (sacrosanct to members only). The doorman wisely let him pass.

Also before the Exchange is the **War Memorial to London Troops** (1920) by Sir Aston Webb and Alfred Drury. An addition was made to include the Second World War.

On a high plinth in Cornhill by the Royal Exchange forecourt is a statue of **James Henry Greathead** (1844–96), Chief Engineer of the City & South London Railway. The first section of this, the earliest electrically operated railway in London, was opened on 18th December 1890 from King William Street to Stockwell. In 1869 Greathead (with P. W. Barlow) had worked on the Tower Hill to Bermondsey foot subway, which was deep-bored through clay using Greathead's Cylindrical Tunnelling Shield, a civil engineering innovation, and lined with cast-iron segments. The tunnel closed when Tower Bridge was built; it now carries water mains. Today Greathead's name is

James Henry Greathead, Chief Engineer of the City & South London Railway, developed the travelling shield that made it possible to cut the tunnels of London's underground railways.

151

The equestrian statue of the Duke of Wellington by Chantrey stands outside the Royal Exchange.

George Peabody's housing still provides homes for the underprivileged.

still associated with the shield, although Marc Brunel had already patented the idea in 1818.

The **Metropolitan Drinking-Fountain and Cattle Trough Association** was founded by Samuel Gurney MP (a nephew of Elizabeth Fry) in 1859, to supply free, pure drinking water to the public to help combat cholera and intemperance. The first fountain survives in the wall of the church of the Holy Sepulchre, Holborn Viaduct. In 1867 troughs were added for horses, cattle and dogs. At the Cornhill end of the passage behind the Royal Exchange, a fountain by J. Whitehead commemorates the Association's Jubilee in 1911. The organisation still maintains drinking-fountains all over London.

Behind the Exchange is a seated figure of **George Peabody** (1795–1869), the American philanthropist and founder of J. P. Morgan Bank, responsible for many housing projects in London. The first Peabody Buildings opened in Spitalfields in 1864. The statue, by William Wetmore Story, a fellow American,

was unveiled on 23rd July 1869 by the Prince of Wales. Peabody was the only American to rest in Westminster Abbey. His remains were then taken to Massachusetts in HMS *Monarch*, an honour specially ordered by Queen Victoria, for interment there.

Some 10 yards from the Peabody statue and near the entrance to Royal Exchange Avenue is a four-sided drinking-fountain commemorating City of London **Alderman William Bartman** (1879). It is surmounted by the bronze sculpture entitled 'Motherhood', of a seated woman with two babies, by Amié-Jules Dalou (1838–1902), a French sculptor who spent much time in England.

A whiskered bust on a granite column by Michael Black (1976) commemorates **Paul Julius Reuter** (1818–99), founder of the news-reporting service, which began at 1 Royal Exchange Building on 14th October 1851.

On the north side of the Exchange is Joseph's statue (1845) of **Sir Hugh Myddleton**, whose

Reuter began his news service in Germany in 1849, using carrier pigeons.

scheme brought pure water from Hertfordshire springs to London at the beginning of the seventeenth century.

Also on the north side is a statue by Carew of **Richard Whittington** (died 1423). Three times Master of the Worshipful Company of Mercers, a City alderman, four times Mayor of London (in 1397, 1398, 1406 and 1419), Whittington was a medieval merchant prince. His wife, Alice, daughter of Sir Ivo Fitzwaryn, predeceased him; they had no children. After 1397 Whittington regularly lent large sums of money to the Crown and was rewarded with trading privileges. After his death his four executors, including John Carpenter, Town Clerk of the City, interpreted his wishes with efficiency, and thus both during his life and after his death Whittington's wealth was directed to such varied causes as the support of the poor and needy; churches and monastic houses; prisoners in London gaols; the rebuilding from 1409 of St Michael Paternoster Royal, his parish church, where he and his wife were to be buried; Greyfriars library; improvements to public works such as the water supply; the rebuilding of Newgate gaol; the Guildhall and its library; St Bartholomew's Hospital; and, a sympathetic thought for a childless man, the establishment of a refuge for 'girls who had done amiss' at St Thomas's Hospital, Southwark. About half of those benefiting from his bequests were asked to offer prayers for the souls of Whittington, his wife and family and certain other persons. The bulk of his great fortune was used to establish an almshouse and college of priests at St Michael Paternoster Royal (the college was dissolved at the Reformation and the name was applied to the almshouse alone). In 1424 Whittington's executors set up the almshouse for thirteen poor persons ('meek of spirit, destitute of worldly goods, chaste of body and of good conversation') of whom one was to be chosen to be tutor. In 1824 the enlarged almshouse moved to Highgate and in 1966 to Felbridge, near East Grinstead. There, a 'village within a village', are twenty-eight houses set among lawns and gardens, with houses for the tutor, matron, assistant matron and gardener, a chapel, a laundry and a dispensary. Whittington's statue, by Joseph Carew (1826), travelled with the almshouse from Highgate. As trustee, the Mercers' Company still administers the almshouse and many improvements have been made over six centuries. The trade of mercer (dealing in luxury fabrics such as taffeta, damask and linens) no longer exists. The Mercers' Company, the City's premier livery company, largely devotes itself to the care of its own charitable foundation and to the many charitable trusts placed in its care by benefactors such as Sir Thomas Gresham, following Whittington's example.

17. The City and north to Islington

In the former churchyard of St Mary Aldermanbury at the junction with Love Lane, EC2, is an obelisk with a bust of **William Shakespeare** (1554–1616) by Charles J. Allen (1895). Beneath it a plaque commemorates **John Heminge** (died 1630) and **Henry Condell** (died 1627), fellow actors and friends of Shakespeare, who were largely responsible for the publication of the First Folio in 1623. This contained all the completed plays except *Pericles*. Both Heminge and Condell were parishioners here and were buried in the pre-Great Fire church. Heminge was said to have been the first actor to play Falstaff. The memorial fell into disrepair but has recently been restored. The church, damaged in the war, was not rebuilt. The ruins were shipped to Fulton, Missouri, and re-erected as a memorial to Sir Winston Churchill.

A little to the north is Aldermanbury Square. The Worshipful Company of Brewers' Hall has existed nearby since the early fifteenth century. It was destroyed in the Great Fire of 1666, rebuilt in 1673, again destroyed in the Blitz of 1940 and rebuilt in 1960. In the square is the Brewers' Company's **Millennium Standing Stone**, dedicated on 12th December 2000. Sculpted by Richard Kindersley, it is of Caithness stone, with riven surfaces on all four sides. The dying words of St Monica, the mother of St Augustine, 'Nothing is distant from God', form the inscription. The dedication ceremony began with opening prayers by the Reverend Gareth Randall, chaplain, Dame Alice Owen's School, followed by readings by the Clerk and Past Master of the Company. The Right Honourable Richard Chartres, Bishop of London, then dedicated the

stone followed by closing prayers by John Weeks, Master of the Brewers' Company, who referred not only to the Company's regulation of the 'noble mystery of brewing' but also to its charitable work and its support of Aldenham and Dame Alice Owen's schools. The ceremony concluded with the blessing and the burial of a time capsule. The Caithness Slab Bench records the Augustinian priory of Spital existed near this spot from 1329 to 1536 and notes the history of the Brewers' Hall nearby since *c*.1400. The fish monogram appears on the stone. The Greek word for fish, *ichthus*, is composed of the initial letters of *Iesous CHristos, THeou Uios, Soter* – Greek for 'Jesus Christ, Son of God, Saviour'. The sign appeared on seals, rings, urns

The memorial to Shakespeare, Condell and Heminge, in the former churchyard of St Mary Aldermanbury.

The Millennium Standing Stone by Richard Kindersley is in Aldermanbury Square.

and tombs in the early days of Christianity.

Outside the new Guildhall Art Gallery, opened on 2nd November 1999 by Queen Elizabeth II, and approached from Gresham Street and through Guildhall Yard, is a series of busts by Tim Crawley, commissioned by the Corporation of London. These include that of **Samuel Pepys** (1633–1703), the naval administrator and diarist.

Here too is a bust of **Oliver Cromwell** (1599–1658). After the Civil War and the execution of Charles I in 1649 Cromwell became Lord Protector of the Commonwealth in 1653. Controversy still surrounds his regime. At best it was benevolent despotism, at worst a military dictatorship. In later years, following disputes with Parliament, Cromwell ruled largely by decree. A man of contradictions, energetic, a brilliant general, of high morals, affectionate, and, given Protestant constraints, surprisingly tolerant, he was never loved by the people and is still remembered for his massacres in Ireland. He died in 1658, to lie in state at Somerset House, where the mob pelted his escutcheon on the gate with dirt. His funeral was princely. His ineffectual son Richard succeeded him but was deposed within six months, paving the way for the restoration of the monarchy in 1660. Cromwell's body, with those of Ireton and Bradshaw, was exhumed to be gibbeted at Tyburn on 30th January 1661, the twelfth anniversary of the King's execution, and decapitated. The bodies were buried in a deep pit at the base of the gallows. Some deplored this act of vengeance: Samuel Pepys wrote in his *Diary* of his distress, 'that a man of so great courage as he was should have that dishonour done him, though otherwise he might deserve it well enough'.

Next is **Sir Christopher Wren** (1632–1723), who, strangely, has been little commemorated. Wren explained his view of architecture, to which he came from astronomy and mathematics, thus: 'Architecture has its political use; public buildings being the ornament of a country; it establishes a nation, draws people and commerce: makes the people love their native country, which passion is the original of all great actions in a commonwealth'. He gained recognition for his work in the classical style after the Great Fire of 1666. This was his opportunity and he embraced it with enthusiasm, working largely in Portland limestone, using over a million tons of it in St Paul's Cathedral alone. His greatest work was the rebuilding of St Paul's (1675–1711) but he also designed over fifty London churches; the Royal Hospital, Chelsea (1692); the Royal Naval Hospital, Greenwich; the Royal Observatory (a rare essay in brick); thirty-six company halls; the Custom House (1669–71); Temple Bar in the early 1670s; and the Monument (1671–7). With surpassing energy Wren supervised work on St Paul's from start to finish. He was forty-three when the

CROMWELL   WREN

Oliver Cromwell and Christopher Wren, together with Samuel Pepys and William Shakespeare, all sculpted by Tim Crawley, front the Guildhall Art Gallery.

foundation stone was laid, sixty-five when the choir was opened and seventy-seven when work ended. It is surely the only major building to have had not only the same architect, but also the same master builder – Thomas Strong – for thirty-five years. The story is told that Wren sent a labourer to fetch a stone to mark the exact centre of the dome; the man returned with a fragment of tombstone bearing the word *Resurgam* ('I will rise again'). Feeling that it expressed the spirit of the whole work, Wren asked Caius Gabriel Cibber to carve this motto under the phoenix rising from the flames, in the tympanum over the south door. Wren is said to have watched progress on St Paul's from Cardinal's Wharf, Bankside. He made weekly visits (nearly eight hundred in all), often on a Saturday; as the cathedral neared completion he was hauled up to the lantern in a basket. He asked his son to perform the ceremony of laying the highest stone in place on the lantern. In retirement in St James's Street he made annual pilgrimages to sit under the dome, as his son wrote: 'Cheerful in solitude and as well pleased to die in the shade as in the light.' He died at the age of ninety-one and was buried in the cathedral under a black marble slab with above it the words *Lector, si monumentum requiris, circumspice* ('Reader, if you seek a monument, look around you').

William Shakespeare also has a bust here, to add to depictions in Leicester Square, Foubert's Place, the old City of London School and the memorial in the churchyard of St Mary Aldermanbury.

Richard Whittington (died 1423), the youngest son of Sir William Whittington, born in Pauntley, Gloucestershire, came to London to seek his fortune in trade. His statue (with his cat) by Laurence Tindall (1998) stands to the left of the row of busts by the Guildhall Art Gallery.

In the churchyard of St Botolph's Bishopsgate, over a former school building now shared by the parish and the Fanmakers' Company, are two Coadestone figures of **charity children** in dark green uniforms. The boy wears an open cutaway coat with waistcoat, knee breeches, white stockings and bands; the girl is in a long green dress with white apron, armbands and mittens. She holds a prayerbook. One of the figures is dated 1821.

At Liverpool Street station, below the **war memorial of the Great Eastern Railway**, a bronze medallion commemorates **Captain Charles Algernon Fryatt** (1872–1916), master of the railway mail steamer *Brussels*. On 28th March 1915, when taking the *Brussels* from Parkeston to Rotterdam, Fryatt was ordered to stop by the German submarine U33. He disregarded the signal and steered for the submarine, which dived and did not reappear after becoming struck. In June 1916 the German navy captured the *Brussels*. Her captain and crew were taken prisoner and Fryatt was tried and shot. In 1919 his remains were exhumed and brought back to England. His funeral at St Paul's Cathedral was attended by the King and Queen of the Belgians. Fryatt was buried at Dovercourt, Essex, where a memorial hospital is named after him.

Bunhill Fields was from 1685 to 1852 the principal burial ground for dissenters – Southey called it the '*Campo Santo* of Dissenters'. The name derives from 'bonehill': Protector Somerset had dumped the contents of the St Paul's charnel house there. South from the main walk is the grave effigy of **John Bunyan** (1628–88) by E. C. Papworth (1851), restored several times. Bunyan was arrested in November 1660 for unlicensed preaching and, refusing to comply with the law, was imprisoned for twelve years until Charles II's Declaration of Indulgence in 1672. During a brief later imprisonment he began *Pilgrim's Progress*, published in 1678. For some years Bunyan's effigy lacked a nose, shot off, it was rumoured by a careless (or perhaps deliberate) bullet from the practice ground of the Honourable Artillery Company next door in City Road. The nose was replaced in a ceremony in 1922, attended by the widow of Dr

John Bunyan's effigy and Daniel Defoe's obelisk in Bunhill Fields.

John Brown, Bunyan's principal biographer. Accompanying panels on the memorial show 'Christian with his Burden' and 'The Burden Rolling from His Back'.

Until 1870 only a shabby stone commemorated **Daniel Defoe** (1660–1731), whose *Robinson Crusoe*, based on the true story of the marooned Alexander Selkirk, was published in 1719. A pillar of Sicilian marble was then erected in Bunhill Fields to Defoe's memory, paid for by the 'Boys and Girls of England', whose contributions were collected by the magazine *Christian World*. At that time the grave was opened and the nameplate found. The skeleton was 5 feet 4 inches in height and the under-jaw massive. Spectators wished to carry off bones as souvenirs but the police intervened and the coffin was reburied in a concrete foundation.

A statue of **John Wesley** (1703–91), paid for by Methodist children, was erected at the City Road Chapel on the centenary of his death. It is the work of J. Adams Acton, 'the Methodist sculptor', and was unveiled by Dr W. F. Moulton, President of the Wesleyan Conference. Wesley's words 'The World is my Parish' appear on the plinth. At Oxford Wesley joined his brother Charles in a 'Holy Club', from which Methodism – life conducted by rule and method – evolved. The first Methodist chapel opened in Bristol in 1739. Wesley's evangelical style attracted crowds of labourers, miners, shopkeepers and the lower middle classes. In April 1777 the City Road Chapel, the so-called 'cathedral of Methodism', was built, with a house for Wesley next door. George III was interested and supplied masts from the royal dockyards for the chapel gallery. Wesley preached widely until late in his life and is said to have travelled 250,000 miles on horseback and to have delivered 40,000 sermons. He died in his house in 1791 and is buried in the graveyard. Wesley wielded much influence and had many admirers. As time passed some who had at first approved came to distrust certain aspects of Methodism – the 'love-feasts', 'enthusiasm', fainting fits, tears, groans and hysteria generated by Wesley's preaching and by what a later writer termed the 'intellectual complacency' exemplified by Wesley's remark that in seventy years he had wasted no more than fifteen minutes, and that only in reading a worthless book. He was a domestic autocrat. His family, rebuked for their non-appearance at his morning's preaching, explained that they had sat up late the night before. He ordered that the whole household should go to bed by nine o'clock and that all, without exception, were to attend his preaching.

Since **Joseph Grimaldi** (1779–1837), the celebrated clown and pantomimist, all clowns have been called 'Joey'. He is remembered by Grimaldi Park, bordering Pentonville Road and Rodney Street, where his grave and headstone are decorated with cast-iron theatrical masks and bronze plaques. Grimaldi first appeared as an infant at Sadler's Wells, and theatres were always packed when he was playing.

This statue of John Wesley was erected at the City Road Methodist Chapel on the centenary of his death.

The statue of Sir Hugh Myddleton and (inset) John Thomas, the sculptor.

Dickens edited his *Memoirs* (1838). In late January each year, clowns gather at Holy Trinity Church, Dalston, for the Clowns' Service to commemorate Grimaldi, the 'Clown of Clowns'.

On Islington Green is the statue of **Sir Hugh Myddleton** (*c*.1560–1631), a wealthy goldsmith, banker and clothmaker, who in 1606 made an offer to Parliament to bring a supply of pure drinking water to London. At that time water was brought round by horse and cart, with resultant disease and inconvenience. The New River Company, formed by Myddleton, piped water nearly 40 miles from the Lea Valley springs in Hertfordshire to the New River Head, where reservoirs still stand. The engineer for the great work was Edmund Colthurst, not yet commemorated in London. The project took four years to complete and from this feat, impressive in any age, grew the Metropolitan Water Board. The statue, by John Thomas, was unveiled by Gladstone in 1862.

By the green at 45 Camden Passage is a memorial plaque by the bewigged head of **Alexander Cruden** (1701–70), a Scot who came to London in 1719, established himself as a bookseller in the Royal Exchange and a 'corrector of the press'. In 1737 he published his *Biblical Concordance*, which remains a standard reference book to this day. Unfortunately Cruden suffered periodic bouts of insanity, during which he felt his mission was to reform society, and he obsessively toured the country expressing his strong views on such matters as Sabbath-breaking. He also had a weakness for proposing marriage to wealthy ladies, whether they wished it or not. Mrs Pain, a widow of means, and Lady Abney's daughter were two of those he selected for this attention. The plaque was put up by the Camden Passage Association.

Alexander Cruden.

160

18.
CORNHILL TO TOWER HILL

The mahogany doors of 32 Cornhill, the offices of Cornhill Insurance plc, have deeply carved panels depicting scenes from the street's history. At the bottom right are depicted **Charlotte Brontë** (1816–55) and **Anne Brontë** (1820–49) talking to **William Makepeace Thackeray** (1811–63) in the offices of the publishers Smith, Elder & Company, at Number 65 until 1868. The Brontës came here to prove they were indeed Acton and Currer Bell. Charlotte's first novel, *The Professor*, was refused by Smith, Elder & Company and others and did not appear until 1857, but *Jane Eyre* came out in 1847 to enduring popularity. The memorial panels, designed by B. P. Arnold, were carved by Walter Gibbon (1939).

The poet **Thomas Gray** (1716–71) was born at 39 Cornhill. In 1996 the BBC's poll to find the nation's favourite poem put his 'Elegy Written in a Country Churchyard' in twelfth place. Its evocative opening lines linger in many memories:

> The curfew tolls the knell of parting day,
> The lowing herd wind slowly o'er the lea,
> The ploughman homeward plods his weary way,
> And leaves the world to darkness and to me.

The house was destroyed by fire in 1748 and the building now on the site bears a memorial tablet with a bronze medallion portrait by F. W. Pomeroy

The Brontë sisters met Thackeray at the offices of Smith, Elder, publishers, in Cornhill. A door panel at No. 32 recalls this encounter.

The Monument.

(1917) and the first line of the 'Elegy'. It was the gift of Sir Edward Cooper, Alderman of Cornhill Ward. The Lord Mayor attended the unveiling on 22nd March 1918.

After many years in the wall of St Swithin's Church the **London Stone** is now set in the wall of 111 Cannon Street, opposite Cannon Street station. It is believed to be a Roman *miliarium*, from which road distances were measured. In Shakespeare's *Henry VI*, Jack Cade the rebel struck his sword on it, declaring, 'Now is Mortimer Lord of this City', suggesting that it might also have had significance in establishing territorial jurisdiction.

A City emblem of the 1980s and 1990s, **The Market Trader** by Stephen Melton, stands at the south end of Walbrook. The bronze statue of the young, confident futures trader, in his characteristic jacket with identification tag in lapel, dealing slips poking from his pocket, is shouting into his mobile telephone. The figure, commissioned by the Corporation of the City of London at a cost of £40,000, was erected in 1997 and unveiled by Jack Wigglesworth, Executive Chairman of LIFFE, the London International Financial Futures and Options Exchange.

James Hulbert (died 1720), Prime Warden of the Fishmongers' Company (1718–20), is remembered by a marble statue by Robert Easton, which since 1978 has stood in the courtyard of Fishmongers' Hall, opening on to the river walkway by London Bridge. Hulbert's will provided for an almshouse for twenty poor persons. South Sea stock was sold at the right moment and the Court of Fishmongers found itself in command of £9,467 2s 5d, enough to accommodate forty persons: £2,000 secured the building; investments provided benefits; residents were warm and dry, with a stuff gown each, 3 shillings a week and a Christmas bonus, an annual visit from the wardens and services in their own chapel. They doubtless felt – and rightly – that fate had been kind to them.

A little to the north, the fluted Doric column of the **Monument** commemorates the Great Fire of London in 1666, which destroyed five-sixths of the medieval timber-and-thatch London and did four times more damage than the Blitz. It started in Master Robert Faryner's bakehouse in Pudding Lane and, with a north-east wind blowing, spread rapidly, destroying 13,200 houses. Booksellers, believing the crypt of St Paul's to be safe, put their stock there. They were wrong. Charred leaves from their books were found in Windsor, 20 miles away, and lead from St

'The Market Trader', symbol of the modern City of London, in Walbrook.

In his Seething Lane garden Pepys buried his Parmesan cheese during the Great Fire. His bust was erected on the site of his garden in 1983.

Paul's roof flowed down Ludgate Hill like volcanic lava. The cathedral was a ruin; eighty-seven churches were lost along with forty-four livery company halls and the Royal Exchange. Landmarks vanished. A Frenchman, Robert Hubert, employed by Faryner, confessed to starting the fire and was hanged. The tallest isolated stone column in the world, the Portland stone Monument, 202 feet high (supposedly the exact distance from the fatal bakehouse where the fire started), was erected to the designs of Sir Christopher Wren and Robert Hooke in 1671–2. A winding stair of 311 steps leads to the top platform, encased in an iron cage in 1842 after six people had jumped to their deaths. A statue of Charles II was planned as a finial; this proved too expensive and a flaming gilt urn was substituted. Round the base are intricate reliefs by Caius Gabriel Cibber; among the profusion is 'London being raised by Father Time'. Offensive inscriptions blaming the papists for the disaster were removed, both from the Monument and from the Pudding Lane bakehouse, with the passing of the Catholic Emancipation Act in 1829. These had given rise to Pope's lines: 'When London's column pointing to the skies, like a tall bully, lifts its head and lies'. The **Worshipful Company of Bakers** set up a commemorative plaque in Pudding Lane to mark the five hundredth anniversary of the granting of their charter by Henry VII in 1486.

At Trinity Square by Tower Hill, Muscovy Street leads into Seething Lane. In the garden of his Seething Lane house **Samuel Pepys** (1633–1703), naval administrator and diarist, dug a hole when the Great Fire threatened and hid certain state papers – and his precious Parmesan cheese. There is a bronze bust of Pepys by Karin Jonzen (1983) in Seething Lane Gardens on the site of his old home. During the Republic, Pepys's patron and first cousin Edward Montagu, a Cromwellian statesman and admiral, developed Royalist sympathies. After the Restoration he rose, taking Pepys with him as Clerk of the Acts to the Navy Board, responsible for the civil administration of the Navy. The Clerk's official lodgings were in Seething Lane and it was from here that Pepys watched the Great Fire. It began on Saturday 2nd September 1666. At first no one appreciated the danger. Pepys himself went back to bed; but he later alerted Charles II, who personally and efficiently organised fire-fighting among the panic-stricken population. Houses were blown up to make firebreaks, thatch was pulled from roofs. But not until the following Wednesday did rain and quieter weather make control possible. The fire swept the City from the Tower to Fleet Street. From 1660 to 1669, when he feared his eyesight

On Tower Hill is the site where Sir Thomas More and many other prisoners from the Tower were executed. Behind is the Merchant Seamen's War Memorial, to which a sunken garden was added after the Second World War.

was failing, Pepys kept his *Diary* in a cipher, which defied resolution until 1825. It is an unexcelled picture of contemporary life, revealing Pepys's own loveable character. In 1673 he was appointed first Secretary to the Admiralty. Now an MP and leading civil servant, by 1678 he had turned the Navy into a powerful, disciplined force. But in the confused politics of the time he was accused of complicity in the Popish Plot and imprisoned in the Tower, although charges were later dropped. He was then out of office for five years until Charles II, concerned about naval efficiency, made him Secretary for Admiralty Affairs, a post he retained under James II. When James was dethroned, Pepys was accused of treason and Jacobitism. He resigned, retired into private life and died at Clapham on 26th May 1703.

In Trinity Square on Tower Hill a small paved area with chains round it marks the **site of the scaffold**, where from 1388 to 1747 many prisoners in the Tower met their deaths. Those of royal blood were usually executed within the Tower; commoners, outside. Lord Lovat, the last to be executed here in 1747 for his part in the Jacobite rebellion of 1745, had his revenge (and, it is said, was amused) when a stand containing a thousand of his Whig enemies collapsed under their weight. Twelve were killed. He commented grimly, 'The more mischief, the better sport'. Others beheaded here included Sir Thomas More, Archbishop Laud and the Earl of Surrey.

The memorial to the men of the **Merchant Navy and Fishing Fleets** who died in two world wars and who have no grave but the sea stands on Tower Hill. The colonnade by Sir Edwin Lutyens was unveiled by Queen Mary in 1928. A sunken garden, designed by Sir Edward Maufe, with sculptures by Charles Wheeler, commemorates those lost during the Second World War. Losses in the Lighthouse and Pilotage Services are included. Ships' names are listed, with only the master or skipper designated by rank. There are 23,857 names in all. The memorial is the focus of wreath-laying on Remembrance Sunday. Individual ships' associations also hold services here. Typically, in June 2000, the HMT *Lancastria* Association laid a wreath in remembrance of the troopship's sinking through enemy action on 17th June 1940, with the loss of over four thousand lives, during the evacuation of St Nazaire. These ceremonies honour the great sacrifices made by the Merchant Navy in the two world wars, carrying vital war supplies and personnel, and saving Britain from starvation.

Trinity House, on the north side of the Square, erects and maintains lighthouses, lightships and other seamarks and is the principal pilotage authority in Britain. The premises were rebuilt in 1793–5 for the 'Guild Fraternity and Brotherhood of the Trinity, most Glorious and Undivided'. On the façade are the corporation's arms and Coadestone medallions of **George III** and **Queen Charlotte** by J. Baker (1796).

Above left: *The emperor Trajan by Tower Hill station and against a section of the Roman wall that once surrounded London.*

Above right: *One of several charity school figures in London, this boy is on the Sir John Cass Primary School, Aldgate.*

A late-eighteenth-century bronze of the Roman emperor **Trajan** (AD 53–117), bareheaded, in the short tunic of the Roman general, stands in Trinity Place by Tower Hill station, backed by the longest surviving section of the original London Wall. Its connection with the neighbourhood is through the Reverend P. B. 'Tubby' Clayton MC, joint-founder with the Reverend Nevill Talbot of TOC H. Clayton, vicar of All Hallows' Church nearby, found the statue in a scrapyard and presented it to Tower Hill Improvement Trust, who placed it here in 1980. All Hallows' by the Tower is the guild church of the worldwide **TOC H movement**, founded to perpetuate the Christian fellowship of the Talbot Houses at Poperinghe and Ypres in Belgium, which provided rest and recreation for troops temporarily withdrawn from the front line in the First World War (TOC H is TH in army signallers' alphabet). The name Talbot House commemorates Lieutenant Gilbert Talbot, killed in action in 1915. On the front wall of 41 Cooper's Row, off Tower Hill, is a bronze medallion of the first **Viscount Wakefield of Hythe** (1859–1941) by Cecil Thomas (1937), with a small bronze TOC H lamp. A plaque notes that in 1937 Lord and Lady Wakefield 'gave this house for good to church and people'. Viscount Wakefield held many public offices and was associated with many City projects. He endowed the TOC H Talbot House at Poperinghe and in 1932 gave the memorial to Admiral Phillip to St Mildred's, Bread Street.

The Minories leads north to Aldgate and Duke's Place, Houndsditch. On the **Sir John Cass Primary School** are figures of a boy and girl from an earlier charity school founded by Cass in 1669 for forty boys and thirty girls. The figures date from 1748 or earlier. While Cass was signing his second will he suffered a fatal haemorrhage and the quill in his hand was stained with blood. For this reason the children of the school wear red plumes on Memorial Day when staff and children attend a service at St Botolph's, Aldgate.

19.
THE EAST END AND DOCKLANDS

Over the door of the Geffrye Museum in Kingsland Road, Shoreditch, is a statue of **Sir Robert Geffrye** (1613–1704), Master of the Ironmongers' Company and Lord Mayor of London 1685–6. Geffrye, who lost heavily in the Great Fire but recovered his fortune, left money for the establishment of almshouses and a chapel. The statue is a replica by James Mande and Company (1913) of the original made for the Ironmongers by John van Nost (1723), which accompanied the almshouses when they moved to Hook, Hampshire. The London buildings became the Geffrye Museum.

Alfred Milner (1854–1925), the statesman, held a number of public offices, including High Commissioner for South Africa, where in 1898 he received Captain Joshua Slocum, who was sailing around the world in the *Spray*. (The Transvaal president, Paul Krüger, believing the world to be flat, refused to accept that this was possible.) Milner was interested in Toynbee Hall, 28 Commercial Street, Whitechapel, the first 'University Settlement' founded in 1885, whose object was 'to educate citizens in the knowledge of one another, to provide teaching for those who are willing to learn and recreation for those who are weary'. It took its name from the economist Arnold Toynbee (1852–83). Viscount Milner became Chairman of its council. On a wall in the courtyard the bronze medallion of him set in a wreath is a replica of the original by Gilbert Ledward (1930) in Westminster Abbey.

Nearby, a tiny mother and child sculpture is inscribed 'Clare Winsten for Jane Adams, USA'. **Jane Adams** worked at Toynbee Hall and returned to Chicago to found a similar institution there in 1889; for this she received the Nobel Peace Prize.

Opposite the Royal London Hospital, Whitechapel Road, is a memorial to

Edward VII (1841–1910), erected by loyal Jews of East London. His medallion portrait by W. S. Frith (1911) is flanked by Justice and Liberty, with cherubs holding a book, with a steamship and a motor car.

In the courtyard of Toynbee Hall are memorials to Jane Adams and Viscount Milner.

Queen Alexandra's finely detailed statue at the Royal London Hospital.

In the Royal London Hospital courtyard garden is a huge bronze statue by George Edward Wade (1908) of **Queen Alexandra** (1844–1925). She was a tireless supporter of London hospitals and in 1900 'introduced to England the Finsen Light cure for Lupus and presented the first lamp to the hospital'. Unfortunately the treatment was afterwards found to be of no value, and indeed dangerous.

On 3rd March 1943 the stampede at **Bethnal Green Underground station** of those seeking shelter in an air raid had tragic consequences. One woman tripped and fell, others following were unable to stop and 173 people were killed in the worst civilian tragedy of the Second World War. Their memorial at the entrance to the station was erected in 1993.

In Cyprus Street, Bethnal Green, off Old Ford Road, is a most unusual war memorial to the **men of Cyprus Street**. It was erected by the Duke of Wellington's Discharged and Demobilised Soldiers' and Sailors' Benevolent Club, the Duke of Wellington being a local pub. Twenty-six names of those killed in the First World War are listed, with four added for the Second World

War. This rare street memorial, against a house wall between two attractive shuttered windows, is beautifully cared for and is treated with the greatest respect, with a flower box and wreaths. The Union Flag is hoisted over it daily. The loss of thirty men from one short East End street brings home the appalling cost of the two world wars.

In the communal garden of a small housing estate west of the Regent's Canal in Roman Road is a bronze group by Elizabeth Frink (1957) of **The Blind Beggar and his Dog**, figures in Bethnal Green lore, ballads and plays since the fifteenth century. Bessee, the beggar's beautiful daughter, was courted by four suitors – a knight, a gentleman of fortune, a London merchant and an innkeeper's son. She told them they must first obtain the consent of her father, the Blind Beggar, who had been blinded at the battle of Evesham in 1265. At this, three slunk away, leaving only

The Blind Beggar and his Dog.

167

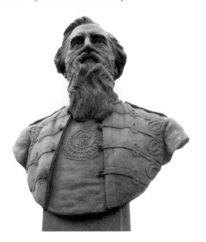

William Booth has both a bust and a statue in Mile End Road, where his services in 1861 were the start of the Salvation Army.

the knight, who asked for Bessee's hand. The Blind Beggar gave her a dowry of £3000 with £100 for a wedding dress and at the wedding feast cast off his rags and revealed himself as no beggar but Henry, the son and heir of Simon de Montfort.

Another reminder of wartime is a plaque erected by English Heritage on 13th June 1985 on the railway bridge in Grove Road, E3, where the **first flying bomb** fell on the night of 12th–13th June 1944 and destroyed an earlier bridge, killing six people. On Hughes Mansions, Vallance Road, is a memorial on the site of the **last V2 rocket** to fall on London. It killed 134 people on 27th March 1945.

Grove Road continues north to Victoria Park, which was established in 1845, covers 217 acres and had 110 football pitches, more than any other sports ground in Britain. **Baroness Angela Georgina Burdett-Coutts** (1814–1906), the philanthropist, who inherited the banking fortune of her grandfather, is remembered by an elaborate fountain by A. Darbishire, which she gave to the park. She was made a peeress in 1871, the first baroness in her own right. For nearly seventy-five years she lived in a bow-fronted brick house at the corner of Piccadilly and Stratton Street. At the window on the top floor Queen Victoria liked to sit watching with child-like pleasure the stream of traffic below in Piccadilly. 'Yours is the only place where I can go,' the Queen told the Baroness, 'to see the traffic without stopping it.' More by accident than design the Baroness was the last person (apart from the Unknown Warrior) to be buried in Westminster Abbey. Cremation was planned: at the last moment her husband changed his mind. It was too late to amend the arrangements and inhumation took place.

Restoration of Victoria Park began in 1988; the Chinese pavilion (part of the Chinese exhibition in Knightsbridge in 1847) and Victorian gas lamps were repaired. Here, too, by the cricket pitch are two **alcoves from Old London Bridge**. In these box-like structures at the side of the bridge foot passengers

Edward VII's bust in Mile End Road.

could take refuge from horses and carts.

At the corner of Cambridge Heath Road and Mile End Road a bronze bust by George Edward Wade of **William Booth** (1829–1912), the founder of the Salvation Army, was added in 1929 to a commemorative stone laid in 1910 by Commissioner Rees. Booth's open-air services on Mile End Waste in 1861 were the beginning of the Salvation Army. In 1979 a fibreglass replica of Booth's statue at Denmark Hill was erected a hundred yards east, painted grey and filled with concrete. It has since lost its right hand.

A further forty yards east along Mile End Road, on a marble plinth is a bust of **Edward VII** 'Erected by a few freemasons of the Eastern District of London 1911'. By Harris & Son, it also reads 'Peace hath her victories no less renowned than war'.

To the east Mile End Road becomes Bow Road. Outside Bow churchyard a bronze statue of **William Ewart Gladstone** (1809–98) by Albert Bruce-Joy was erected in 1882 to mark Gladstone's fifty years as an MP. It was the gift of Theodore Bryant, a prominent Liberal and a member of the match-manufacturing family, whose works was nearby.

At 39 Bow Road, the corner of Harley Grove, a small garden commemorates **George Lansbury** (1859-1940), the Labour politician. Lansbury entered Parliament as MP for Bromley and Bow in 1910, resigning in 1912 to fight a by-election as a Women's Suffrage candidate. This brought the suffragette

Sylvia Pankhurst to Bow, where she founded the East London Federation of Suffragettes. From 1912 to 1922 Lansbury edited the Labour newspaper, *The Daily Herald*, and in 1919–20 was Mayor of Poplar, being imprisoned, with others, for refusing to authorise payment of the county rate. He re-entered Parliament in 1922 and became Chairman of the Labour Party but resigned in 1935, when his pacifist views were not acceptable to his party. In the first Labour Government of 1929–31 Lansbury was First Commissioner of Works and was responsible for the establishment of 'Lansbury's Lido', the bathing-place on the Serpentine in Hyde Park.

This memorial outside Lansbury House commemorates the Labour politician George Lansbury.

169

100 yards apart, the elaborate Gothic memorial to Marian martyrs and the simple classic obelisk to Samuel Gurney in Stratford Broadway.

Bow Road continues to Stratford-le-Bow. In the churchyard of St John's Church in Stratford Broadway is a memorial (1879) to eighteen **Protestant martyrs** burnt at the stake in Stratford and Bow. They include the thirteen martyrs of the Marian persecution burnt at Stratford Green in 1555–6, the largest group martyrdom.

Also in the Broadway, at the junction with West Ham Lane, an obelisk set up in 1861 by fellow parishioners and friends commemorates **Samuel Gurney** (1786–1856), the local banker and Quaker philanthropist, who lived at Ham House, Upton, from 1812. Crowds attended Gurney's funeral in the Friends' Cemetery, Barking. He was the brother of Elizabeth Fry, the prison reformer, and had himself been active in the reform of prisons and the criminal code. He made gifts to the Irish poor and was also an efficient banker. He once refused to prosecute a man who had forged his signature, knowing that the penalty for one found guilty was death. The inscription reads 'When the ear heard him then it blessed him'.

In Arthingworth Road, Stratford, is a 3 foot high granite plaque to **PC Nina Mackay**, who died here on 24th October 1997. The memorial, unveiled by the Prime Minister, Tony Blair, on 22nd October 1998, is one of a number erected by the Police Memorial Trust to London police officers who have died in the course of duty. A paranoid schizophrenic stabbed PC Mackay when she tried to arrest him for breach of bail.

We turn south, back to the riverside. The streets were packed for the funeral at Trinity Chapel, Poplar, of **Richard Green** (1806–63), shipowner, shipbuilder (at the Blackwall Yard) and philanthropist. So great was his popularity that on his death all the ships in the Thames, not only his own, showed the conventional maritime marks of respect. 'I had no time to hesitate,' was Green's favourite saying, typifying a man noted for clear thinking, quick decisions and business acumen, who devoted his short life to the betterment of the seaman's lot. He built East Indiamen, for which his yard was famous, and ships for the

Richard Green, shipbuilder and philanthropist, with his dog Hector.

Australian Gold Rush. His good works included the establishment of a Sailors' Home, navigational instruction for officers and men, work for Poplar schools, the Merchant Seamen's Orphans' Asylum, the Dreadnought Hospital, and more. He was interested in the Naval Reserve and was the chief mover in the Thames Marine Officers' Training Ship. Contributions towards the statue, which stands by the former Poplar Baths in East India Dock Road, came from all over the world. The statue by Edward W. Wyon was unveiled only three years after his death and shows Green seated, with his dog Hector beside him.

Many historic voyages started from the Thames. A plaque at East India Dock to the **Virginia Settlers** records what was virtually the beginning of the United States of America. In December 1606 John Smith and a party of 105 adventurers left here to found the colony of Virginia at Jamestown, fourteen years before the departure of the Pilgrim Fathers. Despite hardships they survived. They sailed in the *Susan Constant* (100 tons), *Godspeed* (40 tons) and *Discovery* (20 tons) and landed at Cape Henry, Virginia, in April 1607. In 1928 the Association for the Preservation of Virginian Antiquities presented the plaque, which was first mounted on the wall of the dockmaster's house, near where the voyage began. In 1951 the Port of London Authority set up an attractive memorial on the East India Dock pierhead, the **Virginia Settlers' Memorial**, incorporating the plaque. It was ceremonially unveiled by Lord Waverley, then Chairman of the PLA. But vandals stole the mermaid that crowned it and later the site was redeveloped. Now the memorial (without the mermaid) is again in place on the pierhead with a cast of the original plaque, which is now in safe-keeping.

An East End tragedy of the First World War is recalled in Upper North Street, Poplar, at the former **London County Council School**, where on the 13th June 1917 a bomb dropped by a Gotha aircraft (some accounts say a Zeppelin) killed eighteen children, most only five years old. A memorial fund was launched by the Mayor of Poplar and in 1919 a memorial was unveiled in the school playground by Queen Alexandra. It took the form of a Gothic obelisk, with a list of names, topped by an angel of Sicilian marble and Aberdeen granite. There is now a plaque on the site in their memory. The impressive memorial survives in good condition, now in Poplar Recreation Ground, south of East India Dock Road, between Hale and Woodstock Roads.

The West India Dock, on the Isle of Dogs, within a loop of the Thames, was the first enclosed dock where ships could berth alongside in tide-free waters, protected against thieves by massive walls. Since the 1980s the London Docklands Development Corporation has changed the scene dramatically. The 800 foot Canary Wharf Tower at 1 Canada Square now dominates the London skyline for miles. Development of the former dock includes offices (particularly those concerned with financial services and newspapers), shops, hotels and restaurants. A bronze bas-relief of **Michael von Clemm** (1935–97),

Michael von Clemm, pioneer of euromarkets, is remembered at Canary Wharf in Docklands.

an investment banker and pioneer of euromarkets, whose vision helped to create this vibrant financial centre, was unveiled by Eddie George (now Sir Edward George), Chairman of the Bank of England, on 28th December 1998, in the gardens by 15 Cabot Square. It is by Gerald Laing.

On the wall of Heron Quays platform of the Docklands Light Railway a plaque marks the spot where on 27th June 1982 **Captain Harry Gee** of Brymon Airways landed his DHC Dash in a flight aimed at proving the feasibility of a Docklands airport; London City Airport followed.

Another figure who, in his day, strongly influenced this area was **Robert Milligan** (1746–1808), a driving force behind the opening of the West India Dock in 1802, and Deputy Chairman of the West India Dock Company. Richard Westmacott's bronze statue of him was placed by the sugar warehouse at West India Quay and stood there until 1875, when it was moved a short distance away. In 1947 the PLA removed it from public view. The Museum of Docklands acquired it in 1984. Milligan has now been returned to stand again by the Sugar Quay Warehouse, designed by George Gwilt in 1802 with cast-iron columns added by John Rennie in 1814.

As well as Robert Milligan, George Hibbert (1757–1837) was instrumental in establishing West India Dock and was Chairman of the West India Merchants until 1831 and agent for Jamaica. In addition to his commercial interests he was a patron of the arts and a collector of pictures, books and exotic plants at his home in Clapham. (When his library was eventually sold, the sale took forty-two days.) His portrait by Sir Thomas Lawrence hung in the boardroom of the East and West India Dock Company. The ornamental **Hibbert Ship Gate**, the main gate to the dock, pierced the high wall of the West India Dock. It was decorated with a 12 foot long bronze and Coadestone model of one of Hibbert's full-rigged West India ships. The archway was demolished between the wars to give greater access to traffic and the ship was placed in a Poplar park, from where it disappeared. Exactly two hundred years after the dock's founding, when Prime Minister William Pitt the Younger was rowed across the West India Dock to lay the foundation stone, the Mayor of London, Ken Livingstone, repeated this journey and unveiled a 32 foot replica of the Hibbert Ship Gate at Hertsmere Park, the landscaped area to the north-west of the wharf, near the Milligan statue. This ceremony took place on 12th July 2000 in the presence of the High Commissioner of the West Indies, whose islands

Robert Milligan is back in the docks that he developed.

The statue of Labour Prime Minister Clement Attlee is outside Limehouse Library.

were intimately connected with the dock's history. The gate's inscription reads: 'The West India Import Dock began 12th July 1800. Opened for business 1st Sept. 1802'.

Also reinstated is the original **Dock Dedication Plaque** for the West India Dock, dated August 1802. This was on Number 5 warehouse until 1935; it was then stored but is now again in place on the west wall of the Ledger Building, West India Quay.

On 30th November 1988 Lord Wilson of Rievaulx (Harold Wilson) unveiled a statue by Frank Foster outside Limehouse public library of **Clement Richard Attlee** (1883–1967), Britain's first post-war Labour Prime Minister, and Deputy Prime Minister in Churchill's wartime Cabinet. Attlee was a former Mayor of Stepney and MP for Limehouse. His government nationalised railways, mines, the steel industry and utilities. The National Health Service was begun, educational reforms made and independence granted to India and Pakistan. Earl Attlee is portrayed speaking, his left hand characteristically holding his lapel. Unkindly, Churchill once called him 'a sheep in sheep's clothing'. Despite his modest demeanour, Attlee relished his advancement, writing with droll self-assessment:

> Few thought he was even a starter,
> There were many who thought themselves smarter,
> But he ended PM, CH and CM,
> An Earl and a Knight of the Garter!

Attlee could turn a dry phrase. Lord Milford, a declared Communist, took his seat in the House of Lords in 1962 with a strident maiden speech, including a demand for the abolition of the Upper House. As leader of the Labour peers Earl Attlee offered the usual congratulations on a maiden speech, observing, 'There are many anomalies in this country. One curious one is that the views of the Communist Party can only be heard in this House. That, of course, is an advantage of the hereditary principle.'

In King Edward VII Memorial Park between the Highway and the river at Shadwell is the **Navigators' Memorial**, set up by the London County Council. The inscription reads: 'This tablet is in memory of Hugh Willoughby, Stephen Borough, William Borough, Sir Martin Frobisher and other navigators who, in the latter half of the 16th century, set sail from this reach of the River Thames near Ratcliff Cross to explore the northern seas'. Missing from the memorial is Richard Chancellor's name. He sailed as Pilot-General with Willoughby in 1553. The ships were dispersed by gales, Chancellor missed a rendezvous, arrived in the White Sea, travelled overland to Moscow, and there met the Tsar, negotiating valuable trading rights, leading to the founding of the Muscovy Company, first of the chartered companies of Merchant Adventurers. The memorial, signed 'Carter & Poole 1922', is surmounted by depictions of ships in full sail.

The Navigators' Memorial is on the river side of the King Edward VII Memorial Park.

A column on a stepped terrace in the park displays a medallion of **Edward VII** by Sir Bertram Mackennal, unveiled by George V in 1922 and paid for with surplus funds from the Waterloo Place statue, also by Mackennal.

THIS TABLET IS IN MEMORY OF SIR HUGH WILLOUGHBY, STEPHEN BOROUGH, WILLIAM BOROUGH, SIR MARTIN FROBISHER AND OTHER NAVIGATORS WHO, IN THE LATTER HALF OF THE SIXTEENTH CENTURY, SET SAIL FROM THIS REACH OF THE RIVER THAMES NEAR RATCLIFF CROSS TO EXPLORE THE NORTHERN SEAS.

ERECTED BY THE LONDON COUNTY COUNCIL, 1922

By St John's Church, Scandrett Street, Wapping, on the central pediment of a school building, are statues of **charity children** with the inscription 'Founded AD 1695'.

River watchers might here see a floating memorial, the **patrol boat** Gabriel Franks. The Thames Division of the Metropolitan Police, with headquarters at Wapping, in 2000 named the boat after a 22-year-old officer shot in 1798 when a crowd attacked Wapping police station in a protest over the arrest of coal thieves. Franks was the first uniformed police officer in the world to be killed in the line of duty.

At St Katherine's Dock is the **Coronarium**, made up of seven large white columns from a former dock warehouse supporting a circular stone roof. Suspended within is a 2 ton perspex block depicting the Imperial Crown, by Arthur Fleischmann. It stands on the approximate site of the original royal and collegiate chapel of St Katherine-by-the-Tower and was unveiled by Queen Elizabeth II in celebration of her Silver Jubilee.

London was the world's ivory market until the export of ivory was banned. Elephant tusks, rhinoceros horns, even mammoth tusks found in frozen Siberia and the occasional narwhal horn, were laid out for auction, destined to become piano keys, billiard balls and paper knives. A whiff of tradition lingers on: at **Ivory House**, St Katherine's Yacht Haven, gates are decorated with fibreglass elephants designed by Peter Drew (1973).

Above: *One of the two ivory elephants on the gate piers of Ivory House.*

A replica Hibbert Ship Gate was set up at Hertsmere Park, West India Dock in 2000. It was unveiled by the Mayor of London, Ken Livingstone.

The Hobbs Gates and the brick sculpture of Len Hutton at the Oval.

20.
Kennington to London Bridge

At Kennington Oval, home of Surrey County Cricket Club, where the game has been played since 1845, gates commemorate the great **Sir Jack Hobbs** (1882–1963), who at the time of his retirement in 1935 had the highest score ever achieved in first-class cricket of 61,221 runs and 197 centuries. Hobbs was knighted in 1953; his modesty, discipline, integrity and charm gained him wide affection.

Alongside the gates a brick sculpture by Walter Ritchie remembers **Sir Leonard Hutton** (1916–90), another player of legend. A marble scorecard of the Fifth Test in 1938 shows how each of the 364 runs was scored by Hutton in an historic innings.

The grounds of the former Bethlem (Bethlehem or Bedlam) Hospital were bought in 1936 by Lord Rothermere and given to London County Council as a park in memory of his mother **Geraldine Mary Harmsworth**. The central

block of the old hospital became the Imperial War Museum.

On the north side of the museum is a black bronze column surmounted by a bell with symbolic arms and head, commemorating the 27 million **Soviet citizens,**

Soviet citizens who died 1939–45 have their memorial by the Imperial War Museum.

The Tibetan Peace Garden leads to an inscribed obelisk, but close by (right) is the much older obelisk commemorating Brass Crosby.

servicemen and women who died for the Allied Victory in the Second World War. The memorial was paid for by public subscription.

On the south side of the museum is the **Tibetan Peace Garden**, a walled circular enclosure with a central bronze device and a path leading to a 12 foot obelisk with an inscription in English and Tibetan. It was unveiled by the Dalai Lama in 1999.

The obelisk erected in 1771 commemorating **Brass Crosby** (1725–93), Lord Mayor of London, is now back in St George's Circus. Older residents recall its being a bus stop announced by conductors with a rousing shout of 'Obliss!' Inscriptions on the plinth give the distances from London Bridge, Fleet Street and Palace Yard, Westminster. Crosby, a friend of John Wilkes and a staunch upholder of liberty, was once committed to the Tower of London for refusing to convict a printer who published Parliamentary proceedings and for declining to back 'press-warrants', which permitted Royal Navy press-gangs to operate in the City.

In the churchyard of St Mary-at-Lambeth (now the Museum of Garden History) stands the table tomb of the **Tradescant family**, who gave their name to the plant tradescantia. Here lie John Tradescant (died 1638), his wife Jane (1634), his son John (1662) and grandson John (1678). The Tradescants were royal gardeners to Charles I and Henrietta Maria, and Charles II. The tomb's devices – classical ruins, animals, including a crocodile, trees and shells – are emblems of their travels and plant-collecting. The inscription reads:

> Beneath this stone lie John Tradescant, grandsire, father, son …
> These famous Antiquarians that had been
> Both Gardiners to the Rose and Lily Queen.

Pineapples, which the Tradescants introduced into England, appear in compliment among the decorations on Lambeth Bridge.

Also in the garden is the Coadestone table tomb of **Vice Admiral William Bligh** (1754–1817) with his coat of arms and a flaming urn. He is described as 'the celebrated navigator, who first transplanted the bread fruit tree from Otaheite to the West Indies, bravely fought the battles of his country and died beloved, respected and lamented on the 7th December 1817'. There is no mention of his being cast adrift in the ship's launch on 28th April 1789 off the Friendly Islands, together with eighteen loyal seamen, by the mutinous crew of HMS *Bounty*. Bligh amply confirmed his reputation as a gifted navigator established during Captain Cook's circumnavigation (1775–9) by steering this open boat an epic 3600 miles to reach landfall at Timor, near Java. Bligh lived with his family at 3 Durham Place, now 100 Lambeth Road.

On the façade of the offices of the International Maritime Organisation, 4 Albert Embankment, was unveiled on 27th September 2001 the **International Memorial to Seafarers**, sculpted by Michael Sandle. It takes the form of the prow of a massive bronze cargo ship, surmounted by a seafarer. It is placed as though bursting through the front wall of this office building and, unusually, is as impressive from the inside as from the outside of the building. The 10 tonne sculpture commemorates all members of the mercantile marine lost at sea. Despite modern navigational aids four hundred men are still lost each year. The sculptor, regarded as one of the leading public sculptors of the day, has a seafaring background. His father was a chief petty officer in the Royal Navy and he himself was christened in HMS *Ark Royal.*

The Albert Embankment leads along the Thames to St Thomas's Hospital, which has statues brought from the earlier hospital in the Borough. Outside on the terrace, with his back to the hospital shop, **Edward VI** (1537–53), refounder of St Thomas's after its closure by Henry VIII, was the central stone figure of the old hospital gateway, sculpted in 1682 by Thomas Cartwright, the hospital mason. Edward VI, concerned about the poor and sick, gave funds to hospitals, made certain ecclesiastical reforms and defeated the Scots at Pinkie during his short reign (1547–53). A second statue of the King, of brass, by Peter Scheemakers, was erected in 1737. This is now indoors, near the hospital's Central Hall.

Another benefactor, **Sir Robert Clayton** (1629–1707), a wealthy broker and scrivener, left a fortune by his uncle, became Lord Mayor of London in 1679, MP for the City of London 1678–81, and President of St Thomas's. His statue, one of two outdoor statues in London by Grinling Gibbons, was first erected in 1702. It stands in a small memorial garden near the Embankment opened by Princess Margaret in September 2000.

Finally, and inevitably, since she had much to do with the design of the hospital and the Nightingale School of Nursing there (closed in 1997), there is a statue of **Florence Nightingale** (1820–1910) in the hospital's Central Hall (open to patients and visitors). The plaster original by A. G. Walker was the model for a bronze version commissioned by the hospital in 1955. This was completed by Frederick Mancini and erected outside in 1958. It disappeared. A further version was put up in 1975 and has now been moved inside. The statue is flanked by cases of Nightingale

Florence Nightingale founded the Nightingale School of Nursing at St Thomas's Hospital.

Edward VI and Sir Robert Clayton were both benefactors of St Thomas's Hospital.

The Coadestone Lion once decorated the river frontage of the Lion Brewery. When the brewery was demolished, it was moved to Westminster Bridge.

brooches, presented to 'Nightingale Nurses' and returned when their recipients died.

Also in the Central Hall are ten busts of **medical men** connected with St Thomas's and a seated marble statue of **Queen Victoria** by Matthew Noble (1873).

Across Westminster Bridge is the **Coadestone Lion** (12 feet high, 13 feet long and weighing 13 tons), which once decorated the river frontage of the Lion Brewery on the South Bank. The brewery was demolished in 1948 to make way for the Royal Festival Hall. This lion, like the Twickenham Lion, was preserved at the wish of George VI and moved here in 1966. It was designed by W. F. Woodington; a paw is inscribed '24th May 1837. W.F.W.' When the Lion was cleaned a sealed bottle with William IV farthings and a Coade tradecard was found. It had been hoped it would have included the elusive formula for the stone. Eleanor Coade (1733–1821), an astute businesswoman with classical tastes, set up in Belvedere Road, Lambeth, to manufacture an artificial stone said to be the most durable of its kind. Mrs Coade called her company the Lithodipyra Manufactury, linking the Greek words for 'stone', 'twice' and 'fire'. When the factory closed in 1840 the secret was lost. Modern analysis suggests that the formula for the stone consisted of a mixture of ball clay, flint, fine sand and soda-silicone glass fired and ground down, then pressed into prepared moulds, released and fired again. Eleanor Coade and her nephew and partner John Sealy used the best designers and sculptors and worked for leading architects. Coadestone was widely used. There are many examples in England and others as far afield as Gibraltar, Rio de Janeiro and Montreal. The Lion was made by William Croggan, who took over the works in 1813. Émile Zola, staying at the Savoy Hotel across the river from the brewery, saw the Lion early one morning rising through the mist off the water, and called delightedly to his wife, 'Come and see, here's the British lion waiting to bid us good-day!'

This handsome entrance to Waterloo Station forms the London & South Western Railway's First World War memorial. Theatres of war are listed on the arch.

The memorial to the International Brigade who fought fascism in the Spanish Civil War is on the South Bank.

In December 2001, after two years of scientific research, Chris Cleere and Stephen Pettifer announced their rediscovery of the Coadestone process. The first new piece of Coadestone to be seen by the public since the 1840s is an hourglass to complete the figures known as the 'Pelican Group', which stood over the entrance to the Pelican Life Insurance office in Lombard Street. These figures, said to be the finest examples of Coadestone in the world, are now in the Museum of London.

Along the South Bank from the Lion, by the London Eye, is Ian Walters's memorial to over 2100 volunteers who fought in Spain in the **International Brigade,** 1936–9, during the Spanish Civil War.

Further north, between the Hungerford railway bridge and the Royal Festival Hall, is a large bust, also by Ian Walters (1985), of **Nelson Mandela**, the anti-apartheid campaigner and President of South Africa from 9th May 1994.

At the top of the steps leading up to Waterloo station is the **Victory Arch** war memorial, erected when the station was part of the London & South Western Railway. To the left of the arch the figure of Bellona, goddess of war, is marked '1914' and to the right is Peace, marked '1918'. Four bronze tablets list the names of the 585 company servants who died in the war. King George V was to have unveiled it on 21st March 1922 but he was ill and Queen Mary took his place, entering from York Road, ascending the steps and cutting a silk cord to unveil the memorial and to inaugurate the new Waterloo station.

The site of the Elizabethan **Globe Theatre** was later occupied by a series of breweries including from 1758 to 1781 that of Henry Thrale, Samuel Johnson's friend. At the corner of Park Street and Bankside a tablet marks the site of the theatre, where Shakespeare, Condell and Heminge were licensed to act by James I in 1603. In 1613 the theatre burnt down, when two cannons fired during a performance of *Henry VIII* set the thatch alight. One enterprising theatregoer doused his burning breeches with a bottle of ale. The theatre was rebuilt the following year. The memorial tablet on the site was unveiled by Sir Herbert Beerbohm Tree, the actor-manager. 200 yards west is the new Globe Theatre, opened in 1995, the first thatched building to be built in central London since the Great Fire of 1666. In the foyer is a bronze memorial tablet to the first Globe with a bust of Shakespeare and a view of the Globe and the Thames. The inscription reads: 'Commemorated by the Shakespeare Reading Society of London and by subscribers in the United Kingdom and India'. Shakespeare is particularly revered by Indian scholars.

The bronze statue of **The Ferryman** (holding a wooden oar) stands within the theatre precincts, by the entrance to Shakespeare's Globe Exhibition. The figure also provides drinking water and was commissioned by the Metropolitan Drinking Fountain Association as a gift to mark the re-opening of the Globe

Nelson Mandela.

Theatre in 1997. The inscription reads: 'The players on the Bankside and round the Globe and Swan will teach you tricks of love ...' The sculptor was Mark Coreth. Thames watermen survive to this day, if in reduced numbers. In the reign of Elizabeth I there were three thousand at work between Westminster and London Bridge and many ferried playgoers across to the Globe at Bankside. Every year young watermen still race against the tide 4¹/₂ miles from London Bridge to Chelsea Cadogan Pier on or near 1st August for the prize of 'a coat of orange livery' and a heavy silver badge bearing the prancing horse of Hanover, 'representing Liberty'. The race was founded by Thomas Doggett (died 1721), a comedian and joint manager of Drury Lane Theatre, and the prize commemorates 'King George's happy accession to the British Throne'. The Doggett's Coat and Badge Race is an important event in the London calendar.

Watermen and ferrymen were the taxi-drivers of the Thames, alert for a shout of 'oars' from customers waiting on the piers and water-stairs of the river. Dibdin wrote poignantly of an old waterman about to retire from his trade:

> Then farewell, my trim-built wherry!
> Oars and coat and badge, farewell,
> Never more by Chelsea ferry
> Shall your Thomas take a spell ....

The table tombs of Bligh of the Bounty and of the Tradescants are at the Museum of Garden History at Lambeth.

181

21.
LONDON BRIDGE TO ROTHERHITHE

In the courtyard of Guy's Hospital in St Thomas Street at London Bridge is a brass statue by Peter Scheemakers (1734) of **Thomas Guy** (1645–1724), a bookseller who made a fortune by selling Bibles and speculating (partly in South Sea stock) and used it to endow the hospital in 1722. The statue's face is probably taken from his death mask. Guy's frugality was legendary: he was said to have used old proof sheets in place of a tablecloth, and to snuff candles during conversation, for which he said one did not need light. Nevertheless, there was another side to his character. One day he was leaning over Old London Bridge watching the tide when a passer-by, thinking he contemplated suicide, pulled him back and pressed a guinea into his hand. Guy reassured his new friend, asked his name and returned the guinea. Later, seeing his benefactor's name on a list of bankrupts (through no fault of his own), Guy set him up again in business in Newgate Street. He also gave generously to Protestant refugees driven from the Rhine Palatinate and to St Thomas's Hospital, to pay for the care of the sick and disabled among them.

In another courtyard is a statue of **William Richard Morris, first Viscount Nuffield** (1877–1963), the car-maker and philanthropist, who made many donations to Guy's Hospital. Lord Nuffield began work as a cycle repairer at Cowley, Oxford, turned to car manufacture and made a fortune. By 1938 he had given £11.5 million for research, education and charity but kept his modest, unaffected way of life. The Nuffield Foundation was established in 1943 with an endowment of £10 million – one of the largest charitable trusts ever conceived, with an annual income of £400,000. By 1957 he had given away £57 million.

Here too is another **alcove from Old London Bridge**, set up here in 1861. Like the two in Victoria Park, it shows the Bridge House Mark or Southwark Cross, an annulet ensigned with a cross patée, interlaced with a saltire conjoined in base, carved on the underside of the key-stone. Dickens had David Copperfield linger in such an alcove while waiting for King's Bench Prison to open and for his interview with Mr Micawber.

On 22nd June 1861 a timber store at Cotton's Wharf, Tooley Street, near London Bridge, caught alight and soon the whole south waterfront of the Upper Pool was ablaze, causing enormous damage. The ruins smouldered for six months. As the blaze was tackled a wall collapsed, killing **James Braidwood**, the respected chief of the London Fire Brigade. A memorial, by S. H.

Thomas Guy in the courtyard of his hospital.

182

The alcove from Old London Bridge in the inner courtyard of Guy's Hospital.

Gardner, was erected to Braidwood in 1862 on the wall of 33 Tooley Street, at the corner of Hay's Lane. A marble slab depicts burning buildings, with firemen's helmets and fire-fighting tools. An inscription within the wreath tells the manner of Braidwood's death. His mutilated body was not recovered until two days later. His funeral was the largest civilian funeral seen in Victorian England. In his honour firemen were nicknamed 'Jimmy Braiders'. The memorial has been removed temporarily and will be replaced when redevelopment is completed. The new site is not yet decided.

The Danes attacked London in 1014. King Ethelred of the English, with his ally, **King Olaf** of Norway, demolished London Bridge (at the time the only one over the Thames) by ingeniously tying ropes to the piles and using boats and rowers to pull them from the river bed. The Danish forces were thus divided and London was saved. The battle of London Bridge was the basis for the future

'King Alfred' in Trinity Church Square. The church is used as a recording studio.

nursery rhyme 'London Bridge is falling down'. Olaf, who was canonised and became Norway's patron saint, has (as St Olave) left his mark on London in Tooley Street (a corruption of St Olave's Street) and in the names of churches and schools. St Olave's Church, in its 1740 form, was demolished in 1928 when the Hay's Wharf headquarters was built. St Olaf House, now part of London Bridge City, took its place in 'Art Deco splendour'. The architect was Goodhart-Rendel. It has gilded faience relief panels by Frank Dobson on the Thames frontage, and on the angle of the Tooley Street elevation is a black and gold mosaic figure of St Olaf by Colin Gill.

The **Dray Horse**, a life-sized bronze horse by Shirley Pace on a plinth in the centre of the Circle residential development in Queen Elizabeth Street, north of Tooley Street, commemorates the **Courage Brewery Dray Horse Stables**, which stood here. The statue was flown over London by helicopter before being placed in position in October 1987.

In Borough High Street, the **Southwark War Memorial** commemorates the 'men of St Saviour's, Southwark, who gave their lives for the Empire 1914–18' (St Saviour's is Southwark Cathedral). A bronze figure of a soldier with tin hat and rifle marches through mud, with figures of a knight in armour and a weeping woman and child. One bronze panel depicts battleships and the other biplanes in aerial combat. It is the work of P. Lindsey Clark (1924). Nearby is a large wall-mounted bronze memorial with sprays of hops to the **hopmen of London** killed in the First World War. Southwark and the Borough have long been noted for hop factors and breweries. Some survive today.

Below left: *The memorial to 'The Men of St Saviour's' in Borough High Street. St Saviour's is better known now as Southwark Cathedral.*

Below right: *Colonel Samuel Bourne Bevington was Bermondsey's first mayor.*

Born in Winsford, Somerset, Ernest Bevin created Britain's largest trade union and controlled the nation's labour force throughout five years of total war.

On the side of Southwark Town Hall is a stone and brick memorial and garden dedicated to the 925 **people of Southwark** who died in the Second World War. Over sixty members of the civil defence organisation, along with residents of Camberwell and Bermondsey, are also commemorated.

The **royal arms from the Great Stone Gate** at the foot of the bridge on the Southwark side, painted in heraldic colours, also survive as the inn sign of the King's Arms in Newcomen Street, which runs east of Borough High Street.

Borough High Street leads via Trinity Street to Trinity Church Square, with a statue believed to be of **King Alfred** (849–99), brought from the old Palace of Westminster in 1822. It probably dates from about 1395. Trinity Church was built in 1823 on land given by Trinity House Corporation and is now much used as a recording studio.

East of Elephant and Castle, the New Kent Road has, opposite Rodney Road, a memorial garden to Dickens's **David Copperfield**, with a stone cherub blowing into a conch shell. Dickens wrote: 'I came to a stop in the Kent Road at a terrace with a piece of water before it and a great foolish image in the middle blowing on a dry shell'. The water has gone and the shell is missing. The memorial was erected in 1931 by the Dickens Fellowship.

By the south end of Tower Bridge is a statue of **Colonel Samuel Bourne Bevington** (1832–1907), whose leather factory was an important source of employment in Bermondsey. A popular man in the borough, in 1900 he became Bermondsey's first mayor. A local leader in social reform and education, he was also a colonel in the Volunteers. His bronze statue by Sydney Marsh (1910) shows him in mayoral robes.

Next to Bevington is a bust of **Ernest Bevin** (1881–1951), a man of humble beginnings and self-educated, who became one of the most admired Foreign Secretaries of the twentieth century. He created the Transport & General Workers' Union, was chairman of the Trades' Union Congress and Minister of Labour in the War Cabinet. His bronze bust by E. Whitney Smith was put up in 1955. Bevin is remembered as a champion of the dockers: the memorial is inscribed 'The Dockers' KC'. Bevin, who did not allow his left-wing views to cloud his common sense, was noted for pithy sayings. Of the Council of Europe he said: 'If you open that Pandora's Box, you never know what Trojan horses will jump out,' and when told that another Labourite was his own worst enemy, Bevin is said to have replied briskly, 'Not while I'm alive, he ain't!'

On the Thames Path upstream from Cherry Garden Pier, Bermondsey (where ships signal their wish to have Tower Bridge raised to allow them to pass), is the bronze sculpture **Dr Salter's Daydream** by Diane Gorvin (1922). It depicts the seated figure on a bench of Dr Alfred Salter, a Quaker, local doctor and MP for Bermondsey. His young daughter Joyce leans against the river wall. Both worked to alleviate poverty and disease in the area. Joyce's cat sits on the wall. The memorial is approached from Cherry Garden Road, a turning off Jamaica Road. A panel describes Dr Salter's work. The surrounding area, a show-piece

Dr Salter fought poverty and disease in Bermondsey, for which he was MP. His statue is on Cherry Garden Pier with that of his daughter Joyce.

development by Culpin and Bowers, is now the Dr Alfred Salter Conservation Area. Centred on Wilson Grove, the garden-city cottages are white-rendered with tiled roofs and have gardens planted with birch trees.

It was on Cherry Garden Pier that Turner sat in 1838 to paint *The Fighting Téméraire*, showing her being tugged to her last berth. This famous ship, on her way to be broken up at John Beatson's yard at Rotherhithe, had fought as second in the weather line astern of HMS *Victory* at Trafalgar.

Near the river, on the eighteenth-century Amicable School House by the churchyard entrance of St Mary-at-Rotherhithe, are figures of two **charity children** in blue uniforms, he with orange stockings, she with a white apron. Both hold Bibles. The inscription between the corbels reads: 'Free School 1742, removed here 1797, supported by voluntary contributions'.

22.
GREENWICH AND WOOLWICH

Major General James Wolfe (1727–59) lived at Macartney House, Greenwich. His statue, with tricorne hat and military cloak, by Dr Tait Mackenzie (1930), the gift of the Canadian people, stands on a terrace adjoining the former Observatory. It was unveiled by the Marquis de Montcalm, a descendant of Wolfe's opponent at the battle of the Plains of Abraham in 1759. Wolfe captured the fortress of Quebec after his troops had scaled the cliffs using a secret path. Britain's control of Canada was secured. Like Nelson, Wolfe was mortally wounded in the hour of victory: a soldier to the end, his last words were 'What, do they run already? Then I die happy.' Wolfe's body lay in state at Greenwich. He is buried in St Alfege's Church. James Wolfe, strict but humane, combining verve with prudence, was a commander of genius. When a courtier suggested to George II, an admirer, that Wolfe was mad, the King retorted, 'Mad is he? Then I wish he would bite some of my other generals!'

The granite statue of **William IV** (1765–1837), the 'Sailor King', in King William Walk, at the foot of Greenwich Park, came from King William Street in the City. By Samuel Nixon, it shows the King in the uniform of Lord High Admiral, with the Garter. William IV entered the Navy in 1779 and saw service in America and the West Indies. His unassuming private life was much admired (a tactful veil was drawn over the twenty years when he had lived with Mrs Jordan, the actress, who bore him ten children). In agreeable contrast to George

James Wolfe, victor of Quebec, and William IV, the 'Sailor King', at Greenwich.

Busts of famous sailors on the former Royal Naval College buildings, Greenwich.

IV, he hated pomp and ceremony. In a period of popular democracy he was the only European monarch to survive. While other countries in Europe were in turmoil, Britain went steadily forward, passing the Reform Bill in 1832, abolishing slavery in the colonies in 1833, reforming the Poor Laws in 1834 and enacting municipal legislation in 1835, led by a man who, in his youth, had been best man to Captain Horatio Nelson when he married Frances Nisbet on the Caribbean island of Nevis in 1787.

On the riverside east of the *Cutty Sark* is an obelisk commemorating those officers and men of the Royal Navy and Royal Marines killed in action during the **New Zealand Maori Wars** of 1863–4. The monument was erected by the survivors of the campaign. The inscription on the obelisk, which stands on a plinth with a rope twist and chain decoration, lists the names and ships of the casualties.

Facing this, on the colonnaded wall, at the west end of the Royal Naval College buildings (now the tourist information centre) are busts of **Britain's greatest naval commanders**, from Drake to St Vincent.

In January 2002 **Sir Walter Raleigh** (1992–1618) made the journey from Whitehall, where he was first placed in 1959, to his new home outside the Greenwich Visitor Centre. The figure is by William Macmillan RA. The Elizabethan courtier, poet and explorer was beheaded in 1618. Raleigh showed admirable *sang-froid* on the scaffold, for he poised the execution axe on his thumb to test its sharpness, remarking: 'This is a sharp medicine but it will cure all diseases.'

Further east, on the riverside walk, near Greenwich Pier, a 35 foot red granite obelisk is

Lieutenant Bellot joined the hunt for Franklin. His memorial is on the riverside walk at Greenwich.

Between the Royal Naval College and the river is a statue of George II, its face eroded by the weather.

inscribed 'Bellot'. **Joseph Réné Bellot** (1826–53), a lieutenant in the French navy, volunteered to join as second-in-command Captain William Kennedy's expedition in the *Prince Albert* to find Franklin, missing while searching for the North West Passage. No trace was found but Bellot discovered the narrow strait between Somerset Island and Boothis Peninsula which was named after him. In June 1853 he joined a further expedition of search under Captain Inglefield. Carrying dispatches to Admiral Sir Edward Belcher, whose ships were trapped in the ice, Bellot and two sailors were carried away on an ice floe in a gale and never seen again. Bellot was a much-respected officer. His memorial is by Philip Hardwick (1855).

A block of marble captured from a French ship ended up as a statue of **George II** (1683–1760) by John Michael Rysbrack (1735), which stands in the quadrangle between the former Royal Naval College and the river. The King is in Roman dress. Notable events of his reign were the 1745 Rebellion, the capture of Quebec in 1759, the French defeat in India, the rise of Methodism and the golden age of letters, of Stern, Smollett, Goldsmith and Johnson. George II achieved personal distinction by being the last British monarch to lead his troops into battle, at Dettingen in 1743. Unfortunately the King's face has been completely eroded by the weather.

At the far east end of the college buildings (in the north-east corner of the grounds) is a memorial to the **Royal Naval Division**. In 2000 plans were announced to move it back to Horse Guards, where it was first set up and dedicated in 1925. When the Citadel was built at the start of the Second World War the memorial was sent to Greenwich and re-erected and re-dedicated there in 1951. It is formed by an obelisk standing in a fountain bowl, on a plinth, and is the work of Sir Edwin Lutyens. On the south side are the words of Rupert Brooke (of Hood Battalion): 'Blow out your bugles over the rich dead'.

Across Romney Road, at the east end of the National Maritime Museum, inside the entrance to the east wing, is a marble statue of **Admiral Sir Edward Pellew, Viscount Exmouth** (1757–1833), by Patrick Macdowell (1846). Pellew's most memorable exploit was the destruction by night and in heavy seas of the French *Droits de l'Homme*. He was 'the *beau ideal* of the frigate captain, and, as an admiral, officers were proud to serve under his command'.

Also inside the east entrance is the marble statue by William Theed (1860) of

Captain Sir William Peel VC (1824–58), third son of Sir Robert. Captain Peel was in command of the naval brigade at Sebastopol, where he threw a live shell, its fuse burning, over the parapet of his battery. During the Indian Mutiny he formed the naval brigade, which pulled 8 inch guns to Lucknow, where he was fatally wounded on 9th March 1858. Weakened, he died from smallpox at Cawnpore on 28th April, aged thirty-three. Colonel Malleson wrote of him 'He was really great'.

Round the building, along the colonnade through the Queen's House, is a statue of **Captain James Cook** (1728–79) facing Royal Observatory Hill. Sculpted by Anthony Stones, it was presented in 1994 by Arthur Weller CBE.

Under the colonnade, flanking the new entrance to the museum, west of the Queen's House, is a statue by Sir John Steell of **Admiral Lord James de Saumarez** (1757–1836), a Guernseyman, who was second-in-command to Nelson at the battle of the Nile (1798) and enjoyed a long and distinguished career in the Royal Navy. He was raised to the peerage in 1831: 'A man of admirable qualities and admirable judgement'. Among his battles was one off Guernsey in 1794 in the *Crescent*. He asked his pilot, Jean Breton, if he was sure of his seamarks as they passed through a needle's eye in the reefs of Vazon

By the Queen's House is the statue of Captain James Cook.

Admirals de Saumarez and Sidney Smith flank the entrance to the National Maritime Museum.

Bay. Breton, a sturdy island democrat, replied, 'Quite sure, Sir, for there is my house and your house in line,' pointing to Saumarez Park and Breton's cottage – words which passed into Guernsey folklore.

Here, too, is the statue of **Admiral Sir Sidney Smith** (1764–1840), who entered the Navy in 1777, did well at the battles of Cape St Vincent and the Saints and became a captain at the age of eighteen. He spent time in the Baltic as advisor to Gustavus III and was knighted by the Swedes. Fellow officers afterwards referred to him sarcastically as 'the Swedish knight'. After Channel

The Titanic Memorial Garden and the Dolphin Sundial.

operations he was captured and imprisoned by the French, but escaped two years later. A born negotiator, plotter and secret agent as much as he was a naval officer, he next went to the Mediterranean and aided the Turks during the siege of Acre. Napoleon was forced to raise the siege and return to Egypt. He was next sent to South America, having escorted the Portuguese royal family to Brazil when Napoleon attacked Spain and Portugal, but behaved so arrogantly that he was recalled. He later became engaged in various causes including the 'Anti-Piratical Society' to free white slaves from the Barbary states. When posted to Turkey he equipped himself with a beautifully bound passport mentioning his Swedish knighthood and describing himself as *Ministre Plénipotentiaire de sa Majésté Britannique*, giving rise to another soubriquet, 'The Great Plénip'. Nelson commented dryly, 'We are not forced to understand French,' and Lord St Vincent complained, 'The ascendancy this gentleman has over all His Majesty's Ministers is to be astonishing'. With his short dark curls and 'enormous moustachios' he was far from a typical naval officer. His taste for secret letters and covert negotiations, and distaste for protocol, made him a trial to his superiors. His final decades were spent in France, where he felt his personality was better appreciated. He was probably right.

Further west along the south side of the museum, next to the children's playground, is the **Titanic Memorial Garden**, a border of herbs of remembrance. The *Titanic*, judged 'unsinkable', struck an iceberg on her maiden voyage to America in 1912. The garden was opened on April 1995 by the oldest living survivor, Mrs Edith Haisman, who was fifteen when she and her mother were saved. Her father drowned. Of the 705 survivors only four were still alive in 2001. The last male survivor, Michael Narratil, died in France on 30th January 2001, aged ninety-two.

By the Titanic Garden is the **Dolphin Sundial**, designed by Christopher St J. Daniel in 1978 to commemorate the Silver Jubilee of Queen Elizabeth II in 1977. The gap between the shadows of the tails of the two dolphins indicates the time.

In 1929 Devonport House nurses' home, Nelson Road, to the east of the old Royal Naval College buildings and attached to the Dreadnought Seamen's Hospital, was built on the old burial ground of the Greenwich Royal Hospital for seamen wounded in battle and unfit for further service. The Royal Hospital had closed in 1869 when most pensioners preferred to live out, rather than in the institution. The buildings became the Royal Naval College and the infirmary the Dreadnought Seamen's Hospital. This, in its turn, closed in 1986. Next to the nurses' home (under conversion in 2002) is a tall Portland stone monument erected by the Lords Commissioners of the Admiralty (1892) commemorating officers and men of the Royal Navy and Royal Marines, **former inmates of the Royal Hospital**. Some 20,000 men were interred here between 1749 and 1869. The monument has a figure of Britannia on the top and an anchor and flag at the base. The names listed include those of Captain

Visible from Nelson Road is the memorial to Admiral Thompson, one of Nelson's 'Band of Brothers'.

The Crimean and Dickson memorials on the Woolwich parade ground.

Francis Dansays of the Royal Navy, Lieutenant-Governor of the hospital, who died in 1757, and Vice-Admiral Sir Thomas Masterman Hardy, Governor of the hospital, who died in 1839. He is perhaps better known as 'Nelson's Hardy'. In a small, enclosed graveyard behind the monument is a three-bay building recording that the **first pensioner** was buried here in 1749.

Here too, and just visible from the road, is a rectangular stone monument to **Thomas Allen** (1838), Nelson's sailor servant, a boy from the Admiral's home village of Burnham Thorpe, Norfolk, and described as 'black-haired, stunted, uncouth, illiterate and always right'. He was devoted to Nelson and they remained together for seven years. In 1802 he left the Navy and retired to Norfolk to raise a family. He died at Greenwich.

Also on this lawn a broken column commemorates **Vice-Admiral Sir Thomas Boulden Thompson** (1766–1828). Thompson was with Nelson at the attack on Santa Cruz, Tenerife, in 1797 and was wounded, after gaining Nelson's praise in the Admiral's favourite phrase 'An active young man!' Commanding *Leander*, Thompson was in action against *Généreux*. Both Captains Berry and Thompson were seriously wounded. After a hard-fought battle *Leander* was captured. When the French eventually released him, Thompson was court-martialled for the loss of his ship, but was acquitted, commended and knighted. He fought at Copenhagen in command of *Bellona* but unluckily the ship went aground and, helpless, was raked by intense fire from the Danish shore batteries. Thompson lost a leg and wrote despairingly, 'I am now totally disabled and my career is run through, only at the age of 35'. In 1806 he was created a baronet and appointed Treasurer of Greenwich Royal Hospital. From 1807 to 1818 he was MP for Rochester.

In 1875, when the railway tunnelled under Greenwich Park and the old burial ground (despite the objections of the Astronomer-Royal), it became necessary to move three thousand bodies to the East Greenwich Pleasaunce, a garden in Chevening Road, which had opened in 1857 as the **burial ground of Greenwich Hospital**. A wall plaque records the names of those who lie there: 'They served their country in the wars which established the Naval Supremacy of England, and died the honoured recipients of her gratitude'. Many original stones remain, including those of Midshipman Parker, who served in the *Belle Isle* at Trafalgar, Captain Mark Halpen Sweny, who served in the *Colossus*, also

Gleichen's moving memorial to the artillery dead of the South African and Afghan wars.

at Trafalgar, and who died in 1865, and James Sherard, a Crimean veteran, who for eighteen years was boatswain's mate on the royal yacht *Victoria and Albert*.

Woolwich is as famous for its military associations as Greenwich is for its maritime ones. A number of its monuments speak of past campaigns and glories. Although within the boundary of the barracks, to which access is usually restricted, most monuments may be seen by following an anti-clockwise route round the barracks itself, along Artillery Place, Repository Road, Ha-ha Road and Great Depot Road. At the junction of Artillery Place with Repository Road, right of the camp gates, is a large boulder from Lüneburg Heath commemorating the affiliation within the NATO alliance of **British and German artillery regiments** in 1969. (It was on Lüneburg Heath that Field Marshal Montgomery accepted the surrender of all German forces in north-west Germany, Holland and Denmark on 4th May 1945.)

From Repository Road the parade ground can be seen, and two monuments. To the east is the **Crimean Memorial** by John Bell (1860). On a tall granite pillar a bronze figure cast from cannon captured at Sebastopol extends a laurel wreath. The monument commemorates members of the Royal Regiment of Artillery who died in 1854–6.

To the west, opposite the Officers' Mess, is the memorial to **Major General Sir Alexander Dickson** (1777–1849) and **General Sir Collingwood Dickson** (1817–1904). Alexander Dickson was Wellington's Commander of Royal Artillery during the Peninsular War. A bronze medallion of him by Sir Frances Chantrey appears on the memorial. In 1920 a further inscription was added to the memory of his third son, Collingwood, who won the Victoria Cross at Sebastopol and became Inspector General of Artillery and Master Gunner, St James's Park, a position held by the most distinguished gunner.

Just off Artillery Place, behind the barracks (1776–1802), with its striking 1080 yard frontage and central triumphal arch, is a memorial to members of the

194

Destroyed by a V1 in the Second World War, the ruins of Old St George's Garrison Church are preserved as a memorial.

Royal Army Ordnance Corps who died in the South African War. On a granite pedestal which serves as a fountain is a bronze figure in the uniform of the RAOC. The memorial, designed by C. M. Jordan, was unveiled in 1905.

Near the end of Repository Road is an impressive granite cairn, 18 feet high, commemorating those who lost their lives in the **South African and Afghanistan Wars**, 1877–81. It bears bronze trophies of Zulu shields, assegais and Afghan arms. It was designed by Count Gleichen in 1882.

Ha-Ha Road is well named for the remarkable dead straight ha-ha on the barracks side, a tribute to military engineering skills. At the junction of Ha-Ha Road with Woolwich Common a granite obelisk with biblical quotations and the remains of a drinking-fountain commemorates **Robert John Little** (died 1861), Staff Captain of the Royal Marines Artillery. Little took part in the Ferrol blockade in 1803 and in the attack on the fortress of Pointe du Ché, near La Rochelle. At 2.30 a.m. on 28th September 1810 a party of 130 marines including Lieutenant Little and a division of seamen stormed the battery. Little pressed forward with the bayonet and the party carried the battery and spiked the guns. But as Little entered the fort he wrested the musket from the French sentry's hands and in the struggle it went off, so seriously wounding Little's right hand that amputation was necessary. He received an award from Lloyd's Patriotic Fund, a pension for wounds of £70 a year, and an appointment to the Royal Marines Woolwich Division (barracked at Woolwich 1805–69). Lloyd's Patriotic Fund was founded in 1803 by the Chairman, John Julius Angerstein, and was generously supported by the underwriters and merchants of Lloyd's Coffee House, conscious of their debt to the Royal Navy for protecting their shipping and mercantile interests during the long war of 1793–1815. The fund gave payments and gratuities to those killed and wounded and their dependants, and swords and items of silver for special bravery. Honorary letters were presented with awards, at first in beautiful calligraphy by the boys of Christ's

Tom Cribb's grave, in the churchyard of St Mary Magdalene, Woolwich.

Hospital but later, as numbers were so great after Trafalgar, an engraved letter was substituted. In 1863 Little's legacy established Major Robert John Little's Charity to aid the families of deserving non-commissioned officers and men killed on active service with the Royal Marines.

Down Great Depot Road is a similar, but red, granite obelisk commemorating members of the **61st Battery, Royal Field Artillery**, killed in the South African War.

Further north on this road are the remains of the Old St George's Garrison Church (1865), destroyed by a flying bomb on 13th July 1944. It is preserved as a memorial garden and contains the ruined west porch and the memorial (1920) to **holders of the Victoria Cross** in the Royal Regiment of Artillery. The memorial once stood over the altar and survived the bomb.

On the Royal Arsenal site nearby, at the old Royal Military Academy building, is a statue (1904) of **Queen Victoria** (1819–1901), in state robes, with crown, sceptre and orb. It stands on a granite pedestal with panels showing incidents in the history of the Academy and the Royal Engineers that occurred in her reign.

The churchyard of St Mary Magdalene, Woolwich, now a public garden, has a memorial to **Tom Cribb** (1781–1848), England's finest bare-knuckle boxer. Cribb came to London at the age of thirteen, worked as a bellhanger, wharf porter and sailor, started fighting and winning in 1805 and defeated all the finest fighters of his day – Maddox, Belcher, Horton, Gregson and Molineaux. His only defeat, in 1805, was at the hands of George Nicholls. In 1821 he received the title 'Champion for Life' and was made a bodyguard at the coronation of George IV. With his winnings he bought a pub in London but it was unsuccessful and he returned to live with his son, a Woolwich baker. In 1851 this handsome monument to him was set up, a life-sized lion, paw raised, set upon a tall plinth, amid lawns and trees.

In Danson Park, Bexleyheath, is a memorial to **all who died fighting the Japanese** in the Second World War and to those who died in prisoner-of-war camps. When it was unveiled on 21st November 1985 the memorial was covered with a Union Flag that had been hidden in a prison camp and signed there by 124 prisoners. The memorial is in the form of twenty oak trees, with an explanatory bronze plaque.

The South African War Memorial in Great Depot Road.

23.
South London

Cannizaro Park on Wimbledon Common is entered by the main gates off West Side Common. In a dell behind the aviary close to the main house (now an hotel) is a large grey stone bust of **Haile Selassie** (1891–1975), Emperor of Ethiopia, 'Lion of Judah', who visited Wimbledon in 1935 when in exile. His hostess, Hilda Seligman, made this bust. On her death in 1955 it was given to Wimbledon Borough Council in memory of his visit. Mussolini invaded Ethiopia in 1935; the Ethiopians resisted bravely but were finally defeated and the Emperor left for exile in Europe. In 1941 the Allies drove the Italians out and restored Haile Selassie to his throne. It is pleasant to note that when the wartime secretary of the Royal Air Force Benevolent Association unwrapped a heavy brown paper parcel which had come through the post he found a 100 ounce bar of gold from the Emperor with a note thanking the RAF for their help 'in the great fight'. When liberation was complete the Emperor sent a spirited telegram to Winston Churchill: 'We have finished the job. What shall we do with the tools?'

Britain has always been short of tennis heroes but **Fred Perry** (1909–95), whose bronze statue stands at the All England Tennis Club, Wimbledon, undoubtedly was one. It shows Perry executing a majestic forehand stroke and was unveiled by the Duke of Kent on 20th May 1984, the fiftieth anniversary of the first of Perry's three consecutive wins in the All England Men's Championship, in 1934, 1935 and 1936. The statue by David Wynne (1984) stands at the entrance to the Members' Enclosure.

Of all Britain's many immigrants few have brought more valuable skills than the **Huguenots**, Protestant refugees from persecution in Catholic France. Market gardening, cloth working, silk weaving and copper work were among their gifts, and to Wandsworth they brought specifically dyeing, hatmaking (the Roman cardinals ordered their hats from Wandsworth) and calico printing. Their memorial in the Huguenot Burial Ground of Mount Nod, at the top of East Hill, bears the lilies of France and the standard of England, and the inscription: 'Here rest many Huguenots who on the Revocation of the Edict of Nantes in 1685 left their native land for conscience' sake and found in Wandsworth freedom to worship God after their own manner. They established important industries and added to the credit and prosperity of the town of their adoption.' The names of thirty notable Huguenot families of the

While Emperor Haile Selassie was in exile in Wimbledon his hostess, a sculptress, made this bust of him.

The drinking-fountain on Clapham Common shows a woman offering water to an elderly man.

district are appended.

The **Clapham Sect** (or 'Clapham Saints'), wealthy, influential adherents of Anglican evangelism, active from about 1785 to 1830 especially in the humanitarian field, were given their name by Sydney Smith as a mild joke because several of them lived in the then village of Clapham. They promoted missionary societies and the education of the poor and, in particular, opposed slavery. On the south-west corner of Holy Trinity Church, Clapham Common, is a memorial to the group, unveiled in 1919, inscribed: 'They rested not until the curse of slavery was swept away from all parts of the British Dominions'. Their names are listed: Charles Grant, Zachary Macaulay, Grenville Sharp, John Shore, James Stephens, Henry and John Thornton, Henry and John Venn, and William Wilberforce.

On Clapham Common close to the church is a drinking-fountain, the gift of the **United Kingdom Temperance and General Provident Institute** (1884). The fountain is in good condition but in 2002 water was not flowing.

L. Roselieb's 1911 statue of **Edward VII** (1841–1910) in Tooting Broadway outside the Underground station, robed and bareheaded, is one of the most successful of this monarch in London. The plinth carries bronze panels of Peace and Charity. Edward, handicapped as Prince of Wales by his mother's refusal to

Edward VII's statue is colourfully backed by Tooting Broadway Underground station.

One of three typical passengers at Brixton Station.

allow him any role in state affairs, on succeeding to the throne (at the age of fifty-nine and a grandfather) proved an effective King. An intelligent man, he had long been forced to seek occupation in trivia but he quickly showed that he could deal adroitly with state business, particularly foreign affairs. He travelled widely and earned the name 'Peacemaker'. The *entente cordiale* with France was a major achievement. The public admired his interest in racing (he was the first reigning monarch to win the Derby) and yachting, and the colourful rumours about his amours and his love of good food (his soubriquet was 'Prince Tum-Tum') only added to his popularity. He married Princess Alexandra of Denmark, who bore him six children, one of whom succeeded him as George V.

At Brixton Station in 1986 British Rail, with rare imagination, set up statues of **three typical passengers**. The subjects, Peter Lloyd, Joy Battick and Karen Heistermann, volunteered. The statues are by Kevin Atherton and are to be found on the platform.

Sir Henry Tate (1819–99) made a fortune in sugar refining, particularly through the invention of the sugar lump. As well as Tate Britain on Millbank (formerly the Tate Gallery), Sir Henry funded the public library before which his bronze bust by Sir Thomas Brock (1905) stands at the bottom of Brixton Hill, along the High Street from the station. He was 'an upright merchant, wise philanthropist,' as the inscription explains.

Behind Tate's bust is a memorial to the **Sharpeville shootings** on 21st March 1960, when South African police fired to break up a demonstration against the 'pass laws'. Sixty-seven Africans were killed and two hundred wounded. Widespread condemnation of the shootings led to South Africa

Sir Henry Tate, inventor of the sugar lump.

199

leaving the Commonwealth and founding a republic. The memorial was dedicated in 1987 by the Reverend Trevor Huddleston.

East of Brixton at Denmark Hill statues of **William Booth** (1829–1912) and his wife **Catherine** (1829–90) stand outside the William Booth Memorial Officers' Training College at Champion Park, by Denmark Hill railway station. By G. E. Wade, they show the Booths in uniform as if preaching. Their evangelical work in the East End began in 1861 among the poor and outcast. At first there was ridicule and persecution but with the introduction of the name 'Salvation Army' in 1878, and brass bands and military-style uniforms, the movement prospered. Booth believed that brutal living conditions and poverty led to sin, and the Army's spiritual work was accompanied by soup kitchens, cheap food shops, hostels, housing, legal aid and model factories. Booth's views were expressed in his book *In Darkest England and the Way Out* (1890). Booth worked until he was eighty-three, travelling and preaching, carrying the gospel to those otherwise untouched by religion. He found friends in high places and among crowned heads. His work was continued by his eldest son Bramwell and his daughter, Evangeline. The Salvation Army enjoys the affectionate nickname 'Sally Ann'.

By the roadside railings of King's College Hospital, also near the railway station but in Denmark Hill, is a statue (1862) by Matthew Noble of **Dr Robert Bentley Todd**, an Irish physician and founder of the hospital in 1839, when it was situated off the Strand. When the hospital moved here the statue came too.

Nunhead Cemetery in Linden Grove has a fine hillside site but recent vandalism has damaged many monuments, although restoration is taking place. Of interest is the **Martyrs' Memorial** (1851), a tall granite obelisk to six Scottish nationalists sentenced to transportation to Australia after campaigning for Parliamentary reform. Another memorial stands on Calton Hill, Edinburgh. Both were erected with funds raised by Joseph Hume MP. The inscription, an extract from the speech in his own defence by Joseph Gerrald, one of the martyrs, reads: 'The experience of all ages should have taught our rulers that persecution can never efface principles'.

At New Cross Gate, Pepys Road runs south to Haberdashers' Aske's School, in front of which stands a Coadestone statue of **Robert Aske** by William Croggan (1825). Apprenticed to a haberdasher and East India merchant dealing in silks, Aske became an alderman of the City of London in 1666 and in 1685 was Master of his livery. His legacy established almshouses for poor freemen of the Haberdashers' Company and a school for twenty boys. He is shown in livery robes with a scroll bearing the school's motto 'Serve and obey'. Another scroll shows the plans of the original almshouses and school.

Loyal residents of Lewisham set up a clock tower at the junction of Lewisham High Street and Lee High Road to mark **Queen Victoria's Diamond Jubilee** in 1897.

On the fringe of London between Bromley and Chislehurst, near the north end of the open space of Petts Wood, is a granite memorial set up in 1927 to **William Willett** (1857–1915), a local resident and originator of 'daylight saving', the expedient of moving clocks forward in spring and back in autumn to gain extra daylight for the working day. During the First World War, when it was necessary to save fuel and light, the scheme came into force on 21st May 1916.

During the enemy attacks of 1944 many flying bombs, or V1s, were destroyed before they reached London. Those that did get through caused appalling damage and loss of life. On 18th July 1944 one fell on the **London Transport Elmers End bus garage**, south of Crystal Palace, killing ten of the staff. Their names are listed on the memorial on the garage that replaced the one destroyed by the bomb.

In the grounds of the Crystal Palace at Sydenham is the memorial to the **Royal Naval Volunteer Reserve,** who, when the Palace was designated HMS *Victory*, trained here during the First World War. Many of the 125,000 men who passed through the establishment were to join the Royal Naval Division. Their memorial, often called the 'RNVR Trophy', is in the form of a bell supported by bronze dolphins, mounted on a teak base. It was unveiled by the Prince of Wales on 6th June 1931.

Until it burned down in 1936 the Crystal Palace was a landmark visible from every part of London. It was the masterpiece of **Sir Joseph Paxton**

Dr Todd, founder of King's College Hospital, moved with it to Denmark Hill.

A gigantic Joseph Paxton overlooks the site of the Crystal Palace.

(1801–65), head gardener to the Duke of Devonshire at Chatsworth and architect, noted for his huge conservatories. In 1850, when 233 other plans for the Great Exhibition had been rejected, Paxton prepared blueprints in a mere nine days, submitted them and was successful. The building was erected in Hyde Park in 1851 to acclaim and Paxton was knighted. In 1853 he superintended the daunting task of moving the building to Sydenham. Paxton was a man of surpassing energy; all this time he was still superintending the Chatsworth gardens and also became Liberal MP for Coventry, a seat he held until his death. He is remembered on the Crystal Palace site by a huge bust, five times life-size, on a red brick plinth, the design of W. F. Woodington (1869). The magnificence of the Palace is well remembered. The £5 coin minted to commemorate the centenary of Queen Victoria's death in 1901 includes in its design the Queen's head within a 'V', surrounded by an image of the south transept of the building.

Something of the scale of Paxton's masterpiece flowed into its grounds. Constructions by Waterhouse Hawkins, supervised by Professor Richard Owen, of **prehistoric monsters**, made of brick and iron and covered with stucco, were scattered in the grounds. In 1853 a high-spirited dinner party for twenty was held in the partly completed iguanodon, with Professor Owen in the chair – in the skull. Twenty-nine of the monsters survive on the islands in the lake. Queen Victoria had opened the 'Dinosaur Park'.

Like Hendon, Croydon was long linked with aviation and never more so than during the **Battle of Britain** of 1940, when Fighter Command squadrons numbers 72, 85, 92, 111, 145, 501 and 607 were stationed there. These squadrons, and the WAAFs, Royal Observer Corps, medical staff and police, who all also served, are commemorated by a 23 foot obelisk topped with a bronze eagle. It stands by Purley Way and was unveiled by Air Marshal Sir William Wratten on 27th October 1991. At night the memorial is floodlit.

Another memorial to the cost in young lives of the Battle of Britain stands by the entrance to Morden Technical College. **Sergeant Peter Kenneth Walley** of 615 Squadron crashed on Morden Park Golf Course on 18th August 1940 after being caught by Messerschmitts during an attack on Kenley aerodrome. He died at the age of twenty in the burning wreckage of his Spitfire. When the college was built local people set a memorial into the wall. The inscription recalls 'with pride' that 'knowing he was about to crash, Sergeant Walley bravely managed to guide his badly damaged aircraft over nearby houses, thereby safeguarding the lives of the residents'.

One of the monsters in the grounds of the Crystal Palace.

24.
WESTWARDS FROM PUTNEY

The start of the University Boat Race between Oxford and Cambridge is marked by the **Universities' Stone** near the Star and Garter pub just west of Putney Bridge. The race has been rowed annually on a $4^1/_2$ mile stretch of the Thames between Putney and Mortlake since 1845, usually just before Easter. Crowds line the towpaths to see Oxford (Dark Blues) and Cambridge (Light Blues) compete in this prime event in the rowing calendar. A memorial at the Mile Post on the Putney–Mortlake footpath commemorates **Steve Fairbairn** (1862–1938), an Australian who rowed for Jesus College and Cambridge University. He is remembered for his innovative coaching in the 'Fairbairn style' and his work to increase understanding of rowing. An 11 foot obelisk erected in 1963, placed where he customarily stood to watch the rowing, was unveiled by Viscount Bruce of Melbourne. It includes a bronze medallion of Fairbairn by G. C. Drinkwater.

Further west, at Barnes, is a memorial to Sir Thomas More's friend **John Colet** (?1467–1519), the reforming Dean of St Paul's, principal Christian humanist of his day and founder of St Paul's School. The statue by William Hamo Thornycroft (1902) shows a robed Colet with two kneeling scholars with books. Colet, a lifelong friend of Erasmus and son of a Lord Mayor of London, was the only survivor of twenty-two children and thus inherited a fortune, which he used to found St Paul's School. It moved from St Paul's churchyard to Hammersmith, and then to Barnes in 1968, taking the statue with it. Field Marshal Montgomery, an Old Pauline, used the school during the D-Day planning. Discipline, austerity and plain speaking marked Colet's character; the two men had something in common.

In the graveyard of St Mary Magdalen, North Worple Way, in Mortlake, stands the mausoleum-cum-memorial to **Sir Richard Burton** (1821–91), explorer, speaker of twenty-eight languages, translator of *The Arabian Nights* and oriental sex manuals (including, said the malicious, pornography), and keeper of Rabelaisian diaries (which an outraged Lady Burton burnt). His instructions by telegram were much quoted by wives of diplomats – 'RECALLED, PAY, PACK AND FOLLOW'. Sir Richard objected to cremation and earth burial. He wanted to 'lie in a tent, alongside my wife'. Lady Burton saw to it that 'He got the thing he wished'. She rented a cottage nearby and oversaw the building in stone and marble, dressed to resemble rippling canvas, of an Arab tent, 12 feet square and 18 feet high. A staunch Catholic, Isabel Burton added an altar and crucifix, and (to the disgust of her agnostic husband's friends) a religious service. Today visitors may peer through a window at Burton's dusty steel coffin, decorated with lions and angels, beside Isabel's plain mahogany, and the remains of Arab lamps and camel bells, ordered by Lady Burton so that Sir Richard might continue 'to hear camel bells in the wind'. The mausoleum is now a listed building.

Inigo Jones (1537–1652) studied Palladian architecture in Italy and brought a new style to England. His work included the Queen's House at Greenwich and the Banqueting House in Whitehall. Beside the outside staircase of the Palladian Chiswick House is his stone statue by J. M. Rysbrack (1729), near one of **Andrea Palladio** (1508–80). There are also busts of **Charles I** and **Charles II**.

To the west of the parish church of St Nicholas, in Chiswick cemetery, is the cenotaph of the Italian patriot **Ugo Foscolo** (1778–1827). He was buried here but after the unification of Italy his remains were re-interred in Santa Croce, Florence. His former tomb is inscribed: 'This spot, where for forty-four years the relics of Ugo Foscolo reposed in honoured custody, will be forever held in grateful remembrance by the Italian nations'.

William Hogarth (1697-1764), 'a sturdy, outspoken, honest, obstinate, pugnacious little man', caricaturist, engraver, painter, depicter of British life, has a bronze statue by Jim Mathiesen at the junction of Chiswick High Road and Annandale Road. It was unveiled in October 2001 by Ian Hislop, editor of *Private Eye* and David Hockney, the artist and patron of the Hogarth Millennium Fund, which raised £50,000 towards the statue. Beside Hogarth is his pug-dog, 'Trump'. Trump's statue was unveiled by Leah James, a pupil at Hogarth Primary School.

Hogarth lived at his Chiswick 'country box by the Thames' (now Hogarth's House Museum, on the busy Great West Road, just west of the Chiswick Flyover) from 1749 until the night before he died at his town house in Leicester Fields (Square), where he is also commemorated. His wife Jane, daughter of Sir James Thornhill, lived on as a widow at Chiswick and in venerable old age was pushed to church in a Bath-chair by a manservant. The mulberry tree in the garden of the house dates from Hogarth's years but Filbert Avenue, where he played ninepins, and a dog's tombstone inscribed 'Pompey' and another to a bullfinch, have gone. Hogarth loathed injustice and identified with ordinary people. His trademark pug-dog expressed this and its homely features would appear among the elegant muzzles of the dogs of Hogarth's sitters. His strong social and moral conscience shows best in the 'Moralities' series – 'The Harlot's Progress' (1732), 'A Rake's Progress' (1735), 'Marriage à la Mode' (1743–5) and 'The Election' (1754). Hogarth's rabidly anti-French feelings were exacerbated by an experience in Calais in 1748. While sketching the royal arms

on the town gate he was arrested as a spy and, amid the jeers of the mob, humiliatingly bundled off to the jetty and home. He retaliated with the drawing 'O, the Roast Beef of Old England etc., or, The Gate at Calais', deftly lampooning Calais's tawdry soldiery, leather-faced fishwives and gluttonous friars. Hogarth is buried in the churchyard of St Nicholas, Chiswick, under a memorial urn on a pedestal, decorated on one side with a smiling mask, a palette and brushes, and a wreath. David Garrick, the actor, wrote the epitaph for his friend:

> Farewell! great Painter of Mankind,
> Who reach'd the noblest point of Art,
> whose pictur'd Morals charm the Mind,
> And through the Eye, correct the Heart.
>
> If genius fire thee, Reader, stay;
> If Nature touch thee, drop a tear;
> if neither move thee, turn away,
> Hogarth's honour'd dust lies here.

Palladio re-introduced the classic style of architecture, which was taken up by Inigo Jones, whose statue is also at Chiswick House.

Hogarth's statue with his dog Trump was erected near his Chiswick home in 2001.

Kew Gardens' bicentenary flagstaff was made from a single Douglas fir from British Columbia. It flies koi carp kites for 'Japan 2000'.

Jane, who died in 1789, aged eighty, is buried beside him.

Upstream from Lot's Ait, in Ferry Lane, Brentford, is the tall granite **Brentford Column**, commemorating events in local history: the brave opposition of British tribesmen under Cassivellaunus to Julius Caesar on his march to *Verulamium* (St Albans) in 54 BC; the eighth-century council of the church held by Offa, King of Mercia; and the battle of Brentford (1642) during the English Civil War. A further inscription notes the discovery in 1909 of the site of the ancient fortified ford, with oak palisades along the bank and in the river-bed.

To celebrate the bicentenary of the Royal Botanic Gardens, Kew, in 1959, and its own centenary, the Province of British Columbia, Canada, gave the gardens a **flagstaff** 225 feet tall, from a single Douglas fir, which weighed 39 tons before shaping. It was craned into place near the Marianne North Gallery by Royal Engineers.

Further west a gaunt 21 foot black Nubian marble obelisk in Gunnersbury cemetery, inscribed 'Katyn 1940' with a Polish eagle, encircled by barbed wire, commemorates 14,500 **Polish army officers and men**, all prisoners of war, massacred by the Russians in 1940. Some 4500 of them were buried in Katyn Forest, near Smolensk. The USSR and Germany had partitioned Poland in 1939; in 1940 Katyn was still in Soviet hands. When Germany invaded the USSR the Russians agreed to return all Polish prisoners of war. This was not done. Only after the Germans overran the Katyn Forest were the mass graves found. The USSR tried to label the Germans the perpetrators of the massacre; only with the end of the Cold War did the Russians admit responsibility. In 1976 a joint committee of Free Poles and Britons (including Winston Churchill MP, Airey Neave MP and Lord George-Brown) succeeded in having the memorial set up. The brevity of the inscription reflects the Labour government's apparent fear of offending the Russians, who it was reported made repeated attempts to have the memorial banned. No British government representative attended the unveiling on 18th September 1976, although the United States of America was represented. Newspapers spoke bitterly of 'appeasement'.

The Twickenham Rugby Football Ground has been the headquarters of the Rugby Football Union since 1910 and is the venue for international matches. On top of the **Rowland Hill Memorial Gate** (commemorating Sir George Rowland Hill, knighted for fifty years of service to rugby) is a gilded **Coadestone lion**, which, like the Westminster Bridge Lion, came from the Lion Brewery on the South Bank. It was presented to the RFU by Sir Desmond Plummer, then Chairman of the Greater London Council, in whose yard it had rested since its removal from the brewery. It was unveiled at Twickenham on 29th April 1972. In 1991 for the World Cup games it was given a coat of gold leaf, at a cost of some £6000, to be a gleaming symbol of the national rugby football team, the British Lions. The Twickenham Lion, like that at Westminster Bridge, owes its preservation to the personal intervention and interest of King George VI.

Now peaceful and grassy, Bushy Park in Teddington was the scene of momentous wartime decisions. General Eisenhower moved his headquarters here to oversee Operation Overlord, the D-Day invasion. A cluster of Nissen huts, tents, an airstrip and three thousand men formed **Supreme Headquarters Allied Expeditionary Force** (SHAEF), which worked in low buildings, poorly heated, with cement floors. Eisenhower's office was in Building C. Every important Allied figure came here: Churchill, his Cabinet, Alanbrooke, Montgomery, Bradley, Patton, Marshall, Alexander, Harris, Portal, Leigh-Mallory and Tedder (Eisenhower's deputy). Generals were so numerous they had their own mess. The fate of Western Europe was decided here. In 1962 local residents were shocked when the camp was demolished and the site grassed over. There was no memorial to SHAEF or to General Eisenhower. In 1994, the fiftieth anniversary of the Normandy landings, action was at last taken. Traces of the floor of Eisenhower's office were found a foot below ground, with parts of his pot-bellied stove. The 20 foot square floor was reinstated, a circular bronze embossed plaque unveiled on 30th May 1994 and a new pedestrian 'SHAEF Gate' installed at the former camp entrance in Sandy Lane.

Between Chestnut Avenue and Sandy Lane, on a five-pointed star stone and brick base, within low railings, is a memorial to the **United States Army Air Force**. The stone marks the site of the European headquarters of the USAAF

The Katyn monument in Gunnersbury cemetery recalls the massacre of Polish prisoners of war in 1940.

from July 1942 to December 1944. The inscription on the memorial, donated by the Royal Air Force, includes a quotation from Victor Hugo: 'It is through fraternity that liberty is saved'. Here, at USAAF's Camp Griffis, the thousand-bomber raids on Germany were organised under General Carl Spaatz.

Teddington may not mean 'Tide-end-town', as claimed, but 265 yards below Teddington Lock on the Surrey Bank a **stone obelisk** marks the official boundary between the tidal and non-tidal Thames and thus between the jurisdiction of the Port of London Authority and Thames Conservancy.

Kingston upon Thames was the coronation place of seven Saxon kings, from Edward the Elder (899–924) to Ethelred the Unready (979–1016). The base of the supposed **Coronation Stone** stands in Guildhall Gardens, with a coin of each reign set into the plinth.

On the south front of the former Market Hall is a gilt-lead statue of **Queen Anne** (1665–1714) by Francis Bird (1706), who also sculpted the original statue of Anne at St Paul's and possibly that in Queen Anne's Gate.

Also in Kingston Market Place is a drinking-fountain commemorating **Henry Shrubsole JP**. Three times elected Mayor of Kingston, 1877–9, he died suddenly in his third year of office, 'while presiding on an occasion of public charity', on 18th January 1880. A stone relief portrait decorates the plinth.

Sir Sydney Camm (1893–1966), the designer of the Hurricane fighter of the Second World War, has a memorial in Camm Gardens, Kingston, its centrepiece part of a Hurricane propeller mounted on a teak base. It was unveiled by his daughter on 3rd May 1984. Camm joined the Hawker Engineering Company at Kingston in 1922 and worked for them with distinction for forty-three years. Not only did he design the Hurricane, the RAF's first monoplane fighter, of which 14,500 were built, but he followed it with the Typhoon, Tempest, Meteor and Hunter, at the end moving to VTL (vertical take-off and landing) aircraft. He was knighted in 1953. (Camm Gardens are approached from Albert Road and Church Road, south of London Road, east of the town centre.)

Memorials in Kingston upon Thames are (clockwise from top left): the Coronation Stone, Queen Anne, Sir Sydney Camm and Henry Shrubsole.

25.
NORTH LONDON

Just off the A40, near Northolt aerodrome, a column with a spread eagle and battle honours is dedicated to **Polish pilots** who died serving with the Royal Air Force in the Second World War. Many took off from Northolt. When the memorial was designed by Mieczyslaw Lubelski in 1948 only five hundred names could be inscribed, but increased funding in 1996 allowed a further eight hundred to be added to a wall behind the memorial, which was recently restored.

At Stanmore, in the grounds of the Royal National Orthopaedic Hospital, Brockley Hill, an obelisk remembering a much earlier conflict was erected in 1750 by William Sharpe, secretary to the second Duke of Chandos, to mark the supposed site of a battle **between the Catuvellauni and the invading forces of Julius Caesar**, although modern historians believe that Caesar was victorious, rather than the Catuvellauni as stated in the inscription. The slender, 25 foot column is west of the main hospital, by the Biomedical Engineering Centre.

The name Hendon, where the first London aerodrome was established in 1911, was long synonymous with British aviation. Under a chestnut tree, to the north of the main gates of the Royal Air Force Museum, iron memorial gates with the name 'Grahame-White Aviation Co. Ltd' commemorate **Claud Grahame-White** (1874–1959), pioneer aviator and aircraft manufacturer, based at Hendon. Impressed by Blériot's cross-Channel flight, he worked in

Conflicts two thousand years apart are commemorated by the Catuvellauni obelisk and the Polish war memorial.

Memorial Gates at the RAF Museum commemorate Claud Grahame-White, the aviation pioneer, closely associated with the early Hendon Aerodrome.

Blériot's factory and in 1910 became the first Englishman to receive the pilot's licence of the French Aero Club. Grahame-White won many prizes, including one for flying round the Statue of Liberty in New York harbour. He sought government recognition for the aeroplane, with the enthusiastic support of Winston Churchill. The first military display at Hendon was in 1911. During 1912–14 Grahame-White organised aviation 'Derbys', joined the Royal Naval Air Service in 1914 and from 1915 was engaged in aircraft design and manufacture. Eventually the government bought Hendon aerodrome, a name Grahame-White had made world-famous. It was announced in November 2000 that, thanks to a National Lottery grant, the old Grahame-White works at Hendon, in which the Sopwith aircraft were made, will be moved to the museum site.

Sir Robert Peel (1788–1850) established the Metropolitan Police Force in 1828. Fittingly, his statue by William Behnes, which stood in Cheapside, then in Postman's Park until the 1930s, stands at Peel Centre, the Metropolitan Police training establishment at Hendon in Aerodrome Road, just south of the Royal Air Force Museum. The statue can be glimpsed from the road.

On 25th October 2001 the Queen opened the **Memorial Garden** in the grounds of the Peel Centre in honour of the members of the Metropolitan Police Service who have lost their lives in the line of duty. The Queen said 'The recent terrorist outrages in the United States have reminded us all in the starkest possible way of the debt we all owe, day in and day out, to the police and other emergency services'. The garden is in memory of 876 London police officers killed during the force's 170-year history. The Queen laid a wreath and signed a book of remembrance noting, 'The first entry dates from June 28th 1830, and the most recent is March 14th this year'.

South of Great North Way, half a mile north-east of Hendon Central and to the east of Sunny Hill Park, at the junction of Ashley Lane and Parson Street, is the archway entrance to Hendon Hall Hotel. Through it may be seen in the courtyard obelisks commemorating **William Shakespeare** and **David Garrick**, the actor. Garrick purchased the manor and advowson of Hendon and presented his nephew to the living of St Mary's in 1776. He is also said to have owned Hendon Hall although he seems never to have lived there.

In Gladstone Park, Dollis Hill Lane, stands a memorial by Fred Korma to **prisoners of war and victims of concentration camps**. It was unveiled on 4th May 1969 and depicts five bronze figures in attitudes of terror and despair. This moving memorial can be approached from the car park in Dollis Hill Lane.

The **First World War Memorial** by the green in the centre of Golders Green is in the form of a clock tower with bronze plaques. An open stone book was added to commemorate the men and women of Golders Green, Hampstead Garden Suburb and Childs Hill who died in the Second World War.

In St Pancras and Islington cemetery, on High Road, East Finchley, is the memorial to **Henry Croft** (1862–1930), first of the Pearly Kings. On his grave is his effigy in top hat and pearly suit. Pearly Kings and Queens, so called from the countless pearl buttons adorning their clothes, were the aristocrats of costermongers, maintaining Victorian coster customs. Today they devote themselves to fund-raising for charity through the Pearly Kings' and Queens' Association. They hold their 'Costermongers' Harvest Festival' in early October each year at St Martin's-in-the-Fields Church.

A dramatic bronze memorial commemorates the German defeat at the **battle of the Marne** in September 1914. *La Délivrance*, by Emile Guillaume, stands at the junction of Finchley Road and the North Circular Road. The gift of Lord Rothermere, it was unveiled by Lloyd George in 1927. A naked girl, on tiptoe, arms outstretched, symbolises the emotion inspired when the French and British defeated the invading Germans. Its unabashed nudity caused embarrassment, vehemently expressed in local papers.

Another battle on the outskirts of London is commemorated in Barnet at Hadley Highstone, north-east of the church. An obelisk erected in 1740 by Sir Jeremy Sandbrook marks the field of the **battle of Barnet** in April 1471 during the Wars of the Roses. The Yorkist Edward IV returned from exile, marched on London, was joined by his brother Clarence, and captured Henry VI. At Barnet, in a thick fog and with only two thousand men, he defeated the Lancastrians led by Richard Neville, Earl of Warwick ('the Kingmaker'), who was killed. Edward's army marched on to decisive victory at Tewkesbury. The obelisk stands within a fork of the road, north of Hadley Green.

A little to the south, at Livingstone Cottage, Hadley Green, Barnet, is a plaque with a relief portrait of **David Livingstone** (1813–73), the explorer, who lived here in 1857, before leaving the following year to continue his African exploration. Livingstone began life as a mill-worker, studied medicine and theology at Glasgow and went to Africa as a missionary in 1841, travelling north and discovering Lake Ngami and the Victoria Falls. On a second expedition he discovered Lake Nyasa and explored the Zambesi. On a third journey he sought to discover the sources of the Nile, but ill-health and finally death overtook him.

A conflict of the 1990s is recalled by the memorial in Alexandra Palace Park, Wood Green, to two **Gurkha soldiers** killed in Kosovo. Lieutenant Gareth Evans and Sergeant Bala Ram Rai died when an unexploded NATO bomb they had removed from a school exploded. The memorial was unveiled on 2nd April 2000.

There are two Richard Whittingtons. The real-life Whittington (*c*.1358–1423), a mercer of great wealth, was four times Mayor of London, a

The nudity of La Délivrance, commemorating the first battle of the Marne, 1914, aroused some local disapproval when it was set up in 1927.

The memorial in Gladstone Park, Dollis Hill, to prisoners of war and victims of concentration camps.

generous benefactor to charity and a provider of loans to four kings. But from 1605 his story was transformed. Dick Whittington became the hero of a nursery folk tale, recounted in chapbooks, ballads, plays and a pantomime dating from 26th December 1814, when the clown Joey Grimaldi played Dame Cicely Suet (the cook) in *Harlequin Whittington* at Covent Garden. The story of a poor boy and his cat who acquired a fortune is found in several countries, including Persia. The Mercers' Company, when choosing a new site for Whittington College in 1822, sought one 'as near as possible to Whittington's stone'. An early-seventeenth-century print by Renold Elstrack showed Whittington with his hand resting upon a skull. Public opinion forced the artist to substitute a cat for the skull. The **Whittington Stone** at the foot of Highgate Hill is the third stone to be placed on the spot where Dick heard the bells and turned back to London and fortune. The inscription is incorrect: Whittington was four times Mayor and was never knighted. The figure of the cat was added in 1964.

Beribboned wreaths of red flowers, left by enthusiasts, adorn the monument to **Heinrich Karl Marx** (1818–83) in Highgate Cemetery. The colossal, leonine bronze bust, four times life-size, sculpted by Lawrence Bradshaw (1956), commemorates this Communist thinker who lived in London and spent the last twenty-seven years of his life in St Pancras. Quotations decorate the plinth: 'Workers of all lands unite', from the *Communist Manifesto* of 1848, and 'The philosophers have only interpreted the world in various ways, the point, however, is to change it'. The number of wreaths laid here is reported to have fallen sharply since the collapse of the USSR and other Communist states.

In Waterlow Park, a fine open space on Highgate High Street, is a statue of **Sir Sydney Hedley Waterlow** (1822–1906). The park was once the garden of his home, Lauderdale House, which he gave with 30 acres to London County Council in 1889. The statue, by Frank M. Taubman (1900), shows Sir Sydney carrying his umbrella, a soft hat in one hand, keys in the other. Sir Sydney was

This monument to Heinrich Karl Marx is in Highgate Cemetery.

213

Sir Sydney Hedley Waterlow is commemorated by a statue in Waterlow Park.

Lord Mayor of London, Treasurer of St Bartholomew's Hospital and Master of the Stationers' Company. The statue was paid for by funds collected mainly from the people of the district. Collecting boxes were set up in the park and realised as much as £18 in a single day, nearly all in pennies.

Behind Lauderdale House, now a community centre, is a **sundial**, whose plate is said to be on a level with the cross on the dome of St Paul's Cathedral.

Abney Park Cemetery, Stoke Newington, off Stoke Newington High Street, has a memorial to all **those who lost their lives in the borough in the Second World War**, with names, dates and, unusually, addresses. The longest list is for Coronation Avenue, where a bomb fell on an air-raid shelter on 13th October 1940, killing nearly a hundred people. A water main burst and many were drowned.

Here too is a statue by E. H. Baily of **Dr Isaac Watts** (1674–1748), the non-conformist pastor and hymn writer. It stands on the site of his favourite seat. Abney Park (later to become the cemetery) belonged to Sir Thomas Abney, a leading non-conformist, who sheltered Watts for much of his life. Watts died 'at the end of a somewhat protracted visit of thirty-five years'. Hackney Council bought the cemetery in 1978 and began restoration. Many of Watts's hymns, such as 'O God, our help in ages past' and 'Jesus shall reign where'er the sun', remain popular today. Even as a child it was natural for Isaac Watts to speak in

The statue of Dr Isaac Watts in Abney Park stands on the site of his favourite seat.

rhyme. This irritated his father, who vowed to beat him if the habit persisted. Isaac fell to his knees in tears with the words: 'Pray, father, do some pity take, And I will no more verses make'. It is said that his father wisely gave up the struggle.

An 8¹/₂ foot bronze statue of **Winston Churchill** (1874–1965) was erected on Woodford Green, east of the junction of High Road and the Woodford New Road, facing Wensley Avenue in 1959 by his constituents, when he had represented as their MP from 1924 until 1959. The sculptor was David McFall. It was unveiled by Field Marshal Montgomery, in the presence of Sir Winston and Lady Churchill.

At The Broadway, Woodford Green, a small open space was named Pankhurst Green in 1995 in memory of **Sylvia Pankhurst**, 'who lived in Woodford from 1924–1956. One of her homes, West Dene, 3 Charteris Road, stood near this sign'; a wooden board bears the name of the green and the details. Pankhurst (1882–1960), the younger daughter of Dame Emmeline Pankhurst, worked for women's suffrage and was involved in many fiery campaigns. Her vocal opposition to the First World War led to public repudiation. She later enthusiastically embraced the Russian Revolution and the campaign for Abyssinian independence. She was a life-long pacifist. In December 2000 Westminster Council approved plans (with the proviso that the council would not have to maintain it) for a statue of Sylvia Pankhurst on College Green, Westminster, a project strongly supported by Margaret Beckett MP, then President of the Council and Leader of the House of Commons. However, it is not yet certain that the Pankhurst statue will achieve this site.

On the eastern fringe of London in Pole Hill Park, near Hawk Wood, Chingford, a 10 foot high white-painted obelisk erected in 1824 marks the

Greenwich meridian, the direction of true north from Greenwich. Unfortunately, at an international conference in 1884 calculations were rechecked and the meridian was realigned to run some 19 feet east of the pillar. The meridian is an imaginary great circle passing through the poles at right angles to the equator; the Greenwich meridian is the point from which longitudes are calculated. The obelisk is reached from a footpath from the top of Woodberry Way and Mornington Road.

Winston Churchill stands 8 feet tall in bronze on Woodford Green.

BIBLIOGRAPHY

Blackwood, John. *London's Immortals: the Complete Outdoor Commemorative Statues*. Savoy, 1989.

Boorman, Derek. *For Your Tomorrow: British Second World War Memorials*. Author, 1995.

Borenius, Tancred. *Forty London Statues and Public Monuments*. Methuen, 1926.

Brown, F.B. *London Sculpture*. Pitman, 1934.

Byron, Arthur. *London Statues: a Guide to London's Outdoor Statues and Sculpture*. Constable, 1981.

Cooper, C.S. *The Outdoor Monuments of London*. Homeland Association, 1928.

Curl, James Stevens. *A Celebration of Death*. Constable, 1980.

Darke, J. *The Monuments Guide to England and Wales*. Macdonald, 1991.

English Heritage. *Twentieth-Century War Memorials: Central London*. English Heritage leaflet, 2000.

Gleichen, E.W. *London's Open-Air Statues*. Longmans, 1928.

Hill, T. W. 'Open Air Statues of London'. *Home Counties* magazine, volume XIII, 1910.

Hudson, Roger. *The Immortals*. Folio, 1998.

Light, Alfred W. *Bunhill Fields*. 1913.

Lindley, Kenneth. *Graves and Graveyards*. 1972.

London County Council. *The Return of Outdoor Memorials to London*. 1910.

Mannheim, F.J. *Lion Hunting in London*. Caducens Press, 1975.

Saunders, David. *Britain's Maritime Memorials and Mementoes*. Patrick Stephens, 1996.

Sitwell, Osbert. *The People's Album of London Statues*. Duckworth, 1928.

Smith, David. *Britain's Aviation Memorials and Mementoes*. Patrick Stephens, 1992.

Sumeray, Derek. *Discovering London Plaques*. Shire, 1999.

Thompson, Geoffrey. *London Statues*. Dent, 1971.

White, P.W. *On Public View: London's Open Air Sculpture*. Hutchinson, 1971.

This obelisk was intended to mark the Greenwich meridian but missed it by 19 feet.

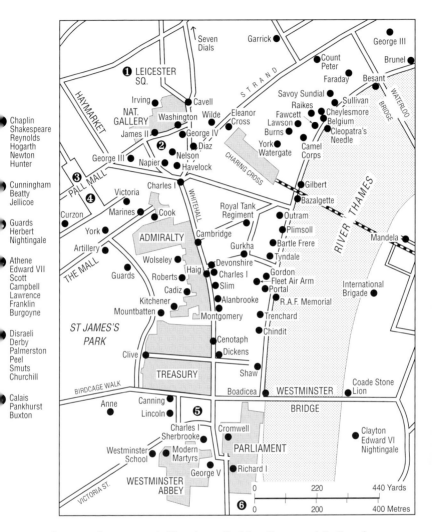

Statues and monuments in Westminster, Trafalgar Square and the Strand.

217

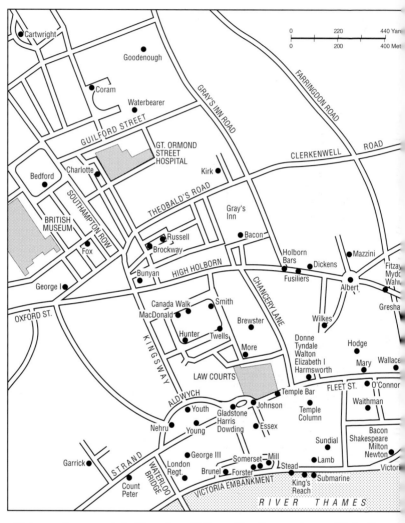

Statues and monuments in Bloomsbury, Holborn, Fleet Street and around St Paul's.

William
Wallace
Martyrs

Wesley

Henry VIII
Golden Boy

ST BART'S

amb

Postman's
Park

Millenium
Standing
Stone

Hill

Guy of
Warwick

Richards
St Paul's Cross

CHEAPSIDE

People of London
Wesley

ST PAUL'S
CATHEDRAL

Anne

Smith

Becket

Phillip

Blitz

ALDERSGATE STREET

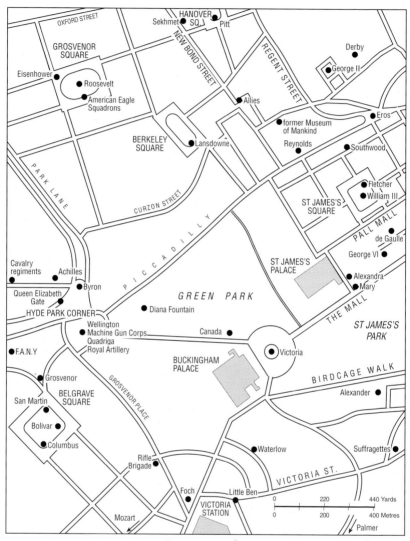

Statues and monuments in the West End and Belgravia.

INDEX

INDEX

INDEX

INDEX

A representation of the Commonwealth Gates as they will appear, framing Constitution Arch, at the top of Constitution Hill.